Unorthodox Judaism

Norman B. Mirsky

# Unorthodox Judaism

Ohio State University Press: Columbus

Some of the material in this book has been published previously in somewhat different form and is reprinted here by permission of the original publishers: chapter 1, "Evolution and the Stork," as "Reform Judaism: Evolution and the Stork" in *Judaism,* vol. 23, no. 3 (1974); chapter 2, "To Solemnize or Not to Solemnize," as "Mixed Marriage and the Reform Rabbinate" in *Midstream,* vol. 16, no. 1 (1970); chapter 6, "Unbinding Isaac," under the same title in the *Journal of the Central Conference of American Rabbis,* vol. 21 (1974); chapter 8, "The Jesus Hang-up," as "The Jesus Jews" in the *Reconstructionist,* vol. 39, no. 9 (1973); chapter 12, "Yavneh versus Masada," as "Yavneh versus Masada: The Uses of Myth and Legend in the Formation of American Jewish Identity" in *A Bicentennial Festschrift for Jacob Rader Marcus,* ed. Bertram Wallace Korn (New York: Ktav Publishing Co., 1976); and chapter 14, "I Think I'd Rather Work!", as "Shabbat, Work and Play in Contemporary Society" in the *Journal of the Central Conference of American Rabbis,* vol. 16 (1969).

Excerpts from *Fear of Flying: A Novel,* copyright © 1973 by Erica Mann Jong, are reprinted with the permission of Holt, Rinehart and Winston, Publishers; Erica Jong, c/o International Creative Management; and Secker and Warburg, Ltd. The selection is reprinted from *Childhood and Society,* by Erik H. Erikson, 2nd Edition, Rev., with the permission of W. W. Norton & Company, Inc. Copyright 1950, © 1963 by W. W. Norton & Company, Inc. Acknowledgment for permission to reprint is also made to The Hogarth Press and the author.

*Library of Congress Cataloging in Publication Data*

Mirsky, Norman B    1937–
  Unorthodox Judaism.

  Includes index.
  1. Judaism—United States—Addresses, essays,
lectures. 2. Jews in the United States—Identity—
Addresses, essays, lectures. I. Title.
BM205.M57          296'.0973          78-8683
ISBN 0-8142-0283-7

..................................................................

For Elaine, Rebekah, and Aaron

## Epigraph

When the gifted young Jew, still flexible in respect of his mental habits, is set loose among the iron pots of [the] mechanistic orientation [of modernity], the clay vessel of Jewish archaism suffers that fortune which is due and coming to clay vessels among the iron pots. His beautifully rounded heirloom, trademarked "B.C.," goes to pieces between his hands, and they are left empty. He is divested of those archaic conventional preconceptions which will not comport with the intellectual environment in which he finds himself. But he is not thereby invested with the gentile's peculiar heritage of conventional preconceptions which have stood over, by inertia of habit, out of the gentile past, which go, on the one hand, to make the safe and sane gentile, conservative and complacent, and which conduce also, on the other hand, to blur the safe and sane gentile's intellectual vision, and to leave him intellectually sessile.

The young Jew finds his own heritage of usage and outlook untenable; but this does not mean that he therefore will take over and inwardly imitate the traditions of usage and outlook which the gentile world has to offer; or at the most he does not uncritically take over all the intellectual prepossessions that are always standing over among the substantial citizens of the republic of learning. The idols of his own tribe have crumbled in decay and no longer cumber the ground, but that release does not induce him to set up a new line of idols borrowed from an alien tribe to do the same disservice. By consequence he is in a peculiar degree exposed to the unmediated facts of the current situation; and in a peculiar degree, therefore, he takes his orientation from the run of facts as he finds them rather than from the traditional interpretation of analogous facts in the past. In short, he is a skeptic by force of circumstances over which he has no control. Which comes to saying that he is in line to become a guide and leader of men in that intellectual enterprise out of which comes the increase and diffusion of knowledge among men, provided always that he is by native gift endowed with that net modicum of intelligence which takes effect in the play of that idle curiosity.

Thorstein Veblen,
"The Intellectual Pre-eminence of Jews in Modern Europe"

# Contents

# Preface

.................................................................

Why have I written this book on unorthodox Judaism? I do not suppose that I know all of the answers, but I do know some of them. I am a Reform rabbi with a Ph.D. in humanistic sociology, teaching at a Jewish seminary that has a tradition of its own. I am a father worried about the future of Judaism and the Jewish people, yet longing for his children's total self-fulfillment as American Jews. I therefore want to clarify for myself what the term "Jewish identity" signifies. I am sure that I am not alone in confronting this question and in craving a meaningful answer.

It is my hope that my exploration of existent Jewish and American phenomena may in some way shed some light on paths presently shrouded in darkness and confusion. Perhaps this effort of mine will help illumine the way for others groping toward a positive American Jewish resolution to conflicts inherent in the identity crisis of our age.

In this book I have employed my understanding of the Jewish past and two methodological systems that have proceeded from the behavioral sciences. One approach is that of sociologists represented by Kai Erikson, Howard S. Becker, Everett Hughes, and Erving Goffman. These men employ theories of deviance, not so much to establish the cause of deviance, but rather to enable deviants to determine for us, by the reactions they arouse among the "normal," the strengths and weaknesses of the static and fluid boundaries of the collectivity. Since Judaism has the aspects of both an eternal value system and an entity that has survived by means of adjustment and flexibility of its values—and since America is a land ever in flux and the home of the world's largest Jewish community—the application of theories of deviance as spelled out above seems highly promising in determining the direction in which American Jews are moving.

The second methodological approach I have recourse to in this book relies heavily on the theories and case histories of ego psychoanalysts such as Heinz Hartmann, Erik Erikson, and Jacob Arlow. These analysts probe identity formation on the biological, conscious, and unconscious levels, thereby providing us with tools with which to examine not only how Jews are striving toward an integral identity, but also how this striving can be either abetted or set awry through legend, fantasy, stereotyping, and more concrete phenomena such as child rearing, sexual experimentation, and intrafamilial as well as intrainstitutional transactions.

If this book seems the work of a dangling man seeking to find his footing, I hope that its struggle with paradoxes and dilemmas will be of help to others. As the well-known expression goes, "It is hard work to be a Jew."

## Acknowledgments

· · · · · · · · · · · · · · · · · · · · · · · · · · · · · · · · · · · · · · · · · · · · · · · · · · · · · · · ·

Like most of the work in this book, what I am about to express is immeasurable. Love and gratitude are subjective, and expressing them involves a risk, for there is always a danger of expressing them inadequately. Rabbi Stanley Chyet of the Hebrew Union College deserves special thanks. Through periods of mutual and private angst we labored together. His was the voice of reassurance, no matter how troubled. His was the steady craftsman's hand, though much of the time both of us were feeling tremors. Even if the project fails, the labor has succeeded. For both of us it was a labor of love.

The same can be said for those closest to me physically and in spirit: my wife, Elaine; my children, Rebekah and Aaron; our Jewish families, which include not only the supportive live, but the inspirational dead—my mother, Florence Poneman Mirsky, and her parents, Dora and Frank Poneman. Among those toward whom gratitude melts into love are my students at the Hebrew Union College in Cincinnati and in Los Angeles. In Cincinnati they were Reform rabbis-to-be; in Los Angeles they also include those who will soon serve as communal service workers and teachers for the entire Jewish community.

Some who receive my special thanks as teachers are Everett C. Hughes, Ellis Rivkin, Philip Slater, and B. Z. Sobel. They are exempt from all but praise, as are Rabbi Sherwin T. Wine and the congregants of the Birmingham Temple, and Rabbis Charles Lipman, David Glazer, and Earl Kaplan, who gave me their willing cooperation by sharing with me their ideas, time, and work. I hope this book reflects positively on them in an orthodox way.

# Introduction
............................................................

By way of introduction I feel that I owe my readers some autobiographical reflections that might increase their ability to
evaluate the sense of American Jewish realities I intend this book
to convey. When I was eight or nine years old, my father was a
buyer for a large Cleveland department store. While waiting for
him to take the family home, I would wander through the store
and would invariably be drawn to one display in particular—the
display featuring religious goods. Since this was the mid-1940s,
still a time when Jewish religious items were rarely, if ever,
marketed beyond the confines of Jewish neighborhoods, what
made the display so irresistible, although it caused some guilt on
my part, was the store's collection of crucifixes. When I would
return home from these encounters with the dying Christ, I would
set about reproducing them in modeling clay or in crayon
sketches.

Soon enough my mother began to be manifestly distressed with
my fascination for such an overtly un-Jewish symbol; she tried to
provide my apparent interest in religion with a more respectable
orientation. She bought me books on Judaism, but not wishing to
squelch my ecumenical spirit totally, she included among them a
book entitled *One God: The Ways We Worship Him,* by Florence
Fitch.[1] The book introduced the young reader to the various forms
of Judaism and Christianity. Much to my own and my mother's

chagrin, as hard as I tried to identify with the Judaism presented in the book, I found myself staring again and again at a picture of a life-size crucifix installed in a convent garden.

My family's connection with institutional Judaism was tentative. Both of my parents were second-generation American Jews whose basic Jewish allegiance was to Zionism. To be sure, I was sent to a weekday Hebrew school and occasionally spent a morning at Sunday school if my mother, who taught kindergarten, was able to get a job substituting at a synagogue. I knew nothing about Judaism, but I had no doubt that Jesus was supposed to be alien to me. Although my mother was college-educated, she was close enough to her European roots to refer to Jesus as *Yoshke,* to priests as *gallochim,* to a crucifix as a *tzalem,* and to a convert to Christianity (the worst thing a Jew could be) as a *m'shumed,* a term whispered with the utmost contempt.

My grandparents, who had emigrated to America in 1905, had witnessed several pogroms in their native Russia. These outbreaks, they maintained, always followed religious processions in which the cross was prominently displayed. They would speak of how as children they had habitually crossed the street opposite a church to avoid being kidnapped by a priest, a monk, or a nun. In America they lived and worked among non-Jews, but they never lost their fear of the clergy and of the symbols of the Catholic church, whether Eastern Orthodox or Roman.

Even if my parents and grandparents were nonobservant and rather disinterested Jews, they nevertheless managed to convey to me, however covertly, a sense of fear and awe where orthodox Christianity was concerned. Consequently, when I began to exhibit a preoccupation with crucifixes, I was filled with a sense of guilt on the one hand and of treason on the other.

Their attempt to direct my religious urge into more suitable channels soon took hold, and by the end of my ninth year I had determined to become a rabbi—though, in fact, I had probably had less than one hour's contact with rabbis up to that point in my life. And seventeen years later I actually did become a rabbi. Thus it might be said that Jesus led me into the rabbinate.

But, of course, this explanation is hardly adequate. My knowledge of psychology convinces me that there are far more complex reasons to account for my attraction to and rejection of the crucifix than the distaste my ordinarily permissive parents showed for my childish interest in that symbol.

To begin with, my parents at that time were in the process, first, of striving to save their marriage and, then, of dissolving it. The likelihood, therefore, is that my sudden religiosity was a function of my turning away from them to look for a more stable and less flawed parentage. It has since occurred to me that I may have been drawn to the spread-eagled figure on the cross because I myself was suffering the torment of being pulled in two opposite directions by the collapse of my parents' marriage.

Next, it is undoubtedly true that the tortured figure on the cross appealed to my childish sense of the macabre and the grotesque. There is for children a fascination in seeing a man in the throes of agony. The sight did not differ very much of course from the virtually ubiquitous comic book depictions of men and women hanged in dungeons, or stretched out on the rack in torture chambers, only to be saved by Superman or Batman. Such imagery has always appealed to children, probably because in it the adult is the victim—and what child can resist such a fantasy? Furthermore, children of my generation *knew* that in the end the forces of Good would prevail and the victims would be saved or at least avenged. Thus, it is relatively easy to account for my own fascination with the man on the cross. However, it is another matter to account for the anxiety this fascination caused my parents.

It would be too simplistic to suggest that their historical knowledge of the relationship between Christians and Jews made them see in my attraction to the crucifix some potential treason or apostasy. For my grandparents, who had actually been witness to the murderous activities of cross-bearers, this explanation might suffice. Christian religious fervor was for them synonymous with the suffering they had seen visited on Jews in Europe. True, my parents, reaching maturity in the Great Depression, had borne the brunt of anti-Semitism, particularly in the economic sphere; equally true, they had heard a priest, Father Coughlin, continually preach widely broadcast praises of Hitler's works coupled with denunciations of the Jews.[2] My parents themselves, however, had never been the objects of persecution in the name of Christ, though of course they were very well aware of the history of such persecutions.

The matter, I think, goes deeper. The fear of Jesus has roots in the Jewish psyche, especially in two respects: the psychological notion of attraction-repulsion and the basic psychological appeal of the Gospels. We know that, psychologically, love and hate are closely linked. To love and to hate both call forth the same emotions. Neither is the product of apathy or indifference. It is common enough to find good friends becoming bitter enemies or former spouses or lovers violently attacking each other. It is equally common to see former enemies become lovers. Paul of Tarsus ardently persecuted Christians, then became one of their chief apostles.[3] Former Marxists like Will Herberg have become faithful and conservative Jews. Former clergymen have become persecutors of their previous faith: Stalin, it is worth recalling, had studied for the priesthood; Rabbi Solomon Levi, of fourteenth-century Spain, became the rabidly anti-Jewish ecclesiastic Paul of Burgos.[4]

Attraction-repulsion is part of the same phenomenon. Perhaps it is illustrated nowhere better than in the process of toilet training. Before children are toilet trained, they take great delight in their feces. They are attracted by the fecal smell and texture. The distaste for feces has to be learned. The child's attitude toward his own feces has to be actively changed from one of love to one of hate. Once this happens few children remain indifferent. Often they come to find their excrement utterly repulsive; they have to defend themselves against its basic attractiveness, which is socially so unacceptable, by developing a hatred for it. Nevertheless, the attractiveness remains, and we find children needing substitutes like Silly Putty, Play Dough, and the like. The makers of perfume have always been aware of the attraction-repulsion phenomenon. The very substance produced by certain female glands that we spend millions of dollars a year neutralizing through deodorants because we have been conditioned to be repelled by it is extracted from animals for use in the making of alluring fragrances for which the same people pay millions more.

It can be argued that certain Jewish attitudes toward Jesus—and, of course, certain Christian attitudes toward Jews and Judaism—are functions of the same attraction-repulsion syndrome. This is not to say that the syndrome is biological in the case of the two religions; on the contrary, it is sociopsychological, as Freud was well aware when he wrote *Moses and Monotheism*.[5] Nearly from the moment of awareness, American Jews confront two sets of values. On the one hand, Jews who live in a Christian culture are bombarded with Christmas, with Easter, and with schools and media that present belief in Jesus as normative, so that in a sense it is un-American to dissociate oneself from Jesus.

On the other hand, in a world where Jews and Christians are presumed to be equal—and in law *are* equal—one of the few universally shared Jewish values is that Jews are not expected to believe in, or even to admire, Jesus.[6]

Jesus is one of the few features of the pluralist American scene that a non-Orthodox Jewish child is generally denied by his parents. Even in the days when the work ethic prevailed—that is, when one was supposed to show that he had earned everything he possessed—no amount of money, prestige, or power entitled a Jew to accept Jesus Christ as his Messiah, his Savior, or even his friend. When Jewish leaders have made positive statements about Jesus in public, they have emphatically not been relating to the Savior Christ, but to the human Jewish prophet from Nazareth.[7] In short, to have anything but an intellectually detached attitude toward Jesus has been to risk excluding oneself from the Jewish community. Even so, all the time that Jewish parents and Jewish institutions continue denying Jews access to Jesus, the larger culture goes on insisting that to deny him is to be abnormal, asocial, and unworthy of the rewards of this world or the next. An American who refuses to accept the spirit of Christmas is seen, and might even see himself, as a latter-day Scrooge.

When this psychosocial configuration is compounded by more traditional Jewish attitudes that maintain that churches are taboo places for Jews, a Jew, especially if he is not Orthodox, is confronted with a situation in which he is denied access to a set of beliefs that the culture has made attractive to him as a child. He is also denied access, in a psychological sense, to certain omnipresent and often physically attractive buildings since he is impelled to regard them as territory forbidden to Jews. What results, I believe, is internal as well as external pressure to resist attractive beliefs and edifices in order to remain in good standing in the Jewish community. To defend himself against the basic lure of the Church, the Jewish child may be forced (unconsciously) to repress his attraction and to develop strong negative feelings, bordering on repulsion, toward Jesus and His Church. Hence the violent response of so many Jews, particularly older Jews, toward Jesus, Christianity, and the Church.

There is, however, another quite potent dimension to the Jesus problem. In the myths presented in the Gospels are several themes that relate to human beings at various stages of the life cycle. Let us take first the Nativity stories in the form best known to us from school plays, Christmas carols, and the media. In this form, which is a composite of several Gospels, a young woman, who is married but still a virgin, is told by an angel that she will bear a child. This child, she is told, will be the Messiah. Toward the end of her gestation period, she and her husband are forced to travel to Bethlehem (the birthplace of their ancestor, King David) to comply with governmental requirements. Upon their arrival, with the mother in labor, they can find no place to stay and are forced to bed down in a stable; whereupon, surrounded by soft downy farm animals, she gives birth to a boy child named by the angels Jesus, a Greek version of the Hebrew word for salvation.

For the child of later generations, it is a kind of salvation in an oedipal sense. Psychoanalytic literature has been able to demonstrate that children are much troubled by and try to escape from the consciousness of sexual intercourse between their parents. Furthermore, psychoanalysis tells us that the child's desire to be dissociated from the superego-imposing parents often finds an outlet in fantasies in which the child identifies with the displaced offspring of royalty.[8] Furthermore, children because of their size see a special relationship between themselves and domesticated animals such as fleecy lambs and soft-eyed, milk-giving cows.

At a later stage in the life cycle, the figure of an early adolescent Jesus besting learned authority is undeniably appealing to the pubescent male whose budding body is constrained by school—and to Jewish lads attempting to achieve their manhood in a *cheder*.[9] The suffering righteous Jesus has an attraction for nearly all adolescents who regard themselves as Holden Caulfields at war with society, its institutions, and its hypocrites and who see in Jesus a person who consorts with and loves those who have been relegated to the periphery of respectable society. (Is it too much to suggest that adolescents, so many of whom have skin problems, are attracted to the Jesus who cures lepers?)

At an even later stage in the human life cycle, we can identify with the surrender of Jesus to society, his readiness to render to Caesar what is Caesar's, and his negation of his own ego in order to sit at the Right Hand of Power. No Eriksonian could achieve more.[10] Anyone willing and able to immerse himself in traditional Jewish sources could certainly find material of comparable appeal. However, Jesus Christ *is* a superstar, while the fantasy-fulfilling heroes of Jewish tradition lie all but totally lost, embedded as they are in foreign idioms and the special preserve of institutionalized religion.

How the Jew remains a Jew against the immense magnetic forces emanating from the larger non-Jewish society around him, the traumatic soul searching, the wrestling match between Jacob and the unarmed angel, is the subject matter of this book. Jews are indeed a peculiar, stiff-necked people, a mixed multitude of souls in conflict. Nevertheless, they continue to wrestle within and without to preserve their mystical covenant—even if it leads to unorthodox Judaism.

# PART ONE

............................................................

## On the Frontier

...............................................................

## chapter one

# Evolution and the Stork

Of all the attributes associated with the Judaeo-Christian tradition, those that come to mind most readily involve the human body. Rabbinic Judaism not only regulates the sexual activities of the Jew but also restricts his choice of food and drink, presents him with a need for ritual bathing, and even goes so far as to provide him with a benediction to be recited after he eliminates bodily wastes.[1] Traditional Christianity, too, pays much attention to the body. It constantly warns of the temptations of the flesh and bids the true believer, through ritual and through identification with the crucified Christ, to rid himself of the body he has had since birth and to be born again in Christ.[2] It seems odd, therefore, that the chief institutionalization of non-Orthodox Judaism, Reform Judaism, heavily influenced by both Rabbinic Judaism and the Christianity of the last 150 years, has paid so little attention to the wants and needs of the body.

If it has been true of Rabbinic Judaism that it leaves no human activity unregulated, and of Christianity that it sees the behavior of the body as having a great deal to do with the status of the soul, it is equally true that unorthodox Judaism in the garb of Reform seems nearly totally unmindful of man as a physical being. One searches in vain through the annals of Reform thought for more than the vaguest references—and even these are rare—to the human body. The traditional synagogal liturgy is rich in allusions to both external and internal organs.[3] It provides instructions for various bends of the knee, for prostration before the ark, for wrapping the head and arm in phylacteries, and for covering the torso of a male worshipper with a prayer shawl. In contrast, the Reform liturgy eliminates nearly every reference to human organs, presents man as almost wholly cerebral, and provides instruction only as to when one should stand, sit, speak, and be silent.

Notably, however, Reform as a movement—if not invariably Reform Jews as individuals—has been constant in taking a liberal position on the rights of workers, the equality of the sexes, and such matters as birth control and abortion. Reform Judaism cannot be accused of indifference to the plight of man when that plight includes oppression of the body. But Reform is guilty of indifference—or, more precisely perhaps, of embarrassment—when confronted with the body in other than political and socio-economic terms.

From what does this peculiar attitude stem? One might suggest many answers, but what seems most inescapable is the fact that Reform was born into a peculiar milieu and more than a century later still finds itself most comfortable in that milieu. Reform, that is to say, was created as a religion for generally upper-middle-class men and women who wished to remain Jewish but did not wish to appear significantly different from upper-middle-class men and women who were not Jewish. To a great extent, this is still true. What has changed are the upper-middle-class values, which now question certain attitudes not previously the object of much thought.

Reform was born into an age of reason, an age when mind was believed to be on the brink of conquering matter. It was a period when each man was conceded liberty to have his own thoughts, but when a great deal of attention was paid to public comportment. Manners were formal, dress was stiff, and sex was virtually unmentionable in polite company. In short, the age of reason was an age when reasonable people were expected to elevate their minds and to leave the discussion of their bodies to those skilled in the biological sciences. It was an age that gave humanity both the theory of evolution and the stork who delivered babies *ex nihilo*.[4]

Historically, therefore, Reform came into being at a time of philosophical idealism, in an age when reason was triumphant and the formalities of behavior and prudery were in full flower. It remained for an atheistic—or at least "ignostic" (someone who does not know the meaning of the word "God")—Viennese Jew, Sigmund Freud, to rescue the human body from the grip of reason—which is precisely what Freud did with his discovery of the unconscious and its roots in human biological drives. But Reform has had surprisingly little to do, intellectually speaking, with psychoanalysis. This has been true for a number of reasons. First, in *The Future of an Illusion*, Freud maintained that the idea of a liberal religion was impossible.[5] Religion, he argued, could not cater to the primitive emotional needs of the believer and at the same time rationally debunk the myths and rituals that answered to those needs. Reform Judaism based many of its claims to Jewish authenticity on its ability to study Judaism scientifically; it lay emphasis on what it construed as "the social outlook" of the Hebrew prophets and de-emphasized the role of customs, ceremonies, myths, and rituals. It was, if Freud was correct, highly vulnerable. Beyond that, the pessimism in Freud's sociological writings about the future of the human race conflicted with the optimism of Reform theologians. Reform preached that a new world was upon us, a messianic era; Freud wrote that there was no guarantee that Thanatos would or could be conquered by Eros.

Finally, at the very heart of psychoanalytic therapy is the matter of the individual's struggle to free his mind and body from the irrational controls of both the id and the superego. Reform simply refused to acknowledge the existence of this struggle, since psychoanalytic thought implied that man was by nature not a rational being but was at birth a lusting, pleasure-seeking animal who had to be tamed through repression. This smacked too much of the Christian doctrine of original sin and spoke too contemptuously of the creature who was little lower than the angels. Thus, while psychoanalytic theory could have provided a means by which Reform rediscovered the human body, it was bypassed for a pseudo-Marxism that seemed more compatible with the Reform view of man and society.

Even if the Reformers had recognized that psychoanalysis could have helped them to a more complete understanding of man as a being with both a body *and* a mind, however, there is a fundamental reason why Reform had to prefer a more one-sided approach to man. It is what we might call the decorum factor. Although at first glance this factor appears trivial, an understanding of how people behave in public, as described particularly in the writings of Philip Slater, Edward Hall, and Erving Goffman, will demonstrate its importance.[6]

When one examines the documents surrounding the earliest attempts at reforming Judaism, even going as far back as Israel Jacobson's first reformist institution, one is struck by the crucial nature of the decorum issue. In his *Prayerbook Reform in Europe*, Professor Jakob Josef Petuchowski says: "Side by side with the publication of reformed prayerbooks, and in many instances preceding such publication, there arose, at the very beginning of the nineteenth century, the literature of *Synagogenordnungen*. The German word . . . means 'Synagogue Order' and it carries the implication both of authoritative pronouncements and of the order and decorum which the Reformers wanted to see in the synagogue."[7]

In 1810, Dr. Petuchowski tells us, the Consistory of the Israelites of the Kingdom of Westphalia issued a twenty-four-page edict concerning behavior in the synagogue. Among the rules were: "The knocking on the doors and the calling out in the streets, which is customary in several congregations as a sign of the impending worship service, must altogether cease. Instead, the congregations must follow the times of services which will be determined by their rabbi without approval"; and, "Everybody should be dressed as cleanly and as decently as possible when appearing in the synagogue. The prayer leader, in particular, must be decently attired."[8]

In 1838, in Württemberg, similar rules were passed. Some of them are of particular interest:

> The synagogue should be entered with decorum and without noise. He who enters must immediately go to his seat and remain in it as quietly as possible. The sexton should direct foreign Israelites to seats. Any walking around or standing together within the synagogue is prohibited on pain of punishment. . . . As being offensive to the decorum and to the dignity of the worship service, the practice of the following customs is no longer permitted in the synagogue: (a) the kissing of the curtain on entering the synagogue during the service; (b) leaving one's seat in order to kiss the Scroll of the Law; (c) the knocking during the reading of the Book of Esther on the feast of Purim; (d) the malkoth-beating on the eve of the Day of Atonement; (e) the noisy beating of hosanoth on the 7th day of Tabernacles; (f) sitting on the floor on the fast of the Ninth of Ab; (g) removing shoes and boots in the synagogue on that day; (h) the procession with the Torah which is still the practise in some localities on the eve of Rejoicing in the Law; (i) the procession of the children with flags and candles on that festival; (j) the distribution

of food and drink in the synagogue on that festival in localities where it is still taking place.[9]

One could cite pages and pages of similar regulations passed by various Reform Jewish groups in Central Europe. Basically, these rules centered around two themes. Their intention was to fix a time for worship and to make certain the worshipper remained quietly in his seat until the service ended. But it was not the nineteenth-century German Reformers alone who passed rules on decorum. In 1964 the Committee on Guide for Synagogue Decorum of the Central Conference of American Rabbis (CCAR) issued a lengthy set of rules, some of which are excerpted below. For example, funerals:

> The funeral should be planned with utmost simplicity to carry out the Jewish idea that the grave levels all distinctions and all are equal in death. Lavish floral displays and *ostentation* are to be avoided.

Bar mitzvahs:

> The Bar Mitzvah, as a son of duty, attests by his participation in the Sabbath Service that he . . . will continue as a more mature young man to fulfill his obligations as a loyal Jew. . . . Its full religious significance must in no way be diminished by the festivities which surround the event.
>
> We are troubled that, concurrent with the raising of standards in preparation for Bar Mitzvah, there has been a steady and alarming deterioration in the character of the Bar Mitzvah "affair." The extravagant consumption, the conspicuous waste, and the crudity of many of these affairs are rapidly becoming a public Jewish scandal. The Bar Mitzvah party is not entirely a private affair. It is associated with a religious event, and as such should reflect the values of the Jewish religion. When these standards are abandoned, the good name of the Jewish community is lowered, and the value of the Bar Mitzvah itself is called into question.
>
> Judaism stands for the sane and dignified conduct of life. Judaism insists upon good taste, decency, and modesty. It is the Torah that limits freedom of choice for those who, in our free society, choose to accept and be loyal to it. The lowering of standards as reflected in many Bar Mitzvah celebrations is in direct violation of the teaching of the Torah. The trend toward the abandonment of aesthetic standards can lead to the abandonment of ethical standards as well.
>
> The *Kiddush* . . . should be kept simple, and should be held in the temple. Activities of caterers and other functionaries should not intrude the field of religious ceremonial. . . . In short, every aspect of the festivities following the ceremony should be dignified and in good taste.
>
> We urge our colleagues to impress their congregations with the fact that . . . the ceremony of Bar Mitzvah should be held during a

regularly scheduled service, at which time the Torah is read. Invited guests are to attend the service in its entirety.

Gambling:

> The CCAR deplores the use of gambling devices to raise funds for Jewish religious and communal institutions, as being contrary to our faith and tradition. The CCAR calls upon its members to discourage such practices.

Dress in synagogue:

> Since the manner of one's dress reflects the attitude toward the place and the occasion, we urge that all persons entering the temple premises should be so dressed as to reflect proper respect for the temple.
>
> Persons coming to the temple to perform specific duties (such as decorating a *Succah,* or preparing a meal in the kitchen) may be allowed to dress in accordance with those duties.[10]

Even today decorum remains a central issue in Reform Judaism. The CCAR guide raises it to the level of a religious obligation, rare in a movement that makes so few demands of its members. From whence stems this obsession with order, decorum, punctuality, and unostentatious behavior? In his two books *The Silent Language* and *The Hidden Dimension,* Edward Hall gives us more than a clue. Although Hall does not write specifically about Jews, he does write about the ways Americans manage matters of time and space. He points out that, with regard to time, punctuality down to the minute and even the second is a by-product of industrialized countries. Furthermore, Hall makes a distinction between monochronic and dichronic time. In industrialized countries it is expected of those who behave properly that they will engage in only one activity at a time. Other cultures, particularly non-Western cultures, find it perfectly acceptable for a person to do two or more things at the same time. The Eastern European Orthodox Jewish service provides a good example of the dichronic use of time. In an Orthodox *shul,* once a *minyan* is formed and the service is underway, it is perfectly proper to engage in other activities such as a discussion of the day's news. Furthermore, unless one is regularly a part of the original *minyan,* it is not considered impolite to come late. This use of time is alien to Western standards of proper conduct. Thus, from the point of view of a religious movement that is seeking to become westernized, the traditional Jewish use of dichronic time is offensive.

In *The Hidden Dimension,* which is about the use of space in various cultures, Hall again illumines the reason why decorum became so important to Reform. In the Moslem East and in Eastern European countries such as Poland, the attitude toward how space should be used in public has differed radically from that of such Western lands as Germany, England, and America. In the East, public space is thoroughly public. An Arab who finds the theater filled thinks nothing of leaning over the occupant of a seat until the occupant becomes so uncomfortable that he gets up. In the marketplace, a Pole would simply not understand, much less respect, the first-come-first-served rule. He would push his way ahead of as many people as he could. Furthermore, in public there is no restriction on how close a person should get to another person. Touching is not considered a breach of good conduct. Jews used to this Eastern allocation of public space clash radically with Westerners who carefully maintain a distance between themselves and the next person. Hence Jews new to Western culture will inevitably appear pushy and rude. In addition, since in the East one is permitted in public to carry on a conversation audible to everyone else within a given area, it is likely that a Jewish newcomer to Western culture would sound overly loud. He simply lacks the Westerner's orientation toward privacy in public. Thus, Jews—most of whom even in the West are of Eastern origin—are often considered loud. Through Hall, then, we come to understand three attributes that "boorish" Jews are said to possess: notoriously imprecise "Jewish" time, "Jewish" pushiness, and "Jewish" loudness.

In all the regulations concerning order and decorum from 1810 until the present, we see attempts to get Jews to observe Western rules of time and space—not just the rules of the Western world in general, however, but the rules of the Western upper-middle classes. From the vantage point of time and space management, the Eastern European Jew had a difficult road to travel before he came to resemble those native members of the upper-middle classes. Could there be two institutions more antithetical in their management of time and space than the upper-class Protestant church of Germany and America and the *shul* of the Eastern European Orthodox Jew? To the extent that it can be argued that religious institutions attempt to embody the most cherished values of a society, it must be admitted that the upper-class Protestant church has more in common with a theater than with a *shul,*

and that a *shul* has more in common with an informal cocktail
party than with a Protestant church. When a theater event is
scheduled, it begins at a precise time, and the members of the
audience are seated far enough away from one another so that no
one need touch another. Unless one is seated on an aisle, it is
usually difficult and embarrassing to have to leave for even the
most urgent of reasons. Furthermore, once the performance begins, it is supposed to occupy the full attention of the audience;
and unless there is a particularly extraordinary performance, the
audience is expected to participate only by applauding and only at
scheduled times. When the performance is completed, the audience is expected to leave the premises within a reasonably short
length of time. One need hardly mention that what Goffman calls
"creature releases" such as belching, breaking wind, or even loud
yawning are totally inappropriate and must be confined to rooms
designated for such needs. In short, both the Protestant church
service and the theater are examples of what Goffman calls a
*tight* situation: "Here each person present may be obliged to show
constant orientation to the gathering as a whole and constant
devotion to the spirit of the occasion as expressed through all the
avenues suggested."[11]

For a variety of reasons, an Eastern European Orthodox *shul*
provides the setting for a loose gathering, rather like that of an
informal cocktail party. Both at a cocktail party and in a *shul,* one
need not be too precise in observing the stipulated starting time.
One is not late even if he arrived twenty-five minutes or more
past the announced beginning. Furthermore, at a cocktail party,
although there is a host and usually a stated purpose for the event
such as greeting out-of-town guests, there is no reason to focus all
of one's attention on the host or the purpose for the gathering.
Instead, after initial formalities are concluded, one is free to stand
or sit, to move around, to engage whomever one chooses in conversation, and to talk above a whisper even to the point where
one's conversation can be overheard by others not in that conversation. One is also freer to meet his creature needs, either
through an easy exit to the bathroom, or through the use of some
sort of shielding, like a hand to cover a yawn or a handkerchief to
cover a sneeze. One need not be embarrassed by these shielded
creature releases as one would be during a church service or a
theatrical performance. In many ways the *shul,* with its loose
seating arrangements, its tolerance of dichronic time, and its lack
of concern for exits and shielded creature releases, truly resem-
bles the cocktail party.

But there is still another way in which the *shul* and the cocktail party are similar. Both usually involve a segregation of the sexes along with off-stage areas where the mixing of the sexes is permitted to take place. Orthodox Judaism does not allow men and women to sit together during worship. In the old Eastern European—or, for that matter, in any Orthodox—*shul,* women usually sit behind a curtained balcony where they are as free as the men to engage in conversation while the service goes on. It is interesting to speculate on why Judaism chose to segregate the sexes during religious services. In traditional Jewish society at large, women were expected to avoid the company of men and vice versa. With some of the insights given us by anthropologists, we may offer an explanation for this phenomenon. In most societies, though perhaps less in those of northwestern Europe, the mingling of the sexes was viewed as highly provocative. It was thought that the outcome of any unchaperoned meeting between a man and a woman would surely be a sexual encounter between the two. Hence, out of respect for the sex drive, Mediterranean and Oriental societies provided external controls over the meeting of boys and girls and men and women. The strict segregation of the sexes in Judaism undoubtedly is part of this system of external controls. In Western society each individual is expected to have an internalized control over the sex drive. The sexes are expected to mingle quite freely, but they are not expected to engage each other in sexual activity. By and large, even in the West, mingling of the sexes was to take place under highly formalized and highly ritualized circumstances. To use Goffman's term, the mingling was to take place in a tight gathering. But there are gatherings, such as cocktail parties, that are loose. In these gatherings it is common to find that the men group together and that the women form circles of their own. If a man and a woman choose to be together, it is generally at the periphery of the gathering, just as men and women in an Orthodox *shul* mingle outside the space allotted for worship. What one finds, then, is that in Orthodoxy there is a looseness of gatherings that involves, in the case of the liturgy, no attempt to avoid the issue of the human body, but that does involve the segregation of the sexes. In the Protestant and Protestantized religions of Western culture, one encounters tight gatherings, a paucity of references to the human body, and a more or less free mingling of the sexes. With these facts in mind, we are led to a better understanding of Reform's apparent denial of the human body and its lifelong obsession with order and decorum.

Since its inception Reform Judaism, as a westernized and wes-
ternizing movement, has been faced with the task of trying to get
Jews who have been socialized into one set of public behavior
norms to abandon them in favor of a set of nearly opposite norms.
Not only this, but the Reformers have had to attempt this task
through the modification of an institution that traditionally embodied all the old norms: the synagogue, that is to say, has had to
be modified into a temple.[12]

If the synagogue is viewed as an agency of socialization, a better perspective on the issues under discussion is possible here.
Inevitably the unorthodox or post-Orthodox—first the Reform
and then the Conservative—synagogue appears as the agency
through which millions of Jews have passed on their journey from
the *shtetlach* of Eastern Europe (or, a few decades earlier, the
*shtetl*-like *Doerfer* of southern Germany) into the upper-middle
classes of Western society. Its rules of decorum, its emphasis on
solemnity and dignity in worship, its urging that ostentation be
avoided and that excesses of any type be shunned, its post-
Orthodox rabbi who speaks the language of Western culture—all
are indicative of the socializing role that the post-Orthodox
synagogue has played since its Reformist beginnings. It is difficult to imagine Tevya singing "If I Were a Rich Man" in a
Reform context. Would a Jew schooled in a Reform synagogue do
as Zero Mostel does in the Mel Brooks movie *The Producers:*
would he shout out the window to a man in a Cadillac convertible
with his arms around a blonde, "If you got it, flaunt it!"? The
mention of money (filthy lucre) or any other "dirty" subject has no
place in a bastion of upper-middle-class sacred values.

Now, however, Jews find themselves living in a time when the
synagogue is no longer needed as a socializer into Western society, when that society as a whole has come to a more realistic
view of the needs of the human body, when informality has become a respectable mode of behavior, and when men and women
have come to see religion as a vehicle for personal expression and
celebration. The traditional Reform approach to religion may now
be in serious trouble. There has been within the style of traditional (pre-Reform) Judaism the potential to embrace the
religion-seeking human being. Judaism has been a viable counterculture. Has this potential been lost? One hopes not.

And maybe these hopes are not in vain. It is worthwhile noting
that one of the religious rituals seemingly most popular today
with Reform Jewish youth is Havdalah. Havdalah was intended

as a traditional ceremony to mark the end of the Shabbat and the beginning of the secular week, but it seems meaningful even to those who have not observed the Sabbath, at least not in the traditional manner. The reason for the popularity of the ceremony is clear. So is the fact that it is among the youth that it is celebrated. The Havdalah ceremony, with its wine, its braided candles, its spice box, its (admittedly modernist) practice of the clasping of one's fellow-celebrant, male or female, during the singing of songs, involves nearly every human sense. It offers visual, olfactory, tactile, and gustatory stimulation and stands in stark contrast to the normal, traditional Reform ritual, which is void of any sensual stimulation.

Those concerned with revitalizing the liturgical appeal of the liberal synagogue have in fact reflected on the popularity of the Havdalah ceremony.[14] They are today more open to the circumstance that, as a religious movement, Reform has an obligation to take *every* aspect of human life into account.

Perhaps it is truer today than ever before: a religion that lacks a body is one that lacks soul—and soon will lack souls.

## chapter two

## To Solemnize or Not to Solemnize?

The problem of soul is not uncomplicated for those Jews living in the open or pluralist societies of the West—particularly in North America, but in such countries as Israel, too—who have moved well beyond the ambit of Orthodox tradition. Nowhere does the problem find a more troublesome form or a more controversial expression than in the area of marriages between Jews and non-Jews. The more segregated societies of the Old World, whether we are speaking psychologically or geographically, still find this problem more or less inapplicable to their own situation—which only infuriates them the more when they see it unfold within unorthodox Judaism or enacted by unorthodox Jews.

On 1 August 1969 a letter was mailed to eighty-nine members of the CCAR, the organization of the Reform rabbinate in North America.

Dear Colleague:

I am sending you herewith the promised list of those members of the CCAR who will officiate at a marriage between a Jew and a non-Jew without requiring the non-Jew to convert.

The results of my inquiry as of this date are: 89 rabbis asked that their names be included on the list. Seven stated that they follow this practice but they did not want their names to be on the list. Fourteen who I am quite certain routinely follow this procedure did not respond. Undoubtedly there are others about whom I have no personal knowledge who also fall within the last-named category.

Therefore one may say with assurance that well over 100 members of the CCAR are officiating at interfaith marriages without requiring conversion.

I trust that you will find this list useful. But just keeping it to ourselves limits greatly both its usefulness and its influence. There are very important reasons which should be quite obvious to all of us for making this list available to anyone who wants it. I have already received eighteen requests for the list from Reform rabbis who themselves do not officiate routinely at intermarriages. Some of the statements made by these rabbis in their letters of request are very revealing:

"This is my present philosophy, but I am not certain that it will be my philosophy in the future. I have total respect for my colleagues who do perform such marriages and for the philosophy which impels them to do so"; "It's not a matter of shipping the couple off to someone else to 'do the dirty work.' Physicians who are unable, for one reason or another, to be helpful to a patient refer him to other physicians. I do the same thing for mixed marriages and any other kind of rabbinic counselling which I feel someone else is in a better position to handle"; "While I do not routinely officiate at a marriage between a Jew and a non-Jew, I have on occasion done so and certainly have no qualms about recommending other colleagues who are so inclined"; "Although I do not routinely officiate at such marriages, I have the highest respect for liberal rabbis who maintain this position"; "I feel that the men who routinely officiate at intermarriages do so with as much integrity and Jewish understanding as those of us who do not"; "Entering into a debate on the philosophy of 'Rabbis who do and those who do not' or of 'You do what I don't do' is, in my opinion, not relevant here."

It is clear that the unrestricted availability of this list will help to combat the defection of many of our people who are being lost to Judaism because of the spiritual insensibility of so many of our colleagues.

Therefore I now ask you to give me permission to include your name on a second list of rabbis who officiate at intermarriages *with the clear understanding that this second list may be given by anyone who has it to anyone else who needs it.* If you are willing, please fill out the enclosed statement and return it to me *before September first.* If I do not hear from you by September first, I shall assume that you do not intend to reply.

Cordially yours,
(Rabbi) David Max Eichhorn

P.S. If you know of any Reform colleague whose name is not on the list and you think should be, please ask him to write to me before September first and, if he gives me permission, I shall, of course, gladly add his name to the list.

What are the potential implications of Rabbi Eichhorn's letter? Rabbis who would perform mixed marriages (marriages in which the non-Jewish partner has not converted to Judaism) have been known to the profession for years. Even though many ostensibly more stringent colleagues referred mixed couples to them, these rabbis constituted more or less of an underground. Some of them had been performing such marriages for decades, while others had more recently been won over to the justness of their position; almost all of them claimed a justifying ideological position ranging from the universalism of classical Reform to some sociological argument for Jewish survival.[1] Nevertheless, despite the fact that almost every other rabbi knew of their existence, knowledge of who these men were long remained in-group, clandestine information. Since in some areas of the country the attitude of the Reform rabbinate was hostile toward the performance of such marriages,[2] one hesitated to give out the name of a colleague who did perform them, lest he be embarrassed and forced to deny that he did them, or lest he be swamped by requests for his services. It was assumed that even those rabbis who were known to officate at mixed marriages did so reluctantly, had certain objective criteria, and did not solicit such performances.

If we were dealing not with the Reform but with the Orthodox rabbinate, the situation would be equivalent to that of a group of American doctors who publicly favored abortion. Abortion, except under highly specified circumstances, was long illegal in every part of the United States. An M.D. who performed an abortion in violation of the legal specifications was subject to the loss of his license by the state. Similarly, mixed marriages are halachically invalid and illegal; therefore an Orthodox rabbi who performs one is subject to halachic sanctions that may include the loss of his right to perform other marriages through his being placed in *herem*. Even for Orthodox rabbis in the United States, however, the problem is complicated by the fact that there are two sets of laws operating—the Jewish and the civil.

In the case of the Reform rabbinate, the issue has been much more complex. By performing a mixed marriage, the Reform rabbi, bound by halacha only to the degree that he wishes to be bound, could claim, in theory at least, to violate neither Jewish law as Reform Judaism saw it nor civil law (for there is nothing illegal about a mixed marriage). It is as valid in a civil divorce court as a halachically sanctioned marriage. Thus Reform rabbis who perform mixed marriages may violate only the mores or folkways of American Jews. The very fact that it is now believed that mixed marriages violate folkways rather than customs or laws is in itself pertinent to our discussion and deserves further examination.

As Rabbi Eichhorn's letter indicates, even among Reform rabbis (according to the CCAR there are more than one thousand), those who performed mixed marriages in the late 1960s were a small, though growing, minority. And, as his letter also suggested and the CCAR later made quite explicit at its 1973 Atlanta meeting, Reform rabbis were and still are unhappy with those of their colleagues who perform them. Nevertheless, it is quite evident that there is considerable doubt even among those who refuse to perform them. This doubt is manifest, for instance, among certain members of the faculty of Reform Judaism's rabbinical seminary, the Hebrew Union College–Jewish Institute of Religion, and even among the student body, far from resolute in their opposition to mixed marriages. It seems safe to predict that, given the current trends in the Jewish community, the number of Reform rabbis willing to perform mixed marriages will increase, the Atlanta resolutions notwithstanding.[3]

In order to understand this, it is important to survey briefly the opinions of most American Jews about the role that the Reform rabbinate has played in American Jewish life in the last century or so. From the 1860s until the large wave of Eastern European immigrants took root in America—i.e., set up their own religious institutions in this country—the Reform rabbi was the chief religious spokesman of American Jews. Religious leaders of these American Jews, who mostly hailed from Central Europe and were anxious to adjust to their new domicile, were exemplified by men like Isaac Mayer Wise, best described as a halachic pragmatist. Wise very carefully weighed the consequences of each breach of halacha and cautioned some of his more theoretically minded Reform colleagues against going to extremes that they felt were philosophically justified.[4]

After the turn of the century, Reform Jews no longer comprised the majority of American Jews; in a period of about thirty years they had become instead the minority. Reform Jewish institutions and their leaders, which formerly had appeared both very American and very Jewish, were now viewed from an Eastern European perspective and seemed somehow "non-Jewish" and of little religious significance.[5]

Nevertheless, Reform rabbis, though perhaps no longer religious leaders in the halachic sense, were still leaders in areas outside of religious practice. Such men as Stephen S. Wise and

Abba Hillel Silver attained leadership because they addressed themselves to the American public at large. They presented an image that could be admired by non-Jews and emulated by Jews in the secular world. Reform temples could promise status if not salvation. During this period, from about 1910 to 1945, the religious role of the Reform rabbinate in the life of most American Jews was minimal.[6]

After World War II, however, the situation began to change once again. Multitudes of Jews flocked to Reform temples, often joining them simply because they were there. For the most part, these people had no roots in traditional Judaism but were in the habit of calling in rabbis and other Jewish clerics and officiants (cantors, *mohels,* caterers) at life-cycle events. This influx into Reform temples of Jews of Eastern European origin returned the Reform rabbinate to the legitimate religious realm as far as non-Reform Jews were concerned. Reform rabbis now officiated at bar mitzvahs (formerly ignored in American Reform) that non-Reform relatives attended; they solemnized weddings between Reform and non-Reform Jews, again in the presence of non-Reform families, not seldom in conjunction with a more traditional rabbi. Similarly, at funerals, circumcisions, and other life-cycle events, the Reform rabbi was considered a Jewish religious functionary. But although he was no longer thought to be outside the Jewish clerical fold, he was still regarded, quite correctly, as different from other rabbis. Often he wore no head covering in temple or was seen in nonkosher restaurants or riding on the Shabbat. Sometimes his wife was seen buying nonkosher meat in the supermarket. In short, others viewed him as a Jew like themselves, except that he was presumably knowledgeable in the area of Judaism and could officiate at religious functions. Perhaps we should qualify the phrase "a Jew like themselves." In the majority of instances, in public at least, the Reform rabbi was less inclined to flagrantly violate religious norms than the average American Jew. He was less likely to go shopping on the Shabbat or to eat pork in public. And he was far more likely to go to temple than most American Jews. After World War II the Reform rabbi once again became a religious leader for non-Reform Jews—but a religious leader who represented the outer limit, the boundary, beyond which one could not go and still be considered able to meet Jewish religious needs in the general Jewish community. His bar mitzvahs were somehow not *quite* authentic. His *brith*s were Jewish but not *quite* as Jewish as those performed by a *mohel.* His conversions, though valid, were considered somehow less valid than halachic conversions.[7]

On the issue of mixed marriages, one question still plagues us: Are Reform rabbis who agree to perform mixed marriages still within the boundary line of American religious Jewishness, or have they in fact moved that boundary line further than American Jews would themselves have moved it?

It seems that in the past few years the number of people who have married non-Jews has increased considerably. Anyone connected with a college community soon comes to realize that this type of marriage is no longer unusual.[8] A rabbi in a large midwestern city, who will not officiate at mixed marriages and who has a traditional, informed congregation, once confided to me that within a single year, among the children of his congregants, just as many of them intermarried (either with or without conversion of the non-Jew to Judaism) as married within their faith. Assistant and associate rabbis in the large urban temples that serve American Jews and whose job it is to minister to the youth report that most of the marriages they perform (after conversion) are intermarriages. If they were willing to perform mixed marriages, they could officiate at several each week.

Therefore, it is quite obvious that intermarriage is a social reality among American Jews. No doubt most American Jews would prefer to see their children marry Jews, but after the fact they are ready to adjust to a mixed marriage. As the phenomenon grows and as more and more families experience it, especially some of the "model Jews" in a community, the stigma is lessened. It is still regarded as a burden to bear, but the burden appears to be lightened if the marriage is sanctified by a rabbi. It must be remembered that the bulk of American Jews regard Reform rabbis as legitimate officiants at life-cycle events, but beyond that they see them as having a function that Orthodox and Conservative rabbis cannot and need not have as long as there are Reform rabbis—namely, the sanctifying of life-cycle events that are halachically invalid but that the community feels, albeit reluctantly, that it must approve. If we are prepared to look at the American Jewish community as an organic whole, which we must do in order to understand it sociologically, it becomes apparent that the Reform rabbinate, in addition to serving as the legitimate religious authority for Reform Jews, serves the larger Jewish community by sanctifying nonhalachic but communally sanctioned behavior.

These two factors—the tremendous increase in mixed marriages and this view held by most American Jews of one function of the Reform rabbinate—tend to make Reform rabbis more aware of the acuteness of the problem. Reform rabbis simply see more couples who are going to intermarry because of the function they are thought to serve. They are also under extreme pressure to perform these marriages. Most parents, unlike in earlier days, beg the rabbi to perform marriages that they realistically see as inevitable; often enough they even threaten that the marriage will take place in a church if the rabbi refuses to solemnize it.

The apparent solution to the problem of mixed marriage would be the conversion of the non-Jewish partner. The rabbi then would not have to perform a mixed marriage. However, we live in an age when everyone is encouraged to "do his own thing," so that there has been great reluctance on the part of the Jewish partner to persuade the non-Jewish fiancé(e) to give up part of his (or her) identity. Furthermore, and this is a truth we must face up to, Jews have never really thought much of conversion. Jews have tended to regard it as merely an attempt to appear Jewish or as a way of getting a rabbi to marry a couple. Conversion, like mixed marriage, has been viewed mainly as the province of the Reform rabbinate, Jewishly valid, but a slightly less than authentic phenomenon.[9] These, it should be stressed, are the subjective attitudes of the American Jewish community. There is little doubt in my mind that conversion can be real and meaningful to the convert. Rabbi Edwin Friedman, of Washington, D.C., has told me that in over five hundred mixed couples he had seen, the non-Jewish partner, whether he planned to convert or not, saw acceptance into the Jewish family and community structure as a fundamental reason for marrying a Jew. Rabbi Albert Lewis, who undertook an intensive study of converts and their spouses in Dayton and Cincinnati, Ohio, found that the converts unequivocally regarded themselves as Jews, though their mates were seldom convinced that conversion could make non-Jews into "real" Jews. What the Jewish spouse did indicate was that the conversion of the non-Jewish partner made the couple feel more welcome in Jewish communal life.[10]

Thus, it would appear that conversion is a passage rite into Judaism for the non-Jew who converts, but that it is taken less seriously by Jews. That is why many young Jews fail to perceive a Reform rabbi's insistence on conversion as anything but hypocritical. Reform rabbis are generally respected for refusing to submit to a double standard of Jewish observance—one for laymen and one for rabbis. Young people are therefore often shocked to discover that Reform rabbis demand conversion, something that they themselves see Jewish laymen taking quite lightly. Hence, the Reform rabbi's dilemma grows. He does not regard himself as being less Jewish or less of a rabbi than his non-Reform colleagues, nor does he see himself (even if he is seen thus by the majority of American Jews) as the border line between Judaism and secularism. When he does decide to perform mixed marriages, it is in most instances after much soul-searching. He tends to see his performance of mixed marriages, although halachically invalid, as consonant with a higher law: the will of the Jewish people to live, or the universal teachings of prophetic Judaism.

Reform rabbis who contemplate performing mixed marriages must examine themselves in the context of the entire Jewish community. Although it may be painful for them to accept the notion that they are regarded as the sociological boundary line of the Jewish group, and although they rightly feel that there are laws more pertinent than those proposed by either sociological theorists or halachists, reality demands that Reform rabbis see that their actions in the realm of mixed marriage do have far-reaching consequences. By agreeing to perform mixed marriages, by taking the matter from its Marrano-like state out into the open, rabbis who publicize their names—as in the newly founded Association for a Progressive Reform Judaism (APRJ)[11]—are going beyond mere honesty and dissent against the CCAR's anti–mixed marriage resolutions. They are openly declaring that their Jewish boundary line has been extended once again—this time to include Christians.

There are several possible consequences of this extension. If it represents the genuine will of the American Jewish community, which it very well may, the Reform rabbinate will be no weaker for extending the boundaries of religious sanction. In fact, its prestige may be enhanced for honestly yielding to the will of the Jewish people. If sanctioning mixed marriages is not the will of the Jewish people, however, then the entire official Reform rabbinate, which includes members who do sanction mixed marriages, may find that in the eyes of the Jewish community it too has crossed the boundary and has lost its religious validity.[12]

It may be possible here to place in a sociological perspective the stance of those Reform rabbis who have publicly declared their willingness to perform mixed marriages. First, there is a vast difference in the social effect of their acts between keeping sanctification of mixed marriages an underground, or backstage, affair and bringing it onstage. Declaring publicly their willingness to perform mixed marriages implies that a larger audience is now welcome to witness the performance. There may be applause, but there are equally likely to be—indeed have been—cries of outrage, and to neither the fans nor the critics is the rabbi able to say "it is my own private concern," for by making a public statement he has declared that this is not the case.

Furthermore, the fact that this willingness to solemnize mixed marriages might involve a tenth or more of the entire Reform rabbinate removes the matter from the realm of private to that of social dissent. When perhaps one hundred of one's colleagues take a group stand well outside of the traditional norms of Jewish community life, the consequences for the Reform rabbinate are bound to be far more widespread than if one hundred rabbis secretly perform such rites. Perhaps most far-reaching is the effect of this move on other Reform colleagues. Strengthened by the knowledge that they can turn to a national organization, the new APRJ, when under attack by their more conventional colleagues, they can make the decision that laymen have long been pressing them into but that they have heretofore resisted.

Contemporary Jewish history and sociology may guide the CCAR in dealing with this crisis. When over two hundred of its members declared themselves hostile to the idea of a Jewish state, the CCAR allowed these men to remain in good standing in the conference. History accomplished what the majority in the conference failed to do.[13] It gave most of these American Council for Judaism rabbis a choice between joining the Jews and not having a congregation. There are probably more Reform rabbis today who are hesitant to criticize Israel in public than to sanction mixed marriage.

When a few years ago one of the CCAR's members publicly declared that, though he was a rabbi, he no longer planned to have his congregants mention God in religious services, the conference chose to ignore him. The result of this action has been favorable, as the congregants drew closer to traditional Jewish theology than they would have if their rabbi had been made a martyr. Silence has proven an effective weapon in the CCAR arsenal.[14]

Of course, one familiar with the CCAR wonders whether this inactivity is part of a deliberate strategy or if it is the result of paralysis. There is no way of estimating how many Jews were lost to the Reform movement because of its willingness to tolerate American Council for Judaism rabbis in its ranks. There is also no telling how far the religious authority of all Reform rabbis in the entire Jewish community is undermined by the extreme tolerance of the Reform rabbinic body.

It is difficult to determine whether sociology is with or against a rabbinate that defies laws and mores followed by a people for thousands of years. Abraham himself violated the mores of his father's people. Jacob, too, broke the laws of his day. What is clear is that a failure on the part of the CCAR to condemn those of its members who publicly declare that they will ignore the Atlanta resolutions and perform mixed marriages will most likely widen the gap between halachic and nonhalachic rabbis in this country.

However, it can also be argued that, while the more traditional members of the rabbinate may publicly disapprove of this breach of halacha or mores, many of them may be secretly relieved. No one is certain whether mixed marriages spell doom for Jewish survival. Nearly everyone is convinced that couples refused Jewish religious sanction will marry anyway. Rabbis faced with anxious brides- and grooms-to-be and frightened and nervous parents may be comforted in their ability to refer these people to the APRJ and its sympathizers.

. . . . . . . . . . . . . . . . . . . . . . . . . . . . . . . . . . . . . . . . . . . . . . . . . . . . . . . . . . .

## chapter three

# Ill Wind or High Tide?

Even Rabbi Eichhorn, the APRJ, and others of like mind will not deny that mixed marriage is alleged—justifiably or not—to be one of the gravest problems facing American Jewry as a community. The fact that one is well advised to use the term "alleged" constitutes part of the problem: there are, to be sure, widespread and well-articulated fears on the part of a sizable number of American Jews and what might be called outright panic on the part of Jewish institutions (e.g., the rabbinate, the synagogue, and Jewish federations throughout the land); simultaneously, however, as we have already suggested, there is a growing acceptance of mixed marriage on the part of the Jewish masses. In fact, this greater willingness to accept mixed marriage as normal and not as something deviant tends to elicit strong expressions of concern and dismay from individuals and agencies charged with the maintenance of Jewish institutions.

The resolution that the CCAR adopted by a substantial majority at Atlanta in June 1973 reflects a much more severe view of, and a much more outspoken stand against, rabbis who officiate at mixed marriages than did the CCAR's previous resolution.

> The Central Conference of American Rabbis, recalling its stand in 1909 "that mixed marriage is contrary to the Jewish tradition and should be discouraged," *now declares its opposition to* participation by its members in any ceremony which solemnizes a mixed marriage.

Recognizing that historically the CCAR encompasses members holding divergent interpretations of Jewish tradition, the Conference calls upon these members who dissent from this declaration:

1. to refrain from officiating at a mixed marriage unless the couple agrees to undertake, prior to marriage, a course of study of Judaism equivalent to that required for conversion;
2. to refrain from officiating at a mixed marriage for a member of a congregation served by a Conference member unless there has been prior consultation with that Rabbi;
3. to refrain from co-officiating or sharing with non-Jewish clergy in the solemnization of a mixed marriage;
4. to refrain from officiating at a mixed marriage on Shabbat or Yom Tov.

In order to keep open every channel to Judaism and K'lal Yisrael for those who have already entered into mixed marriage, the CCAR calls upon its members:

1. to assist fully in educating children of such mixed marriage as Jews;
2. to provide the opportunity for conversion of the non-Jewish spouse, and
3. to encourage a creative and consistent cultivation of involvement in the Jewish community and the synagogue.[1]

A decade ago, on the other hand, the other major branch of unorthodox Judaism, the Conservative movement, which had never been known for its willingness to accept mixed marriages, received the following majority opinion from the highly prestigious Committee on Jewish Law and Standards of the Rabbinical Assembly, the Conservative rabbinical organization:

A. The Jewish party to the marriage (to a non-Jew) may be accepted to membership in the congregation provided there is a definite agreement that the children of this marriage shall be raised as Jews and shall be converted to Judaism (provided the mother is not Jewish). . . .
D. One who intermarries after he has been admitted to membership shall not be deprived of his membership. . . . If he refuses to give his children a Jewish education and refuses to have them converted, he shall forfeit his membership.[2]

Other items in the report stated that the non-Jewish spouse would not be permitted membership on synagogue boards or auxiliaries, burial in Jewish cemeteries, or honors in the worship service. The Conservative recommendation of 1964 in no way, of course, sanctioned intermarriage without conversion, but (as the minority opinion of the committee pointed out) it *did* give tacit recognition to what was already in the mid-1960s becoming a reality of Jewish life in America, namely, the increasing number of mixed marriages. It also implied that marrying a non-Jew did not necessarily mean that the Jewish partner was a person who denied his or her Jewishness or sought no further links with institutional (in this case, synagogal) Judaism.[3]

So we see that, while there has been some movement toward traditionalism on the part of the Reform rabbinate, there has also been some movement toward liberalism on the part of a more traditionalist segment of the American rabbinate. Both position shifts stem from a number of factors (e.g., the relationship of the Reform rabbinate to its more traditionalist counterpart, the laws governing religion in the State of Israel, and the Conservative desire to "save the children" and perhaps retain important members involved in mixed marriages); at the same time they explicitly reflect a need to take into account the reality of the increasing rate of mixed marriages.

This book is not meant to deal historically with the subject of mixed marriage or to argue the pros and cons of the subject, though I do intend to examine some of the fears as well as some of the promises that an increased rate of mixed marriage evokes. At this juncture I want to explore and attempt to interpret some rather startling data recently gathered by the National Jewish Population Study (NJPS), sponsored by the Council of Jewish Federations and Welfare Funds. The project was under the direction of Fred Massarik, one of American Jewry's outstanding survey-research sociologists. Dr. Massarik was aided in survey-researching the American Jewish community by an equally distinguished staff of experts.[4]

Before I present a summary of the study's findings, a methodological caveat would seem to be in order. The preface to the study states that the NJPS was based on a sample specifically chosen to be representative of the total United States Jewish population. The sample included communities of all sizes and in all parts of the country; random samplings included Jews not on any organizational lists as well as those who were. Unfortunately, the report nowhere supplied a definition of who is a Jew, nor did it specify the actual population size surveyed. Moreover, it offered no comprehensive account of the sampling techniques it employed. Even so, because of the outstanding reputations of the members of the project as well as their conceptualization of the term "basic mixed marriage," one should for the moment overlook their omissions and attempt to interpret their findings.[5]

I propose first to quote the report and then to explain how its concept of the "basic mixed marriage" differs from other formulas. The report states: "We define *'basic'* as a marriage in which one or the other partner describes himself/herself (or is described) as having identified with a non-Jewish cultural viewpoint *at the time that he/she met his/her future spouse.*" The authors then go on to say: "the crucial point considered *precedes the act of marriage itself;* it focuses on each partner's 'original' state of belief (or unbelief), whatever it may have been before being influenced by the relationship leading to marriage."[6] They call this form of intermarriage basic because "it includes the most elemental, general circumstance preexisting to courtship and marriage."[7] Their formulation is important because it broadens the sociological territory that should be considered in evaluating and possibly predicting the impact on individuals not born or raised as Jews marrying those born or raised as Jews.

In most instances, according to the socioscientific literature as well as the writings of religious authorities, a *mixed marriage* is one in which both partners retain the religions they followed before the marriage, whereas an *intermarriage* involves the conversion of one spouse to the religion of the other.[8] These old definitions are confusing and misleading for a number of reasons. First of all, "inter" suggests two outsiders engaged in an encounter (in this instance, marriage). Although "inter" is generally used to cover converts and "mixed" is used for a marriage with no conversion, the literal meaning of "inter" tends to confuse the subject. Second, Jewish law and tradition regard a person who converts to Judaism as a Jew. The convert is "born again," a circumstance signified by the assignment to him of a new name and a new set of "parents"—usually Abraham and Ruth. Thus, in the sense that "inter" means an encounter with an outsider, conversion virtually eliminates the "inter" dimension of an intermarriage.

These simple linguistic and religious facts concerning the meaning of intermarriage have stood in the way of understanding what is meant by intermarriage, for literally it is no different in meaning from a mixed marriage. In short, legally and traditionally there are only two kinds of marriages in Judaism, mixed and Jewish. Since Orthodox Judaism does not consider a marriage to an unconverted non-Jew valid, there can be no such thing as a mixed marriage or an intermarriage for an Orthodox Jew. Two people may mix or interact in ways that the state calls marriage, but this is no valid marriage in Orthodox eyes.

The most useful NJPS definition of a basic mixed marriage is that it throws into focus some of the wider implications of intermarriage, lumps converts and nonconverts together, and draws critical attention to the cultural rather than merely the personal factors that go into the making of an intermarriage. Most vitally, the NJPS definition recognizes that, even where conversion has taken place, the couple's relatives usually remain their old religious or irreligious selves. Thus, the child of a happy marriage between two practicing Jews (one of them a convert) is more than likely to have grandparents, uncles, aunts, and cousins who invite him over to see their Christmas decorations, include him in the festivities (as they have every right to do in religiously tolerant America), and give him a present and perhaps even a blessing. Likewise, the child of a happy marriage between a Christian and a Jew converted to Christianity is not unlikely to experience a Shabbat with his grandparents or look for the afikomen at a seder conducted by his Jewish relatives. Thus, whether there is conversion or not, or whether children are raised as Jews or as non-Jews, important as these factors are in the development of the identity of the individual, they do not suffice to account for the impact an intermarriage has on the Jewish community and its sense of survival, nor, from the Christian point of view, on the survival of values that Christians have long cherished.

Here is a summary of the NJPS findings. Let me try to interpret the data as presented in the summary and then offer a few thoughts of my own on the subject of marriages between Jews and non-Jews.

1. Of all Jewish persons now married, some 9.2 percent are intermarried.
2. The proportion of Jewish persons intermarrying in the period 1966–72 is much greater than corresponding proportions in earlier periods; 31 percent of Jewish persons marrying in this recent time span chose a non-Jewish spouse.
3. The combination of a Jewish husband and a non-Jewish wife is about twice as prevalent as the combination of a Jewish wife and a non-Jewish husband.
4. About one-fourth of all intermarrying non-Jewish females report conversion into Judaism; in contrast, few intermarrying non-Jewish males have converted.
5. Nearly half of marriage partners who were non-Jewish prior to marriage subsequently identify as Jewish, regardless of formal conversion.
6. In a very large majority of cases, when the wife is Jewish though initially the husband is not Jewish, children are raised

as Jewish. On the other hand, when the husband is Jewish and the wife initially not Jewish, about one-third of the children are raised outside the Jewish religion.

7. A belief in the Jewish religion is widely professed, both in intermarried and non-intermarried households, but such belief is somewhat more prevalent among the non-intermarried. There is continuing widespread belief in One God.

8. Regardless of marriage pattern, active participation in temples and synagogues is the exception, not the rule. Somewhat more intensive participation in temple or synagogue life appears for the non-intermarried and in those households in which the wife is Jewish and the husband is not Jewish. Relatively higher levels of involvement in Jewish organizations appear for the non-intermarried, but in absolute terms these levels, too, are generally low.

9. Among non-intermarried, four in ten indicate that they had never dated a non-Jew.

10. Reported parental opposition to interdating is significantly linked to marriage *within* the Jewish group; reported lack of parental opposition to interdating is associated with intermarriage.

11. Non-intermarried couples and those with a Jewish wife report similar patterns in their early upbringing: a majority describe their own childhood upbringing as "strongly Jewish." In marriages with a Jewish husband and a non-Jewish wife, the childhood upbringing is rarely described as "strongly Jewish."

12. The chance that intermarriage will take place is greatest for those who cannot clearly describe their upbringing, but also very high for those who describe their own upbringing as marginally Jewish. Positive Jewish identity in childhood is associated with marriage within the Jewish group.[9]

There are some new and unsettling data in this report. First, given the fact that Jews make up only 2.5 percent of the total United States population, an intermarriage rate of 9.2 percent is really quite small; for if Jews and non-Jews married without ethnic or religious considerations as a factor—that is, at random according to their representation in the United States population alone—intermarriage would constitute about 97.5 percent of marriages involving Jews. Obviously there are religious and ethnic barriers to mixed or intermarriage, but these barriers appear to be disintegrating in a society that claims and, to a large extent, takes seriously the values of tolerance, equality, and freedom of individual choice. It stands to reason, then, as the statistics point out, that to the extent that these values are translated into acceptable behavior, the intermarriage rate will increase, not only between Jews and non-Jews, but also between Protestants and Catholics and blacks and whites. Indeed, this is certainly true for Jews and non-Jews, since statistics show that the longer Jews live in America, the greater their rate of intermarriage.[10]

The NJPS's findings concerning the increase in percentage of intermarriage are perhaps the most disturbing to the Jewish community: between 1955 and 1965 there was a 300 percent increase in the Jewish intermarriage rate; the years 1966–72 saw a rise in the intermarriage rate of about 75 percent over the 1965 statistics. Altogether, then, there has been an increase in intermarriage among Jews of about 500 percent in sixteen years.[11] Small wonder that there is growing concern about the rise of Jewish intermarriage. Small wonder, too, that intermarriage, once regarded as a deviant act, is more and more regarded by the Jewish masses as nearly normative. When what was regarded as deviant, be it the smoking of marihuana, abortion, racial integration, or mixed marriage, suddenly (or even gradually) becomes accepted as normal, the classic arguments against the act lose any potency they may ever have had and become utterly ineffective. This forces people either to accept what they formerly rejected, to develop new arguments against the normalization of a once deviant phenomenon, or, in a more militant way, to seek means to make deviant again what has become normal.

These pages have already cited as an example of the acceptance of the intermarriage phenomenon the growing pressure that the parents of children who have firmly decided to marry non-Jews exert on rabbis to solemnize such marriages. Since Orthodox and Conservative rabbis will not officiate at marriages without conversions, the greatest pressure clearly falls upon Reform rabbis. But this pressure comes from Orthodox and Conservative parents as well as from Reform Jews. It is statistically undocumented but well known to Reform rabbis how many referrals for mixed marriages they get from Conservative rabbis. To a large extent, Reform rabbis have historically, though perhaps unintentionally, led the Jewish community at large to expect them to yield to the Jewish public's will.[12]

As I pointed out earlier, the Reform movement is the branch of Judaism that historically gave religious sanction to what was invalid from the standpoint of halacha but desirable from the nonhalachic point of view of many committed Jews. For example, although Jewish law forbids the remarriage of Jews who have not obtained a *get,* there are virtually no Reform rabbis who refuse to perform a marriage ceremony involving a divorced woman who lacks a *get*. Also, except for extenuating circumstances involving immediate danger to the life of the child, the halacha requires circumcision of the male eight days after his birth, and the rite of circumcision is to be performed by a Jew who is a *shomer shabbat* and *kasher*. When circumcision became routine in American hospitals for non-Jews as well as for Jews, Reform rabbis seldom refused to offer the traditional blessings either before or after the halachically prescribed eighth day and rarely insisted that the person performing the circumcision be a Jew, let alone a halachically observant Jew. The examples could be multiplied almost endlessly—conversion without circumcision or ritual immersion, reciting the *motzi* blessing over nonkosher food at public dinners (such as Rotary Club or Chamber of Commerce), and numerous comparable occasions. What is more, Reform rabbis have apparently received practical approval from all but the ultra-Orthodox Jewish laymen. Why? Because the laymen have agreed with the Reform rabbis that performing halachically invalid, but communally desirable, religious services has helped keep Jews in the Jewish fold. It has allowed these nonhalachic Jews access to religious services and has permitted them to operate within the framework of the American life-style.

This in part explains the June 1973 decision of the CCAR to urge its members not to perform mixed marriages. The pressure from the Jewish community at large to have them officiate at mixed marriages has not diminished, but there is a growing desire among many Reform rabbis to close the gap between themselves and more traditionalist rabbis. There is also a desire not to alienate themselves further from *k'lal yisrael* (which here refers to the State of Israel, since it is usually not American Jews who disapprove strenuously when Reform rabbis officiate at mixed marriages). Reform rabbis who do not wish to solemnize mixed marriages need all the support they can get from other members of the CCAR. Interestingly enough, the lay pressure for mixed marriages solemnized by rabbis also explains the fact that, although the Atlanta resolutions declared opposition to rabbinical involvement in such marriages, the CCAR was at pains to avoid threatening with sanctions any members who chose—as clearly a minority would—to ignore the resolutions.

When what was once considered deviant becomes so frequent as to be considered normal, new arguments and new methods have to be developed to keep the deviance from spreading and gaining even more acceptance. Of course, one can take the position that statistical frequency does not make for normality, let alone desirability. For example, if the rate of venereal disease increased 500 percent in fifteen years, so that 31 percent of the population was afflicted, it might be argued that it was statistically normal to suffer from venereal disease. Nevertheless, it would be difficult to argue that such a statistical prevalence made it desirable or that one ought to adjust to its prevalence and accept it as a fact of life. The same might be said of malnutrition. If in India one-third of the population is suffering from malnutrition, so that malnutrition borders on the normal, it does not mean that malnutrition should be accepted as desirable. Nevertheless, human beings, if they cannot solve a problem and if the problem is extensive enough, seek ways of rationalizing the problem away. To return to the example of venereal disease, before—and even after—a cure for it was available, persons who did not have the disease simply declared those who had it victims of their own wrongdoing. Since one contracted venereal disease though sinning, and since sinners (no matter what their statistical prevalence) were evil, persons free of syphilis, for example, simply decided that syphilitics were not worth much, should be allowed to suffer, and were as much as possible to be excluded from the company of nonsyphilitics. It was God's punishment for illicit sex. Even when relatively easy and cheap methods were developed for treating venereal disease, many elements in the population refuse to "destigmatize" those now cured of the disease. In many states today those who contract venereal disease are forced to give their names, to reveal the names of the person or persons from whom they either contracted the disease or to whom they might have given it, and to be registered in a public record as having had the disease.

In such countries as India, where starvation and malnutrition affect a large percentage of the population, the upper classes employed the caste system to rationalize the situation. Such suffering among a majority of the population was defined as the will of the gods. The unfortunates must have done something evil in a previous reincarnation; otherwise would they not have been born into a higher caste and suffer no want of food? Rather than change the system, the rulers of India used religious concepts to rationalize the status quo.

These two examples have not been selected lightly, for in clear ways they resemble the classic solution that the Orthodox (with considerable help from their friends) offer to the problem of intermarriage. Jewish Orthodoxy has existed since its beginning as a minority religion surrounded by a majority that was thought to be inferior because if that majority was non-Jewish, it was not part of the Chosen People; and even if it was Jewish, its members had broken with the halacha (that is, they had spurned God's will) and, as such, were not worth much thought—except for use as bad examples. In America many of the Orthodox see intermarriage as the calculated result of non-Orthodox Jewish attempts to enjoy the freedom, tolerance, and affluence of America and still pretend to remain part of the Chosen People. Used to always being a minority, but a God-chosen one, the Orthodox, along with other Jews who share their beliefs, are willing to dismiss the Jews who intermarry, no matter how great the increase in their number, as people not worth saving as Jews. Or, sensing the unhappiness of even non-Orthodox Jews over their children's intermarriages, they use the increase of intermarriage as an argument for Jewish isolation and the establishment of Orthodox day schools.[13]

It has been said that when a mixed marriage ends in divorce, two lives are ruined and two religions are vindicated. The argument that intermarriages have a greater chance of ending in divorce is one that has been offered by non-Orthodox Jews who were nonetheless opposed to intermarriage. It is an argument from the heart, so to speak. One says, "Look, I know John Cabot (or Bridget O'Riley) is a fine person. I have nothing against this person and I know you love him (or her). However, even though two people are in love, love is not the same as marriage. Love dulls the intellect. Marriage, even if the love remains intense, involves problems—sickness, economic struggle, raising children. It is hard enough for people who come from common backgrounds. Why add to the burdens of marriage by marrying a person who does not share with you a common history, religion, or ethnic background?" This is a well-meaning argument offered by parents who honestly believe that they are trying to spare their children agony. It also is an argument offered by people who have bought a share of the American dream but who retain a fear for Jewish survival and are beset by another not inconsiderable fear, that of having non-Jewish in-laws. One need not question the sincerity of those who use divorce as an argument against intermarriage. It is, however, reminiscent of the venerable contention that *kashrut* evolved out of the Jew's innate scientific sense. The fact that *kashrut* was developed thousands of years before scientists learned about germs, let alone viruses, did not prevent modern Jews from attempting to rationalize it scientifically by convincing themselves and others that the Jews of antiquity somehow knew that trichinosis comes from diseased pigs.

The analogy holds up for a number of reasons. It is next to impossible to get accurate data on the ratio of divorce among intermarried couples to divorce among Jews. In most states, for instance, divorce records do not state the religion of the divorcing partners. This is the case in California, which has the second largest Jewish population in America and one of the country's highest divorce rates. Moreover, the divorce rate in America, though not as high as it was following World War II, is in many places as high as one of every three marriages. An official of the B'nai B'rith women's auxiliary reportedly stated (without citing the source of her data) that the Jewish divorce rate, nationally, is now equal to that of the country at large.

The longer Jews live in America, the more non-Jews and Jews freely intermingle and share a common experience (e.g., secular education, the reaction to the war in Vietnam), and the smaller the role of religion in the total identity of one's total personality—the more religion as a factor in divorce, just as religion in the choice of selecting a partner for marriage, is likely to decrease. Thus, the argument that mixed marriages are more likely to end in divorce is statistically unverifiable. Even if it were verifiable in the past, it is only likely to be one (not necessarily the most important one) of the many factors that lead to divorce. Even Hollywood demonstrates this: religious or ethnic diversity is not what corroded the Streisand-Redford marriage in *The Way We Were;* religioethnic uniformity could not save the marriage of *The Heartbreak Kid.* Religioethnic factors seem not really relevant in these films.

The most convincing argument against intermarriage is that a religiohistorical community decimated by the Nazi Holocaust and rapidly losing its group identity through assimilation into general Western culture can ill afford the risks to its communal existence that intermarriage seems to pose. Jews 50 percent of whose relatives are not Jewish are less likely to retain their historic ties to the Jewish people. If a couple has a successful marriage and has worked out a way in which their children feel little anxiety from their parents' intermarriage, the couple is perhaps less likely to offer any resistance when their children choose a marriage partner from another religion.

Although the NJPS admits that its data are sparse for the years 1966–72, when the intermarriage rate leaped dramatically from 17.4 percent in 1961–65 to 31.7 percent in 1966–72, they are consistent with what anthropologists such as Margaret Mead and sociologists such as Philip Slater would have predicted. The problem, that is to say, is not specifically Jewish. It has to do with factors in America at large. The generation born after the Great Depression and World War II that reached chronological maturity about 1965 and marrying age between 1967 and 1972—this generation is the product of a different America, an America that saw the civil rights movement flourish, experienced relatively little poverty, saw the Catholic church lose a hold on many of its youth, and encountered virtually no overt anti-Semitism. This generation did not see as its enemy Nazis, Communists, blacks, Jews, or Catholics. Raised as they were to assert their own personal identities, the members of the postdepression, postwar generation tended to view as their enemies the institutions supported and represented by their parents and grandparents—institutions that thwarted their own efforts at self-expression, reflected confusion in the lives of their maintainers, and scoffed at their music, costumery, sex habits, and other attempts to establish their own identities.

This is the situation that produced the anomaly of Jewish youth founding *chavurot* and seeking out the religious (Jewish) costumery and behavior that their parents had laid aside in *their* efforts to gain acceptance in America.[14] Young Jews see their families as stifling their desire to "be themselves," whereas older Jews often enough abandon the political liberalism of the past and seek protection from the radical changes in society and its implied and sometimes observable violence. We are also in an era in which young non-Jews reject what they take to be the coldness and bigotry of their own families and seek in Jews the warmth of family ties and the liberalism that has been associated in America with the Jewish political stance. Thus, both Jewish and non-Jewish young adults seek one another out because they feel that they have more in common with one another than with their separate pasts. The question is: Is all this necessarily harmful to Jewish survival?

Thus far our discussion has focused on Jews in general, but what of Jewish women in particular? The NJPS indicates that, despite the increase in intermarriage, it is still twice as common for Jewish men to marry non-Jewish women as it is for Jewish women to marry non-Jewish men. Why is this so? Why are Jewish women less given to marrying non-Jews? There are many ways to account for the phenomenon, some psychological, some sociological—and most speculative. Before we examine the explanations, however, let the reader be warned that the NJPS is based on who was likely to intermarry, but it did not actually deal with who had intermarried. The survey dealt with intermarriage types rather than with actual intermarriage cases. In 1941–45, the World War II years, when there were fewer men around, four times as many Jewish women as Jewish men were of the "type" to intermarry.[15] The switch from hard data to postulated types can be misleading and does cast findings into some doubt: in this instance, the survey might be interpreted as an indication that the likelihood of intermarriage among Jewish women is increasing, a circumstance that indeed might be encouraging.

Let us examine an interesting fact. Traditionally (here the Reform movement is an exception) Jewish women have been given a poorer Jewish education than Jewish men. They were not prepared for bar mitzvah (bat mitzvah is relatively very new). They were not sent off at age three (as were boys) to the *cheder* or *bet midrash*. They were exempted from all positive time-bound commandments (e.g., praying three times a day). In fact, they were halachically exempted from attending synagogue. Traditionalist men, in their prayers, thank God every morning that they have not been created women; and because women menstruate, the halacha declares them "unclean" for extensive periods in their life. On the argument that Jewish education and institutional involvement reduce the chances for intermarriage, it *should* be true—although apparently it is not—that Jewish women intermarry more frequently than Jewish men.

Next, it might be enlightening (or at least ecumenical) to reverse the question: Why do twice as many non-Jewish women marry Jewish men as non-Jewish men marry Jewish women? This introduces us to the question of choice, which takes us into an unexplored aspect of the question. Perhaps as many as one-third of the marriages in America take place *after* the woman has become pregnant (at least this was probably the case before the enactment of more liberal abortion laws). We know that Jewish women tend to achieve a higher level of secular education, make greater use of medical specialists (gynecologists, for example), and enjoy in general a higher economic status.[16] Thus, should Jewish women engage in premarital sex, their greater knowledge of and access to birth control methods plus their economic ability made them less likely to *have* to marry because of pregnancy. This increased the choice possibility for Jewish women and non-Jewish men. Such advantages to Jewish women are relatively new, but they may well be consequential.

Let us explore the less novel interpretation of the two-to-one phenomenon. Since women, even in the 1966–72 data, represent only 9 percent of those who intermarry, it is still possible to apply to them the deviant measure. One can argue, that is, that those few women who intermarry constitute a small minority, that their act of intermarriage is probably due to individual psychology, e.g., a bad relationship with father or mother, a bad experience with Jewish institutions, an overromanticization of marriage so strong that it defies the reality of the difficult problems involved in an intermarriage, or pregnancy before marriage. Such an argument—coupled with the fact that most Jewish women appear to have strong family ties, tend to respect and love their parents, and have a better chance of financial security married to a Jewish husband—would indeed make deviants of those Jewish women who intermarry. Furthermore, as the NJPS indicates, even when Jewish women do intermarry, whether their husbands convert or not, they are more likely than men (even those whose wives have converted) to see to it that their children are given a Jewish education and to raise their children as Jews. Using the theory of deviance, this finding might suggest that when Jewish women intermarry there is considerable residual guilt. The intermarried women try to compensate for the break with their families by assuring their parents that their grandchildren will be Jews.

This is a tenable argument, especially when it is reinforced by the historical fact that the Jewish community has allowed Jewish women less freedom, that is, has applied more social pressure against them when they dated non-Jews. While Jewish men, too, have always been expected to marry Jewish women, they have had to face far fewer strictures against premarital sexual encounters with non-Jews. Jewish fathers and brothers did not regard with horror a sexual encounter with a *shikse*. Recognizing that the sex drive is strong, and wanting their own women to remain virgins until marriage, Jewish males have tended to look upon premarital sexual encounters between Jewish boys and non-Jewish girls as compensation for the male sex drive; at the same time, of course, the arrangement has offered some insurance that their own daughters and sisters would remain virgins. Furthermore, Jewish girls were more closely watched than Jewish boys, so that any encounter they had with non-Jews would have had to be clandestine. Generally the males initiated the date and called for the girl at her home or frequented places where "nice" girls are not supposed to hang out. If the date was not to be kept secret, the girl had to receive the male at her parental home and thus risk exposure of the fact that her date was not Jewish. Since Jews normally regarded non-Jews as "out for one thing," they made it difficult for a Jewish girl to have anything but a secret meeting with a non-Jew. The secrecy, if the girl was willing to risk it, probably made the encounter more exciting, if also more productive of guilt.

There are strong historical arguments against intermarriage by Jewish women, but it is possible to counter some of them. For one thing, Jewish girls away from home are not subject to the same external control as when they are at home.[17] Dating does not have to be clandestine. The raising of female consciousness has had its impact on Jewish women, so that they, like all Americans, feel that they have a right to be free to be themselves. The statistics on the intermarriage of Jewish women, moreover, may be misleading. In the past, marrying a non-Jew was such a disgrace, and represented for both the girl and her family so sharp a deviance, that she may have dropped entirely out of contact with Jews and disappeared into the non-Jewish world. Hence, there may be many more Jewish women married to non-Jewish men than the statistics gathered by even the most sophisticated sampling techniques would indicate.

This last is only conjecture, but let us turn now to other speculations. Given the relative freedom of today, the raising of female consciousness, the fact that at least 70 percent of Jewish women go to college and are, in secular terms, the best educated group of women in human history, the odds in favor of more intermarriage among Jewish women are likely to increase dramatically. Further, one may add that in non-Jewish America, unlike in traditional Judaism, religion is considered the woman's province.[18] Hence, as the NJPS indicates, a non-Jewish husband is likely to leave the religious upbringing of the children to his wife. This same factor may account for the finding, also reflected in the study, that Jewish men Americanized enough to intermarry are sometimes Americanized enough to let their wives have control over the religious upbringing of their children. Thus, if one is concerned with preserving the children for Judaism, it could be argued that an increase in Jewish female intermarriage, whether or not her non-Jewish husband converts, might not be as dangerous for Jewish survival as the intermarriage of Jewish males (even where the non-Jew converts to Judaism). If a way could be found to reverse the Jewish male and female intermarriage rates (given intermarriage as the wave of the future), the prospects for Jewish survival, through the maternal raising of children and the "womanizing" of Jewish religious institutions, would be more hopeful.

I should like to comment on what I regard as three of the most solvent findings in the NJPS: (1) the prevalence of belief in the Jewish religion and continuing belief in God; (2) the conversion rate; and (3) the rate of participation in temples and synagogues.

The study indicates that nearly all intermarrieds believe in some way in one God or in Judaism. Remember that old saying, "There are no atheists in foxholes"? Apparently there are no atheists in marriages either (the analogy need not be taken too literally). We are confronted with a problem—Jews, Protestants, and Catholics together. When universalism is stressed and all religions seem to be different only in "trivial" ways such as ethnicity, history, customs, and ceremonies (which is the position held by many), then intermarriage is not viewed as a violation of God's will. In fact, it may be justified as a step toward ushering in the messianic era. Consequently, the fact that many intermarrieds believe in God is good news to those who are also believers, but this good news is tempered by the possibility that God's primacy is being accepted at the expense of the particular demands each religion has claimed necessary for His proper service. In that event, a barrier against intermarriage has been shattered. Among Catholics and Protestants there appears to be a decline in belief in the trinity, in the mysteries of the sacraments, and in the rituals of the church in general. Jews, at the same time, with notable exceptions, have accepted the notion that belief in God is something apart from the intricacies of theology and the historical reasons for observing halacha and ritual.[19]

To add a further dimension to the problem, many Christians no longer able to believe in the mysteries of their churches find in the Jewish home—the historically familial and ethnically warm ceremonies and customs of Judaism—a very attractive alternative to the religions into which they are born, which place less emphasis on home celebration and the religious function of the family in general. Thus, in an age in which the traditional theology and mystery and authority of Christianity are no longer taken as a given and in an age that is witnessing the breakdown of family ties, Judaism may well provide a viable alternative to Christianity. Judaism, liberally interpreted, may offer an attractive option to disillusioned Christians. Indeed, many case studies of Christians who marry Jews indicate that the attraction to Judaism preceded the meeting with the future Jewish spouse.[20] Why, then, are the rates of conversion to Judaism and of participation in Jewish institutional life relatively low?

The NJPS does not make it clear who performs or solemnizes the marriages of the more than 75 percent of intermarrieds who do not convert. Theodore Lenn has reported that 44 percent of Reform rabbis officiate at marriages without conversion "under certain circumstances," while a substantial number of Reform rabbis, probably between 200 and 250, officiate at mixed marriages and, at most, impose minimal conditions on the nonconvert.[21] Undoubtedly a sizable number of mixed marriages are conducted by Reform rabbis. In addition, although figures are unavailable, thousands of mixed marriages are conducted by civil authorities, and some (one suspects fewer than those by rabbis or judges) are performed by Christian clergymen.

The question of conversion, however (aside from halachic considerations and Reform rabbinical consciences), may not be as important as one would think. Although the NJPS tells us that about half of the intermarried non-Jews, regardless of conversion, regard themselves as Jews, 75 percent of the women, whose conversion rate is higher than that of non-Jewish men, plan to raise their children as Jews. This is further confirmed by the NJPS data that indicate that, where the male is unconverted, "in a very large majority of cases, when the wife is Jewish though initially the husband is not Jewish, children are raised as Jewish." In contrast to non-Jewish women who marry Jewish men, "few intermarrying non-Jewish males have converted."

What, then, of conversion? As a rabbi I favor conversion and would even go so far as to warn potential converts that, among the Orthodox and in Israel, only conversion under Orthodox auspices is halachically acceptable; without it, couples in which the mother is not of Jewish birth will deny their children the right to be considered Jews. Still, I do have misgivings as to whether an insistence on conversion is any particular guarantor of Jewish survival. My doubts seem to me well founded. People born after World War II in general regard themselves as highly individualistic. They object to being told that they have to abide by particular requirements. They want to *want* to do something. Insistence on conversion seems to them coercive. On the other hand, if the non-Jew considers it a *personal* decision to be Jewish, his or her ego integrity is not felt to be compromised, and the person, as the NJPS seems to indicate, eventually considers himself a Jew and voluntarily raises the children as Jews. The formal act of conversion, although not the intermarriage itself, often creates great anxiety in the parents of the non-Jew (as it certainly does in the parents of Jews when conversion to Christianity is involved). The insistence on conversion will probably not be a deterrent to engaged couples. They will be married by someone, Jewish, civil, or Christian. Insistence on conversion can, however, lead to strong guilt feelings toward the non-Jewish parents; whether consciously or not, the coerced convert may be led into pleasing his parents by declining to join a synagogue and by giving them grandchildren with freer access to non-Jewish institutions.

Finally, the summary of the NJPS states that the more strongly the parents are committed to Judaism, the less likely there is to be an intermarriage; but, conversely, a strong antipathy on the part of Jews toward Judaism is likely to produce an all-Jewish marriage (perhaps due to rebellion against the Jewishly self-hating parents). Moreover, when Jews intermarry, they tend to describe their upbringing as only marginally Jewish and their parents as indifferent to their dating non-Jews. Clearly, it seems that parental attitudes toward intermarriage and toward Judaism constitute the central factor in determining whether or not their children intermarry. Here we are faced, if we view intermarriage as a threat to Jewish survival, with both an insoluble problem and a challenge. To begin with, it is too late to change the "marginality" (admittedly, the term needs definition) of Jewish parents. The acceptance of Jews into the mainstream of American life, the decrease in the notion that adherence to halacha is essential to being a good Jew, the amorphous theology of Judaism, the inherent incompatibility of the Chosen People concept with the American value that "all men are created equal," the experience of anti-Semitism and the Holocaust—all these tend to increase a marginal Jewishness. To this configuration must be added the fact that the synagogue has not proven itself a very satisfying institution for most American Jews. The NJPS shows that intermarrieds are more likely to be active in

Jewish community functions outside the synagogue than within, but this is equally true of Jews married to Jews. Those who intermarry at the highest rate are the products of this marginality-*cum*-nonsynagogalism—plus the post–World War II child-rearing practices and the rapidly changing contemporary society that inspire the young to reach out in an effort to define their own identities. This, one suspects, is an irreversible trend.

But what of the future? Barring an upsurge in anti-Semitism, there is unlikely to be a decrease in the acceptance of Jews into the larger society. Hence, the possibility of isolating Jews from Gentiles, even if desirable (and few American Jews think it is), is remote. Furthermore, the circumstance that Jewishness is ill-defined but does have appealing aspects—such as a strong emphasis on home celebration and on family ties while (among all but the ultra-Orthodox) de-emphasizing dogmas, mysteries, or laws laid down by a distant authority—might make Christians want to join the Jewish group. Our society cannot be expected to change at a slower rate, nor is it probable that the young will be raised less permissively. It seems improbable, too, that parents (in a youth-oriented society) will fail to look to their children as role models, rather than the reverse. The seeking of identity and self-definition is likely to go on. The raising of female consciousness and the tolerance of deviance in the name of self-fulfillment are not likely to decline.

Unless one is concerned with genetic purity, intermarriage in itself need be no threat. Assuming, as the NJPS indicates, that most of the children born of intermarriages are raised as Jews, the threat to Jewish survival is in numerical terms no greater than the decline in the Jewish birth rate among marriages between Jews. The major threat lies in the quality, not the quantity, of Jewish life; that is, Jews must not take their Jewishness for granted. They must be taught that Jewish life, with its stress on family ties, its willingness to take up the challenge of changing times, its attempt to come to grips (not through dogmatic authority but through careful thought) with the needs of Jews, offers an admirable community religion. In addition, Jews (and here the so-called counterculture helps) must be reeducated or reconditioned so that they are able to be emotionally demonstrative, not afraid of challenging God or Jewish institutions, not afraid of expressing joy and sorrow, love and hate, in the context of the synagogue and other Jewish institutions.

The intermarriage of people committed to seeking personal fulfillment and able to find that fulfillment within a Jewish framework will not produce marginal Jews. Perhaps, then, intermarriage among their children will decrease; or if not, at least it will not be the curse that we have been taught to believe it is. It may even be a blessing. If the rise in intermarriage goads us into attempting to seek solutions to Jewish marginality, it could be one of the strange ways in which God seeks to bless the Jews.

··················································· ·······

## chapter four

# Why Me, Lord?

The Good Lord has blessed unorthodox Jews in many ways, not least among them by inspiring in numbers of young people the will and determination to study for the rabbinate. What God's ultimate judgment on mixed marriages might be I would not venture to predict, but it does seem unarguable that God delights in mixed blessings. The process of preparing oneself to become a Reform rabbi, to spend years on the frontier of preordination study and experience, must fall—for the candidate at any rate— well within the category of mixed blessings.

The process of becoming a Reform rabbi bears a good many similarities to other processes of professionalization. As in other professions, the candidate is required, first of all, to earn a bachelor's degree at a recognized university or undergraduate college; then, upon admission to the seminary, he is expected to pass through a five-year course of study concentrating on subject matter deemed professionally appropriate. At some point the candidate must serve "preprofessionally" in a congregation either on a part-time (i.e., weekend) basis or in an internship under the tutelage of someone who has already achieved ordination. Upon graduation the candidate, now an ordained rabbi, joins a professional organization, the CCAR.[1]

The professionalization of a Reform rabbinical student offers certain problems that although similar to those facing other preprofessionals, are unique in certain aspects; but before these can be elaborated upon, it is necessary to discuss the place of the rabbinate within Judaism and the place of Reform Judaism within the framework of other manifestations of the Jewish religious structure.

The rabbinate, which at times has attained great authority within Jewish communal life, has not traditionally gained its authority through the prerogatives normally associated with a priesthood or an ordained ministry. That is to say, a rabbi has not been viewed as a person who, by virtue of either a calling or the certification of his ecclesiastical superiors, is singularly qualified to celebrate the life-cycle events and those days set aside as holy by the religious calendar. The fact is that Judaism includes no rite or holy day that cannot be performed or celebrated by a layman, i.e., by someone lacking rabbinical ordination (*s'michah*). *S'michah* has traditionally been granted to those who, in the eyes of their rabbinical masters, have achieved depth in, and facility with, that vast aggregation of law and lore that historically constitutes the body of Rabbinic Judaism. Usually, but not invariably, one granted *s'michah* was judged qualified to decide cases involving questions of the interpretation of Jewish law. The rabbi, then, was not seen as a priest who held in his hand the keys to absolution or salvation, but as a functionary whose superior facility with the law made him worthy of respect and rendered him an authority in problems growing out of the law.[2]

Reform Judaism stands in a peculiar relationship to Jewish law. In essence, in order to establish itself as an alternative way of practicing Judaism, it declared the law to be binding only upon those who wished to be bound by it. Reform Judaism claimed to be concerned only with the spirit of the law—and if that spirit appeared antagonistic to newer and presumably better insights, either as a result of the zeitgeist or of a holy spirit of some sort operative in science and the humanities, then even the spirit of the old law could be declared unworthy for a Reform Jew. Since, traditionally, a rabbi was one who had greater knowledge of the law—a law now no longer held crucial to the Jewish religion—precisely what meaning could there be to Reform *s'michah*?

Assimilation and the growing place of professionalism in the Western world during the past century offer partial answers to this question. Assimilation played its part by providing modernizing Jews, mostly people of Central European birth or ancestry, with some role models with which to operate. One of these models was the Protestant ministry; a second derived from the university professorship. Protestants generally had no sacraments to be administered only by priests, but they did have a clergy whose responsibility it was to baptize, to solemnize weddings, to conduct burials, and to officiate at services of public worship, whether on the Sabbath or on other holy days. Furthermore, it was the duty of this clergy to preach to the congregation about what God required of them. Yet this was not quite a sufficient model for Jews accustomed to a clergy steeped in religious literature and known for its learning. In the universities of Germany and America, however, they found another model.[3] While it was true that Jewish law was cumbersome and antiquated, it was equally true that Jews entering the world of Western attitudes—primarily through economic pursuits or through migration—found themselves lacking the "culture" of the bright and promising new civilization. They saw the great cathedral-like universities and their secular priesthood, the professors, and they liked what they saw. Surely, it was not too much to expect that their own scholar-clergy class would help them gain access to a culture that seemed to have so much to offer Jews. So, for several decades in the late 1800s and early 1900s, Reform rabbis were given a fairly clear-cut job definition. Reform rabbis were the first among their rabbinical peers to consolidate their new position in Judaism by forming a professional organization that, as in other professions, set standards for all who wished to gain entrance into the profession and kept out impostors, i.e., those not certified by the organization. The professional organization—the CCAR—was to publicize these standards so that an innocent layman might not mistakenly accept services from someone lacking professional credentials.[4]

But the problem was not so easily solved. On the contrary, it was aggravated by time and social realities. For a considerable length of time, the Reform rabbinate could operate in a Jewish vacuum. The Orthodox rabbinate and Orthodox Jews refused to recognize Reform legitimacy, but that scarcely mattered. In terms of prestige and power in American Jewish life, the Reform rabbinate was in the saddle. When outsiders—that is, Eastern European Jewish immigrants and even the new rich—joined a Reform temple, it was on terms laid down, not by Jewish law, but by the bylaws of the congregation. Often these bylaws forbade the wearing of hats and prayer shawls and scorned the use of phylacteries. Boutonniered ushers politely—and sometimes not so politely—enforced these codes. Nearly everywhere it violated the temple's rules to have a *hupah* at a wedding or to observe the tradition of breaking a glass at the conclusion of the wedding ceremony. Decorum and its demigods did away with the loud music provided by the wailing of a cantor or by the boisterous bands that played at traditional wedding celebrations. Schnapps, the morning reward given the pious *minyan*-maker, was thought incompatible with the solemnity required of the worship service, and finally, during Prohibition, even wine, the sine qua non of traditional Jewish ritual celebration, was permitted to be replaced by grape juice. In all this, however, or perhaps because of all this, the status of the Reform rabbi was maintained, and the temple bylaws usually, though not inevitably, gave the rabbi full freedom of the pulpit. Freedom of speech meant freedom to preach, even if it did not mean freedom to chant in the manner traditionally associated with Jews at prayer.

Until the Great Depression the Reform movement and its rabbinate was a self-sustaining, self-validating Jewish "denomination" in America. Its membership was elitist or sought to become so through association with it. Its rabbinate and its professional organization, the CCAR, took stands on social issues that were by contemporary American standards bold and even at times ultraliberal.[5] To the extent that there was movement in any direction, it was toward humanism and away from tradition. Reform's most controversial issue centered on the extent to which the movement wished to acknowledge the nascent Zionism (Jewish nationalism) that was making some headway in Palestine, among the immigrant Jewish masses in America, and even among such notable, well-established Jews of Central European stock as Louis D. Brandeis and Julian Mack. Reform rabbis themselves, to be sure, were increasingly men of Eastern European antecedents, but what was true of the laity was no less true of them: they came to Reform Judaism for what it offered them—an opportunity to gain a position of leadership in the Jewish community, respect from the non-Jewish community, and a platform from which to advance interpretations of Judaism in a manner that seemed to them in keeping with the best, most liberal, most enlightened spirit of the age.[6] During the depression, however, subsequently as a result of the Judeophobic horrors of World War II, and finally through the postwar expansion of synagogue affiliation, the Reform movement underwent strategic demographic changes.

During the depression membership in Reform temples dropped off precipitously. Those who were attracted by Reform's social stance went further to the left and abandoned or ignored the synagogue. Others could not afford the congregational dues. World War II made Reform's universalistic, meliorist position tragically pollyannish in a Western civilization that, either through the Nazi ovens or through general European and American indifference to the Jewish plight, had tried to rid itself of Jews, no matter what religious or social philosophy they held.

The growth of synagogue affiliation following the war and lasting into the early 1960s led the Reform movement into a competition for members with the rapidly expanding Conservative movement.[7] In this race to attract second- and third-generation American Jews of Eastern European descent, the Reform movement could only partially rely on its old allies, universalism and snob appeal. To a large extent it had to demonstrate that it was in the mainstream of ethnic consciousness by meeting its new constituency's demand for more ritualism.[8] One traditional ceremony, the rite of passage known as bar mitzvah, previously dismissed as primitive and unimportant by nineteenth- and early twentieth-century Reform, returned with a vengeance to the ceremonial schedule of Reform temples. Such circumstances made it impossible for the Reform rabbinate to continue representing itself as a clergy different from the other rabbinates of America, although the other rabbinates had meanwhile had their public images reshaped in imitation of their more prestigious Reform colleagues.

From the mid-sixties to the present there has been rather little to differentiate the members of Reform from those of Conservative congregations—with the possible exception, as recent surveys have indicated, that Reform congregants expect their rabbi and synagogue to be less outspoken in demanding conformity with traditional observances. Reform congregants now seem to expect their rabbi to be competent to deal with certain legalistic matters concerning ritual observance, but, as we have already seen in connection with such matters as mixed marriage, flexible enough to bend or even to ignore these halachic prescriptions.[9]

The Reform seminary, the Hebrew Union College–Jewish Institute of Religion, is where a student is supposed to master the skills that will enable him as a novice rabbi to both feel and act like a professional. For a variety of reasons, however, the seminary cannot devote itself wholeheartedly to grinding out professionals. For historical, psychological, and sociological reasons, the Reform seminary (to a very large extent, this is true of the Conservative seminary as well)—counting among its ancestors the

Central European university—has come to imagine itself as mainly a center for the "scientific" study of Judaism. This image enables many faculty members who come primarily from traditional, observant backgrounds either to rationalize their break with tradition on scientific, scholarly grounds or to remain observant and Orthodox while occupying a professorship in an institution that has historically stood at odds with all but the fringe of Jewish law. The school was founded in 1875 at Cincinnati with a pragmatic purpose. Its founder, Isaac Mayer Wise, had in mind initially no Reform seminary; he sought to establish an institution that would train professionals for the pulpits of American—not necessarily liberal—synagogues.[10] Thus, from its very inception the seminary had to acknowledge some obligation to the rabbinate as a public profession, even though most of its faculty have preferred to think of it as a center of *Wissenschaft des Judenthums*, a graduate school of higher Jewish learning.

In consequence, only a minimal portion of the curriculum has been devoted to courses in the practical rabbinate. These courses include classes in public speaking, sermon writing, religious school educational techniques, and human relations, a potpourri that includes the sociology of the Jews, basic concepts in humanistic psychology, and the fundamentals for counseling the troubled. All told, these courses comprise at most 25 percent of the curriculum. The remainder of the course of study, with the exception of a few courses in philosophy, theology, and history, is focused on a painstaking scrutiny of traditional sacred texts. There is no course in traditional or even Reform observance that instructs the student rabbi how to act as decision-maker and officiant. The student is simply expected to acquire this knowledge, so fundamental to his professional role, on his own from his fellow students or through trial and error in the weekend congregation he serves as a prerequisite for ordination.[11]

When, as we said earlier, the Reform movement was self-validating, congregants were willing to accept the rabbi's interpretation of ritual and legal practice as his prerogative. Furthermore, until after World War II, most Reform rabbis had come from Orthodox homes. They knew traditional practice, the laws pertaining to the observance of holy days and life-cycle events, from personal experience. After World War II a paradoxical situation developed in which the Reform movement sent its own sons to be rabbis at a time when more and more of its membership came from homes whose contact with Judaism was through its traditional practitioners. This meant that even though these new Reform Jews were minimally observant of Jewish law themselves, their major experience of weddings, funerals, and bar mitzvahs was through the agency of Orthodox and Conservative clergymen.

Thus, we have the classic dilemma that faces many new Reform rabbis and that I propose to illustrate by an actual experience report presented to a class in human relations by a student serving as a weekend rabbi. The report gives us a poignant picture of a twenty-five-year-old man struggling to maintain himself as a competent professional in the face of a host of problems that threaten his view of himself as both a rabbi and a young, bright, rather good-looking citizen of contemporary America.[12]

On New Year's Eve, 1969, the [student] rabbi of M. "got stoned" (from alcohol) for the first time in his life, while visiting friends on Long Island. He went to bed at about 5:30 A.M., and was awakened by the master of the house at 11:15 A.M. "There's a long-distance telephone call for you from M." The rabbi hurried to the phone. "Hello rabbi. This is Joe Schmo from M. I hate to bother you at an hour like this, but we've had a tragedy down here. S. has done away with herself. It happened at about 7:00 A.M. this morning. Her parents and [her husband] want you to do the funeral, rabbi." The [student] rabbi's heart sank, and his hangover hung even more. His immediate answer was, "Well, what about [M.'s other student rabbi] Rabbi X from HUC in Cincinnati? I'm sure he would be able to come down. And it would be much easier to come from Cincinnati than from New York. Or what about Rabbi Y?" Joe answered: "Rabbi, we already discussed all these possibilities. The family wants you. You know that this is especially tragic because S. was due to give birth next Wednesday."

The rabbi agreed to fly to M., and Joe suggested that he, the rabbi, make the flight arrangements. The rabbi then spent approximately an hour on the phone making reservations, and between calls he sipped a scotch on the rocks to calm his nerves. *This was to be his first funeral.* He became so nervous and mixed up that at one point he had three different sets of reservations. Finally he decided that he would fly into Cincinnati that evening (January 1st), and he called M. to let them know his plans. He would fly to M. the next morning.

The rabbi left his friends and flew to Cincinnati. *There were so many things that he did not know —had the baby died also? Was he expected to give a eulogy? What prayers could he say in a situation like this?* These were only a few of the questions that bothered the rabbi. On arrival at HUC, he saw that one light was flickering in the dormitory (it was still vacation), and he went up to seek advice. It so happened that the friend had conducted several funerals at his own congregation and that his own father had committed suicide.

He advised the rabbi to find prayers as appropriate as possible, not mentioning too often how "she was taken from us." He also advised that the rabbi write a short eulogy which would be nice for almost any funeral. All in all, he felt that every reference to her "life as an example" in any way would be in poor taste. The rabbi really did not know how to start, and it was already 2:00 A.M. So he borrowed a book of eulogies, and from this book, the Reform rabbi's manual,[13] and his own brain, he wrote a one-page eulogy which everyone had thought was completely tasteful.

The rabbi left for M. early on the morning of January 2nd. The flight lasted for about forty minutes, and it was during this time that the rabbi decided how he would arrange the service itself. He used the second service for funerals found in the rabbi's manual, and decided that he would use the prayer for a child which seemed appropriate.

The president of the congregation met the rabbi at the airport and began talking about pertinent matters. The president emphasized that the girl's parents were Orthodox (something which the rabbi later discovered was not true; any adherence to tradition, he later realized, would appear to be Orthodoxy in the eyes of the congregation's president). The baby was still alive, but it appeared that there was brain damage from a lack of oxygen for too long a period of time, and it seemed that the baby would die also. Before entering the home of the parents of the deceased, the president insisted upon paying the rabbi his expenses.

The two of them entered the home and were confronted by all the members of the family. Immediately the phone rang, and the father answered it. He called for the rabbi and said: "Rabbi, you know that S.'s husband is not Jewish. He agrees that S. should be buried as a Jew, but *we* feel that this service should be for him as well. Father John is on the phone here, and he would like to speak with you. He has talked with K., and I think that he would like to take part in the service. But we'll leave that *all* up to you." The rabbi took the phone and introduced himself to the minister, an Episcopalian, who was a personal friend of K.'s but not his minister. (K. is not affiliated with any church and attended services with S. at the Temple. He even sits on the temple board, but has not converted.) The minister said: "Rabbi, I would like to meet you very much, and I want to talk with you. Can I see you soon? Perhaps we could go over to K.'s together." The rabbi agreed that he and the minister would meet at the home of the parents, and that the two of them would go to visit K. together. The night before, the rabbi had read [the] views of Reform's most highly regarded legal scholar, Rabbi Solomon B. Freehof,[14] on the problem of Christian clergy taking part in funerals. The rabbi had always told himself that he would never co-officiate with a minister, but Freehof wrote that it was all right for the minister to take part in the eulogy as long as he did not mention Jesus. But, until the minister arrived, the rabbi had not yet made up his mind.

The rabbi and minister rode in the minister's car to see K. The minister said that he would like to take part in the service, but that if the rabbi did not want him to, he would not. The rabbi said that he would not mind in the least, "as long as you don't mention Jesus." The minister answered that he would of course do no such thing. The rabbi told him that, if he so desired, he could add to the eulogy, perhaps making it a little more personal. When the minister asked if he could read the 23rd psalm, the rabbi answered, "Yes, of course."

They arrived at K.'s house, and he led them into a bedroom. In this room was a bassinet, a copy of Benjamin Spock's book on child-rearing, and a few toys hanging from the ceiling. The two guests sat on the bed, and K. began to talk, although, as he said later, he was under the influence of tranquilizers, and he did not really realize what he was saying. K. was the one who did the talking, and like the parents, he claimed that he did not know why she did it. "On New Year's Eve, she lay on the couch and hugged me and said, 'Honey, you have made this pregnancy so much easier for me. The next year will be so wonderful for us with a baby!' We went to sleep, and she did not appear to be depressed at all. The next thing I knew it was morning, and I heard a shot, and I went into her bedroom and found her. It was so horrible. I never saw anything like it in my life. She was cuddled up in bed like she always is in the morning, but the gun was by her head. And there was so much blood. I'll find out where she got the gun, if it's the last thing I do. I must know. The police don't know yet, but I'll find out. O, God, if I live to be a hundred, I'll never know why she did it."

K. then sobbed a little, and the rabbi tried to comfort him. "K., there are some things we never know. We'll never know why she did it, or where she bought the gun perhaps. We just don't know what goes on in someone's mind." He shook his head affirmatively, he and the rabbi clasped hands, and the minister asked K. what he could do at the funeral. K. said: "Whatever the rabbi here agrees to." The rabbi said that he thought that it would be nice if the minister would read a psalm and add to the eulogy. K. said that this would be all right with him.

Meanwhile, Joe S. had come to K.'s home, and he took the rabbi back to the home of the parents. The rabbi could see that the family was not really Orthodox, he had eaten at their home about one month before, with K. and S., and knew that *kashrut* (dietary laws) was not observed. He asked Mr. O., the father of the deceased, if he wanted any traditional rituals performed. He said that he did not, that he did not even want the rabbi to wear a *kippa* (skullcap). "S. would have wanted it that way, and we must remember that K. would not understand traditional observances." Mr. O. said that he did not even plan to keep any *shiva* (seven-day mourning) period.

Joe and the rabbi then left for the funeral home. But, on the way, Joe felt that he wanted to have the car washed, so they stopped at an automobile car wash establishment. There was a long line of cars, and the hour was 2:45. They emerged from the car wash ten minutes later and raced to the funeral home. The casket was open, even though the rabbi had asked that it be kept closed. The deceased's mother said, however, that since the death, many people had not had the opportunity to visit the family and to get the story straight. So there were all kinds of ugly rumors in the air, such as "she blew her head off." The rabbi thought to himself: "She did shoot herself in the head, so they're not so far wrong. What in the hell do they need an open casket for?"

The rabbi entered the funeral home and went to the clergy room in the back, through the sea of people. He did not go over to the casket, and at no time did he see the body. Somebody came up to him and said: "Did you see her? You could see where the hole was in her head." Someone else approached the rabbi and said that he was in mourning as his brother had died one month ago. Could he attend the funeral according to Jewish Law? The rabbi was very nervous, and he impatiently answered: "Well, you're here already, so it really doesn't matter, does it?" The man's wife then announced that her late father had been a *kohen* (a member of the priestly caste traditionally forbidden contact with the dead), and could she attend the funeral? The rabbi said: "When you got married you gave up your tribe and took your husband's. Of course you can attend! You've been to funerals before, haven't you?" The couple joined the crowd, apparently satisfied.

The funeral home was packed, and several people said that it had been the largest funeral ever in M. K. is a judge, and S. was very active in mental health work, and at one time had been a TV weather girl. The service was short, and everyone assured the rabbi that what he had said was in excellent taste. A majority of the people went to the cemetery afterwards, the service of interment lasting just about ten minutes.

The rabbi was among those who returned to the home of the parents. He made it a point to console members of the family, and since he had mentioned to several people that this was his first funeral, not a few came over to him to tell him that he had done a good job. At one point, after quite a few of the people had left, the rabbi was sitting alone at one end of the room. The deceased's mother came over to him to hold his hand. A peculiar feeling came over him—as if *he* were being consoled by the mourner.

At first, the rabbi planned to leave in the afternoon, but Joe and the president told him that a memorial service was planned for that evening in the house of mourning, and they thought that it would be nice if he would stay on. So he arranged to fly back to Cincinnati the next morning. As the time approached for the memorial service, the house filled up with people. The local shul has a *minyan* every evening, and when someone is in mourning, the *minyan* is held at their home. It was evident that most of the people present were members of the shul, and the rabbi asked Mr. O. whether or not he should make the service more traditional and whether or not he should wear a *kippa*. Mr. O. answered that it should be all Reform.

There were about 100 people at the memorial service. As soon as the service began, Mr. O. slipped a *kippa* on his head, and the rabbi was shocked. After the service, the rabbi went home with Joe, and he spent the night at his home. The next morning, the rabbi flew back to Cincinnati. Just before he boarded the plane, Joe told him that Mr. O. wanted to give him an honorarium and would do so shortly. The rabbi protested, but not too much.

On his next few visits, the rabbi visited the [O. family], and K. came to services at the temple. Mr. O. slipped him an honorarium of a fair amount of money, half of which came from K. He thanked the rabbi for everything and the rabbi in turn thanked him. The baby died within two weeks and was buried by the other student rabbi of the congregation.

The rabbi was very unsure of himself throughout this experience and looked to others to make decisions for him. He let Mr. O. decide the type of service and he told not a few people that this was his first funeral. In turn he was praised, Joe sending a beautiful two-page letter of the highest praise to the Hebrew Union College. The congregation sent another such letter a few weeks later. The rabbi's insecurity must have been rather evident, because as reported above, Mrs. O. at one point came over to him to hold his hand. But the rabbi is no longer afraid to perform funerals. His first experience, in which he apparently was successful, gave him much self-confidence. But he realizes that this self-confidence came as a result of praise which he openly sought.

This episode from the life of a Reform rabbinical student in his last year at the seminary demonstrates problems faced by all preprofessionals—i.e., whether or not he had done the right thing, employed the proper technique, come across as competent to his clientele—but it also illustrates some unique problems faced by a candidate for the Reform rabbinate.

Our student rabbi is secular to the extent that he gets "stoned" on the secular New Year. He is boy enough to be living with his parents; friends have to wake him from his stoned sleep. Yet he is fully aware of his professional responsibilities. Realizing the inherent difficulties that the situation presents, he at first tries to avoid them by suggesting that he step aside for someone more seasoned in the role of rabbi. Failing this, he returns hastily to the seminary where he seeks expertise—but not from a member of the faculty (perhaps due to the late hour, but undoubtedly because he hesitates to show his ignorance in an area that most of the faculty feel is so insignificant that they have omitted it from the prescribed course of study).

After gaining what help he can from a colleague, he goes to a collection of questions and answers about Reform Jewish practice written, not by a current or recent member of the faculty, but by a respected Reform rabbi (a former faculty member, but of decades ago) who, by searching the Jewish legal literature, has provided solutions amenable to the needs of other Reform rabbis. Rabbi Freehof's responsa nearly always find in the literature some traditional rabbi's liberal opinion on the issue in question; Freehof is often able to take it one step further to make the contemporary rabbi's break with the law appear less severe. Even here, though, in the problem of sharing the funeral with a non-Jewish clergyman, Freehof offers a stricture against allowing the Christian to invoke the name of Christ, an eventuality over which the rabbi has little control.[15]

However, even after the student has made his peace with two essentially "illegal" (i.e., untraditional) practices—eulogizing a suicide, who, according to Jewish law, is not permitted burial in sanctified ground, let alone a eulogy, and co-officiating with a non-Jewish clergyman—he is still troubled by other aspects of the tradition. He is expected to honor the wishes of the deceased's family—the wishes, that is, of a father who regards himself as Orthodox but does not want the rabbi even to wear a skullcap, and of an unconverted non-Jewish husband who sits on the Reform synagogue's board of directors. Should he not be sufficiently confused by these facts, he next finds himself having to answer questions of Jewish law posed to him at the funeral itself by relatives of the deceased with some knowledge (or at least experience) of the tradition.

Then, to add to the confusion of what is expected of a Reform rabbi, he is told *not* to cover his head while conducting a service at the house of mourning by the father of the deceased, who slips a skullcap on *his own* head. What is the student rabbi to make of this—that the older man does not wish the rabbi to appear too Jewish to the gentiles? Or that he does not regard the rabbi as authentically Jewish enough to wear traditional Jewish garb?

Thus, we see that although the Reform rabbinate meets all of the criteria of a profession, historical and sociological factors have combined to force the professional into a marginal position. Not blameless in this process is the Hebrew Union College, the Reform seminary, which thus far has failed to meet its full responsibilities—has failed, that is, to provide the requisite skills and, more fundamentally, the requisite sense of adequacy and authenticity so vital to a professional who must meet a demanding public.

But what if the seminary does a better job? Even then the rabbi must confront the ever-changing nature of the American Jewish community, which wants a rabbi to give it roots while expecting him not to stand in the way of what the community feels it wants. The seminary's failure to respond more seriously and effectively to his need for professional self-authentication makes the Reform rabbi's position, already tenuous and insecure, self-defeating as well. In addition, both seminary and seminarians, like the ordained rabbi, are compelled by historic and sociological circumstance to maintain themselves on an exposed and precarious frontier. That is the fate—and at least potentially the glory—of Reform Judaism in contemporary North America.

## chapter five

# A Rabbi Named Sally

The frontier represented by the Reform rabbinate is not a fixed one; the ordination of a woman rabbi in 1973 made it clear that, even sexually, the Reform rabbinate and its constituency feel bound by no past norms. Since then, the Reconstructionists, another active unorthodox group, have ordained a woman, and the Hebrew Union College has admitted several women to rabbinical candidacy.[1]

Rabbi Sally Priesand's ordination by President Alfred Gottschalk of the Hebrew Union College–Jewish Institute of Religion at Cincinnati, in June 1972, generated more interest by the mass media in a Jewish clerical leader than had ever been the case before—something of an index to the impact the first American female rabbi may be expected to have on the American Jewish community. What I propose to demonstrate here is that different groups within American Jewry will greet Rabbi Priesand's ordination in very different ways.

There is one group in particular for whom the emergence of a woman rabbi is singularly fortuitous and a much desired event; for another group of American Jews, however, the ordination of a woman arouses ambivalence much more than enthusiasm; and for still another group the event may prove disastrous. The groups I have in mind are American Jewish organizational women, the Reform establishment, and the American male rabbi.

Before I present my analysis, however, let me provide some background information. In the first place, it is not difficult to surmise why Rabbi Priesand has received so much publicity. Given an American public that grows indifferent even to the second man on the moon, the first *anything* is something of a godsend to the media. As of this moment there are fewer women rabbis than there are people who have been to the moon! Add to this the fact that Priesand's career as a candidate for ordination roughly coincided with the emergence of Women's Liberation as an object of American concern. Although this coincidence between an individual's sacred calling and historical reality is, Rabbi Priesand has insisted, sheer accident, it is certainly a happy accident both for the media and, as I intend to show, for Jewish organization women.

It is also useful here to place the first ordination of a woman within the context of the American Jewish religious scene. As anyone discovers who takes the trouble to undertake a serious probe of the issue in question, there is no clear Jewish legal argument against a woman's becoming even an Orthodox rabbi (unless one accepts the highly dubious dictum that *minhag* has halachic force).[2] Although Jewish women are by Jewish law exempt from the obligation to obey commandments that require a fixed time for their performance, there is no legal obstacle to a woman's carrying out any commandment she so chooses. Even the fact that menstruation makes a woman a source of impurity is no obstacle to her becoming a rabbi. It is only males a woman can render impure, not the ritual objects that a rabbi might have occasion to handle. Furthermore, a rabbi, though an expert in Jewish law and lore, is no administrator of sacraments. The only prerogative that the tradition may be able to deny a woman rabbi is that of validating marriage contracts. According to Jewish law, however, rabbis are not required as officiants at weddings; they are mere decorations when they choose to officiate, so that, halachically, even the loss of this prerogative need not mean much to a woman rabbi. In America, of course, rabbis act as agents of the state at weddings, and there is nothing to prevent a woman from acting as an agent of the secular authorities.

In short, there is no valid *legal* reason why heretofore no American women have been ordained even as Orthodox rabbis. The objection to women rabbis stems not from legal formalities so much as from the social and psychological attitudes preserved by the tradition. To begin with, women are accorded a legal status comparable to that of Jewish slaves and minors.[3] They may be well treated and even respected, but in status they are always inferior to adult Jewish males. Therefore, the classic argument against calling a woman up to the Torah is not that the law denies them such an honor, but rather that strangers might assume that the synagogue did not have enough learned men present to call up to the Torah.

Then, the folklore of Jewish tradition includes what might be characterized as a genuine fear of a woman's innate power. She has the power to lead even the most pious Jewish male astray.[4] She can by her very presence arouse a male and at the least take his mind off his sacred obligations, if not lead him to even greater sins. Women, therefore, have to be segregated; married women must have their heads shaven and be kept isolated from men other than their husbands. If Jewish tradition has allotted an inferior legal status to women, it certainly has not denied that she possesses powers that male Jews are well advised to respect, fear, and attempt to diffuse. Thus, traditional Judaism would be unlikely to elevate a woman to a position of public power and prestige in the religious realm. It is not, therefore, from the seminaries of Orthodoxy that a woman rabbi would have emerged, nor is it from the Jewish Theological Seminary of America, which trains rabbis for the Conservative movement. The Conservative movement, to be sure, long since abolished the segregation of women at worship services and of late abandoned other symbols of women's inferior status: in some Conservative congregations, women may be counted as members of the worship quorum. But although the Conservative movement accepts the de facto will of its members, it is reluctant on the whole to encourage them to dismiss Orthodox tradition.

Consequently, it is from within the ranks of Reform Judaism that one would have expected the first woman rabbi to emerge, as indeed she has. It would, however, be a great oversimplification to claim that the Reform movement has encouraged women to study for the rabbinate, and it would do even greater damage to the truth to suggest that only Reform Jews are enthusiastic about the ordination of "Rabbi Sally."

Certain facts should be acknowledged. First, although Reform Judaism has from its inception accorded women a legal status equal to that of men, has been on record for half a century as being unopposed to women rabbis, and has not hesitated to operate on the basis of its liberal, democratic impulses even when these clashed with tradition, it remains a fact that before June 1973 there were no women ordained as rabbis—Conservative, Orthodox, or Reform. Second, although the Hebrew Union College put no obstacles in Priesand's path when she was a student, it certainly made no special effort to call attention to her newsworthy ordination. It never attempted to push her on the Jewish public, nor was she given nearly as much institutional publicity as had been lavished in the past on a Japanese candidate for the Reform rabbinate. Third, although Priesand's fellow students, future Reform rabbis, may not be said to have acted toward her with any degree of hostility, none may be said to have expressed any overt joy at seeing her fulfill her calling during their tenure as rabbinical students. Indeed, one must marvel at the contrasting responses that the first woman rabbi evokes: on the one hand, she is hailed by the media and by large numbers of American Jews as a truly remarkable individual; on the other hand, she is treated by Reform officialdom and in particular by her fellow students with an indifference bordering on diffidence. She is a genuine heroine to nearly every non-Orthodox Jewish women's organization; she was given financial assistance in her pursuit of rabbinical studies by the B'nai B'rith Women, a group not known for espousing radical causes; and she was received with as much enthusiasm by the sisterhoods of Conservative congregations as by their Reform counterparts. Still, this enthusiasm and excitement have not spread to the broader male-dominated Reform movement on which her pioneering activity has conferred distinction.

The cause of these paradoxical responses flows from three distinct realities that converge in what Rabbi Sally symbolizes. The materialization of a female Reform rabbi at this time is received with ambivalence by the rabbinate of the Reform movement; it wins admiration from the members of Jewish women's organizations; and, finally, it constitutes a definite threat to the sexual identities of American rabbis in general.

I think it necessary to distinguish between the ambivalence felt by the Reform movement, which I see as a sociological problem, and the threat that a woman rabbi poses to the individual identities of rabbis, which I would view as a sociopsychological problem. The Reform movement in America is currently in the throes of a severe identity crisis that directly results from certain historical and sociological situations beyond the control of the movement: (1) the collapse of the ideology of progress, with its concommitant belief in the triumph of universalism over particularism among American Jews; (2) the emergence among committed Reform Jews of a strong drive toward ethnic identification, centered around the State of Israel; and (3) the emergence of the counterculture, which, I have attempted to demonstrate, is potentially devastating to Reform Judaism.

It is fairly easy to see the relationship between the first two points and the ambivalence that the Reform rabbinate has shown thus far toward its ordination of the first American woman rabbi. It is, to a large degree, similar in kind to Reform's internal struggle over mixed marriages, the rites of conversion, and a host of other variables that exemplify points of divergence between Reform and the other branches of Judaism. From its founding until World War II, Reform could be certain that emphasis on the rule of reason and universalism and a corresponding de-emphasis on emotionalism and particularism represented the direction in which all intelligent Americans were heading. A modified Marxism seemed reconcilable with the teachings of the biblical prophets on social justice, and with the aid of Protestant biblical critics it appeared easily demonstrable that there was a direct causal nexus between the lofty social idealism of the prophets and their alleged antagonism to cultic practices. When Reform was sure of the direction in which humanity was moving, it seized the initiative in attempting to mold Judaism and the Jews in the image of a messianic era. If other Jews wished to join them, it would be on Reform's terms. It was in this period of exuberance and confidence that Reform went on record in favor, not only of the full equality of women, but even of the logical outcome of such equality, a woman rabbi.[5]

The Nazi Holocaust put an end to the messianic illusions that the nineteenth century had aroused and that the melting-pot ideals of turn-of-the-century America had seemed to reinforce. Now, after Auschwitz, Jews everywhere began to see themselves as survivors rather than as Elijahs announcing the imminent arrival of the Messiah. Reform Judaism began to regret some of the violence with which it had earlier repudiated ethnicity and tradition. As early as the 1930s, it had begun abandoning its objections to Jewish nationalism.[6] It began searching for ways to move back into what it now felt was normative Judaism. By 1971 its rabbinic seminary was enlarging its new Jerusalem branch to accommodate the requirement that all Reform rabbinical students spend their first year of study in Israel. Some of its rabbinic leaders were urging the CCAR to repress colleagues willing to officiate at mixed marriages.[7] The World Union for Progressive Judaism, Reform's international arm, was moving its headquarters to Jerusalem. An issue of the *Central Conference of American Rabbis Journal* carried an article by no less classical a Reform liberal than Leon I. Feuer calling for a halt to criticism by American Reform rabbis of social problems in Israel—hardly a prophetic stance.[8]

This context—a rabbinate and a fairly large constituency of Jews seeking to strengthen ties with Jews everywhere, especially in Israel—cannot be ignored. It is within this context that our theme of mixed blessing reasserts itself, this time in the guise of a woman rabbi. What a woman rabbi represents within Reform is an impulse toward novelty, democracy, and timeliness; simultaneously, however, she and other women candidates for the rabbinate call attention to the fact that Reform Judaism is not simply a less authoritarian version of traditional Judaism (the image Reform would like to project in Israel). Reform in America is the branch of Judaism expected to help Jews adjust most readily and effectively to the tensions of being Jewish *and* American. This is a difficult role for Reform to play, and most Reform rabbis would just as soon not be reminded that Reform is expected to play it. This is one reason why the Reform rabbinate might view its newest achievement, Rabbi Sally, as something of a mixed blessing.

Rabbis who see it as their responsibility to normalize the position of Reform within the framework of non-Orthodox but people-centered Judaism will tend to be uncomfortable with a woman rabbi.[9] Others, however, will see nothing problematic in the emergence of a woman rabbi; these are rabbis whose openness to innovation makes them recognize that something must be done to fulfill a mandate that more and more Jews seem to be giving to the synagogue: *save our children!* It is clear, we have seen, that there is a growing anxiety on the part of parents that their children are being lost to the Jewish community. Part of this anxiety stems from the visible increase in the rate of mixed marriages, with or without conversion. The anxiety also accounts for the blurred message Jews are giving the rabbis with regard to their solemnizing marriages where one partner has not converted to Judaism (or, more recently, with regard to rabbinical participation in joint wedding ceremonies with Christian clergymen). Jews, including non-Reform Jews, simply don't know what Reform rabbis should do, for they fear that refusing to give the blessing of Judaism to a child who is marrying a non-Jew will break what they know to be at best a tenuous tie to the Jewish group.

There is, however, another reason for their increasing anxiety about their children. Not only Jews but nearly all Americans recognize that their children belong not to them but to their own generation. The life-styles of their children are at such radical variance with their own that they can no longer guarantee that proferred inducements will lure their children back to the values of the parental institutions after a few wild-oat-sowing years. That is, although Jews in America have nearly always had to be child-oriented, since their children were more familiar with the American way of life, American Jewish adults have felt that, by accommodating themselves to American standards of success and by co-opting fashionable life-styles, they would be able to lure their children back from wherever they might have strayed. Although a son might choose not to go into his father's scrap business, he could be counted on to affiliate with Jewish institutions modified to suit third- rather than second-generation Jewish needs.

Jewish institutions, from the family to the synagogue, have been highly responsive to the needs of their members. Within one generation, for example, Jewish family size shrank from an economically burdensome 7 or 8 children to the much more manageable 2.2 children of the upper-middle class.[10] It took synagogues no more than one generation to acquire clean-shaven English-speaking rabbis and decorous religious services that would suit the sense of propriety of an Episcopal deacon. American Jews have heretofore been able to hold their children for Jewish institutions through a combination of rapid adaptation and the colonialization of its more successful young adults. In other words, a Jewish institution would not exclude a Jewish physician or lawyer from membership on its board of directors merely because he publicly flaunted religious norms. A young executive certainly would not be kept off the Jewish Center board because he raced speedboats on Saturday afternoon. The adults of the Jewish community felt that they knew how to manage whatever modifications were needed to ensure the loyalty of their children. Parents might have had to promise their daughter a trip to Europe to get her to go through with her confirmation, or they may have had to pay their son-in-law's tuition to get him to become their son-in-law rather than their daughter's roommate, but this procedure worked. Mr. Patimkin, in Philip Roth's *Goodbye, Columbus,* could always get Brenda to renounce Neil. The Robinsons were not as successful with Elaine, the daughter in *The Graduate,* a movie that could just as well be about Jews as about Gentiles. Furthermore, if adaptation, colonialization, or outright bribery failed, there was always the guarantee that sooner or later Jewish youth would discover that it was only in the Jewish community that they were truly welcome. Even education and wealth could not buy for Jews the status and ego gratification of the non-Jewish world. Now the situation is different, and with their unerring instinct for survival, Jewish adults are desperately worried because they no longer know how to guarantee the loyalty of their children. What financial inducements can be offered children who prefer blue jeans and work shirts to cashmere sweaters and who would rather hitchhike than have their own cars?

Today even the less overtly materialistic rewards for good conduct—a college education, for example—seem hollow. Most students know that schools do not educate, just as they know that churches and synagogues do not inspire spirituality. How is one to convince a person who has viewed the sunrise after taking mescaline or watched and heard the Who while stoned on marihuana that a rabbi's sermon or a temple choir is what a religious experience is all about? In addition, how is one to persuade young men and women who have lived in multiethnic and sexually liberated communes that a person cannot feel comfortable with any other than his "own kind"? Jewish parents turn to their rabbis for help, but their rabbis are helpless because they are more a part of the problem than a part of the solution. Therefore, rather than confront the seriousness of the situation and attempt to come to grips with the depth of the problem, they fall back on the old solutions. They put on rock services once or twice a year. They hire advertising firms to sell their image and point with pride to the fact that Judaism is so "with it," so much in tune with the times, that there are even women rabbis. Thus, although Jews seeking a broader intra-Jewish ecumenism may find it somewhat embarrassing from the standpoint of public relations, a woman rabbi *is* a gift from God, since her existence provides the Jewish public with the notion that its religious institutions are changing to meet the needs of which Jewish parents are so painfully aware.

Although it might be difficult to prove, it is interesting to speculate on the widespread enthusiasm that Jewish women's groups have demonstrated for the first woman rabbi. These groups, a check through their program calendars of the last several years shows, have devoted surprisingly little attention to the Women's Liberation movement. I use the term "surprisingly" because, as we know, middle-class Jewish women are usually in the vanguard when it comes to collecting information. Since they are, by and large, better educated then their non-Jewish peers, and since, according to at least one source, they read more widely than almost any nonacademic group in America, one would expect them to reserve room in their organizational schedules for speakers who represent the various Women's Liberation organizations, especially in view of the fact that these organizations make speakers so readily available.[11]

Yet, if we examine the literature of Women's Liberation in the light of what we know to be the socioeconomic status of Jewish organization women, the apparent lack of interest in Women's Lib is not so surprising. In fact, it is their very position in society that makes them most threatened by Women's Lib. Jewish women, particularly those between the ages of twenty-five and forty, are those for whom the call to freedom might have the greatest intellectual appeal. They are well educated. They are well read. They were encouraged throughout their academic careers, prior to their marriages, to compete with males and, probably to a greater extent than any group of females in history, to develop themselves as individuals. How much more abrupt, then, must be their encounter with the realities of suburban life? How much more difficult must be their acceptance of the relative anonymity of being a housewife? Certainly this is true of women who, typical of the pattern in this country in the fifties and early sixties, got married either while in college or immediately thereafter and then embarked on careers, ostensibly to support the family while the husbands prepared for a profession. For a brief period in these women's lives, *they* were the ones with the careers, while their husbands confronted the sometimes degrading anonymity of graduate and professional school. During this period these women experienced what later had to be rationalized as role reversal, but what at the time was merely an extension of the promise made them when they were encouraged to excel in school. To be sure, while these women were being asked to compete with males in school, they were being socialized at home into the more feminine role that would make them suitable mates. Nevertheless, such a woman must have suffered some loss of self-esteem when once and for all she found herself Mrs. David Goldberg and no longer Alice Schwartz, B.A. *magna cum laude,* teacher of creative arts.[12]

If the socialization into domesticity has been successful, the birth of a first child and the accolades given her as a mother by parents, husband, and synagogue might cause her to suppress temporarily the other socialization she has received. It may also partially account for the tremendous ambivalence she has towards her children. On the one hand, they afford her attention from significant others; on the other hand, they become the measure of her success. Failure as a mother would mean yet another jolt to her identity. This, of course, imposes on her children a burden that, combined with the time she and her children must spend in suburban isolation, must make her role as a mother potentially explosive.

Small wonder, then, that Jewish organization women appear uninterested in contact with the more strident exponents of Women's Liberation. In order to make peace with their lives, they must manifest a certain amount of cognitive dissonance; that is, they must strive mightily to rationalize the conflicts built into their identities—the academic and career competence that measured their success until age twenty-five or so and that of "good Jewish wife and mother" that must sustain them from the first child onward. If the conflict is as severe as one would logically expect it to be, the need to proclaim their own satisfaction and to shield themselves from contrary evidence could be expected to be very strong. But if it is true, as I maintain, that members of Jewish women's organizations fear the aspects of Women's Liberation that relate most poignantly to their own lives, wherein lies their obvious affection for the woman rabbi? It is precisely within the context of their rejection of militant Women's Lib that Rabbi Sally's tremendous appeal finds its center.

From the purely contemporary angle, one might claim that Jewish women are as proud of producing a pioneer, in a period when everyone is women's rights conscious, as Jewish men would have been, had there been a Jewish astronaut when America was space conscious. This, I believe, may account for some of the interest that makes the woman rabbi a celebrity. However, I believe that to mistake enthusiasm for self-congratulation and newsworthiness for sincere admiration is to underestimate greatly the sociological and sociopsychological meaning that the existence of women rabbis holds for organized Jewish womanhood.

First, if it is true, as I would argue, that there is a great deal of suppressed resentment toward the social position that Jewish women find themselves wedded to, and if this social position is demonstrably a by-product of their being Jewish, then to see the rabbinate—that bastion of Jewishness and Jewish male supremacy—successfully stormed should give Jewish women some vicarious feeling of triumph.

Then, because her decision to become a rabbi came many years before Women's Liberation took shape as a movement, Sally Priesand was unconsciously able to ignore whatever broader implications her entering the rabbinate might have. She is a person with a genuine calling. While she recognized the historic significance of her action, she could never be faulted for selecting her career on the basis of this significance.[13] On the contrary, she viewed history as an obstacle to her calling. Furthermore, Rabbi Priesand has manifested so deep a commitment to other aspects of the Jewish tradition that, one is led to suspect, whatever damage she has done to the precedents of tradition is likely to cause her some inner conflict. Furthermore, if anything beyond her calling has been operative in her career as a rabbinical student and an ordained rabbi, it has been a deliberate effort to do nothing that might arouse whatever latent traditionalism or male chauvinism there may be at her seminary and her congregation. Rabbi Priesand, then, from the point of view of a group hesitant to confront the implications of Women's Liberation for their own lives, is the perfect instrumentality for acting out in a non-threatening way whatever sympathies these women might feel for Women's Liberation. In addition, her appearance, while attractive enough, is neither that of a Gloria Steinem nor that of one who eschews the feminine role. She is feminine without being coquettish, and she in no way inspires male disclaimers as to her sexual identity. She is, whatever pejorative connotations some might see in the word today, a lady. She threatens no one. It is not her goal. She is the perfect first woman rabbi.[14]

Finally, the factor that may be the most important—and that may have become lost in our attempt at a deeper analysis—is the strong possibility that the very fact that there have been no women rabbis before in America is what non-Orthodox American

Jews regard as the anomaly. It may be that a woman rabbi is insignificant to all but her male counterparts. There is evidence to support the above contention within American religious life in general and in Jewish life as it has been restructured by America.

I want to elaborate on this somewhat. Not only is there the obvious historical fact that America has given the world what is, to my knowledge, the only major religion founded by a woman, Christian Science, but there is a more subtle psychological fact that lies in the American resolution of masculine feminine conflicts. Whereas all but a few psychological "hard hats" would argue against the view that there is such a thing as a biologically determined set of personality traits that are sex-linked, almost everyone would agree that, prior to the generation of the "flower children," Americans tended to characterize certain traits as masculine and others as feminine. Among the traits American folk wisdom has ascribed to women are emotionality, mercy, sensitivity, intuitiveness, and the prerogative to be inconsistent ("a woman has a right to change her mind"). One other characteristic, although it is not in the same category as the above, should be considered: the right to wear regularly skirt-like garments and to don colors in the pursuit of one's livelihood.

Clergymen have for a long time been the only American males permitted to wear vestments, robes, and cassocks and to manifest emotional responses to situations and to such so-called feminine things as poetry without having their masculinity called into question. Artists, poets, and musicians have always been allowed emotionality, of course, but at the risk of having considerably greater doubt cast upon their manhood than have clergymen; and even for clergy permitted these characteristics (probably because they need by definition to be able to interpret literature and to be receptive to the spirit) there is no little doubt cast upon their manliness. In fact, to this day seminaries are among the few graduate or professional schools that demand rigorous psychiatric and psychological screening of their applicants. A review of the history of this screening quickly reveals that it grew out of a fear on the part of laymen that seminaries were magnets for homosexuals.[15]

Why should laymen feel that homosexuals might be attracted to the clergy any more than to any other profession? This stems undoubtedly from a biased suspicion of priestly celibacy. Men who renounce sexuality and live in societies of other men arouse the suspicion of Americans who historically combine fear of Catholics with homosexual panic. There is, however, an even subtler reason for suspecting that the clergy would attract homosexuals. The American notion is that what a clergyman does is really woman's work that only by historical accident has become the province of men. What do clergymen do? They preach (contrast the ever verbal preacher with Gary Cooper or John Wayne). They work with small children. They visit the sick. They read poetry. They talk about love. They put on flowing robes. And, most important to our argument, they are not supposed to be interested in sex. They are supposed to find sex dirty and embarrassing. They are not even supposed to know about it. Only the most gauche individual tells an obscene story in front of his clergyman. In male-dominated America, all of the above activities are thought to be the activities of women, especially of ladies. Who, the American male layman must ask himself, would want to do woman's work if not a "queer"? Hence the insistence on psychological screening.

It is on this point that American and Jewish traditions part company. The association of sensitivity, emotionality, and impracticality with femininity—along with the association of femininity with a disinterest in sexual matters—is foreign to traditional Jewish custom. On the contrary, in certain Jewish communities where status was based on learning, nearly the opposite standards of judging masculine-feminine behavior were operative. It was the woman who was supposed to be pragmatic, unromantic, functionally illiterate; the men were to be the dreamers, the writers, and even the teachers of very small children. In puritanical America traits associated with femininity are those also connected with the clergy; in Jewish tradition these very traits were supposed to be the ideal for all men. The model man, the rabbi, was to embody these traits to an even greater degree than his lay counterpart.

What I am suggesting, then, is that the assimilation of American Jews can, in part, be measured by the degree to which the masculine-feminine stereotype so integral to the conventional, Puritan-derived American way of life has been grafted onto the American Jewish psyche. There is evidence, I believe, that as yet Jews have not entirely accepted American sexual role assignments. If the participation of Jewish males in the interpretative professions such as the arts and literature is any indication, it appears that conflicts of sexual identity are not produced in Jewish males around the linkage of emotionality with femininity. It is still somewhat amazing to find a Jewish hunter, for example.

Many saw in Barry Goldwater a *goy* less because his family converted than because he emphasized ruggedness and tough talk.
Jewish cowboys, though surely they exist, remain hard to imagine, not because Jews are incapable of getting along in the out-
doors, but because the image of the cowboy as male par excellence
is one of insensitivity and lack of emotion. Jews have not yet come
to typify American machismo, and if the counterculture, with its
devaluation of machismo, becomes embedded firmly enough in
the American middle-class value system, they may never have to.

Thus, it can be argued that, whereas the traits associated with
Christian clergymen are those that put the clergyman in conflict
with the norms of masculine behavior among Americans, these
same traits pose a minimal threat to a rabbi's sexual security. To
the extent, however, that these "macho" values have infiltrated
Jewish norms of masculinity and femininity, the rabbi does suffer
considerable discomfort. For example, the rabbi may see nothing
unrabbinic in his desire to play sports, read poetry, listen to sexual jokes, and, while still unmarried, pursue eligible women; but
he is often dismayed to discover that some of his congregants find
this behavior inconsistent with his career and make it known
that they want the rabbi to resolve this inconsistency by abandoning precisely those activities that are the prerogatives of the
American male. In other words, they would rather have the rabbi
write poetry than be a tennis champion, and they would prefer
him to blush at off-color jokes rather than attempt to top them—
even though they themselves have come to view poetry and sexual diffidence as somehow unmasculine.

Being treated as a lady is threatening to the new male rabbi
and creates an identity conflict that he may attempt to resolve,
but only in counterproductive ways. There are many instances in
which student rabbis serving their first pulpits report a desire to
dress in a deliberately "mod" fashion, use profanity publicly, and
become veritable raconteurs of dirty jokes. Later on, it is not so
uncommon for a rabbi to be surprised to learn that he is actually
an object of sexual desire for his female congregants. In more than
a few instances, rabbis have taken advantage of their newly
discovered (or recovered) charms. It is fairly easy to surmise how
unpleasant it is to learn that, by aspiring to what has been historically the most desirable Jewish male role, one has done so at the
expense of one's American masculine image. The occasional masculine "acting out" associated with rabbis probably can be traced
to this conflict.

The appearance of a woman rabbi is thus an anomaly. It is likely that, in a country that has feminized the clerical role, the actual emergence of a female rabbi represents a very minor shift from mental image to physical reality. On the other hand, to Jewish clergymen who for the first time have found their masculinity impugned by their career choice, the actual existence of a woman rabbi may serve once and for all to confirm what they have often been warned: that being a rabbi is no job for a Jewish boy.

## chapter six

# Unbinding Isaac

Thus far we have discussed the unorthodox rabbinate as a profession. In purely sociological terms, that is precisely what the unorthodox rabbinate is—or, for that matter, the Orthodox rabbinate or any group of intellectual individuals banded together to protect the rights and status of the careers for which they have been schooled. Even so, in the case of the rabbi (no matter how unorthodox), as in the case of anyone ordained, professionalization is often no more than a contemporary way of referring to a sanctified vocation.

The rabbi is more than a professional, even if he or she places the attainment of professional status above any other value. The rabbi is embodied myth, the successor of Moshe Rabbenu, who rediscovered the covenant between God and the patriarchs Abraham, Isaac, and Jacob. The unorthodox rabbi may be fully contemporary in dress, speech, and deed, yet he is primordial in the collective and individual unconscious of the Jew. The rabbi becomes an object of transference in representing the totality of Jewish holy men and women, of feared or beloved parents or siblings, of the entire family that is the Jewish people, past and present.

For this reason I think it essential to interweave myth and modern professional identity, as a reminder to rabbis and laymen alike that the two realms are in fact one and inseparable. Knowl-

edge of this truth would be a mighty step toward reasonable fulfillment of the expectations of both rabbis and laymen. We are
dealing here with a memory basic to Jewish identity—and again
a mixed blessing.

When I discovered that the veterinarian to whom I had been
taking my cat was Jewish, I said to him, "You must really love
animals to be a vet." He said to me, "Some animals I like—some I
don't. Just because you're a rabbi, do you love every Jew?"

Until we become professionals ourselves, we often fail to realize
that a professional's identity and his occupational role are not one
and the same. Even after we come to understand that rabbis or
professors have identities separate from their rabbinical or
academic roles, we find it hard to include other professions in this
generalization. Our needs and our expectations are such that we
cannot, for instance, allow our surgeons, nurses, and objects of
heterosexual fantasies much distance between the behavior we
expect to accompany their professional roles and the actual selves
that lurk beneath those symbols of competence, rank, and status.
To meet our own needs, we join together in our minds their roles
and their identities.

It seems to me that much of what Jewish tradition does with
the patriarch Isaac is similar to what is done with rabbis. In order
to make Abraham the hero of the Akedah—or to make God less of
a villain—Jewish tradition had to either see Isaac as totally non-
descript or turn him into a Jesus voluntarily accepting his fate.[1]

Both the tradition and the rabbis themselves need Isaac as an
object in their search to find some meaning in God's mysterious
acts, but is it fair on this basis to deprive Isaac of his own subjective response to his experiences? May Isaac not be permitted an
identity of his own apart from the mythic role our tradition has
assigned him? Can Isaac not be permitted to speak after his final
victimization—after the wife he did not choose has helped the son
he did not choose rob him of his blessing?[2]

The blessing that was to be Isaac's only reward as the son of
Abraham has been wrested from him, and now he lies sick and
blind upon his bed, complaining to whoever is the Eliezer[3] of his
old age. In the following dialogue we imagine what must have
taken place.

"You know what troubles me most about my binding? Not that
my father almost killed me, not that I was so frightened that I, a
thirteen-year-old boy, become incontinent like a baby, not the

looks we gave each other when he answered me by saying what neither of us believed, that God would provide the lamb.

"Those things don't bother me. What bothers me more is that, when I realized what was happening, I was fully willing to die. I was so imbued with my father's wishes that if he needed to sacrifice me, I *needed* to be the victim.

"I couldn't even dream of struggling. Where was the impulse to come from? When the two of us walked together, it was really two of *him*—not father and son, just Abraham present and future.

"And now, dear friend, as I lie here, wondering if your hand is even your hand, I wonder also what I might have been if I had not been the Single One—an Ishmael[4] whom I used to tag after until they drove him away or an Esau whom they wouldn't let me bless. It is too late to change my life—but, dear friend, might I change my fantasies?"

The servant Eliezer might choose to deal with Isaac's complaint in a number of ways. Being a loyal servant of Abraham, he might help Isaac accept what history has ordained for him. Through long hours of intense analysis, Isaac may come to imagine that the servant is Abraham. When this finally happens, there is a good possibility that Isaac will find himself in the same bind. Now, however, he won't complain, because he'll have been convinced that what is wrong with him is not that he was willing to die then, but that he is bothered about it now.

Perhaps that is the proper tack to take. History would be on his side, for the fact is that, although Isaac himself appears to have been something of a shlemiel—nearly killed by his father, tricked by his wife, cheated by his son—he nevertheless served Judaism well by acting as a transitional figure between Abraham, who made the break with the past, and Jacob, who wrestled with God and man to become Israel.[5] Isaac was the antihero between two heroes, the bridge over which the B'nai Abraham passed to become the B'nai Yisrael. So, although history seems to have gained nothing from Isaac's existence except time, history nevertheless is not unappreciative. It accords Isaac his place among the patriarchs. His name is mentioned thrice daily in the Amidah between his father and his son.[6] Indeed, one could be convinced that Isaac had better adjust and slip quietly and passively back into Torah and *tfilah*.

Some Jews, in fact, would become angry with Isaac were he to seek a change in his destiny. Some would say to him: "You have no right, granted your opportunity on behalf of the Jewish tradition, to seek to assert yourself. Learn to accept your fate. Some people are innovators. Some people are conservators. Each role is important, and when the history books are written, there is room for both. What history has *no* room for are the unfulfilled fantasies of the role players."

A very good case could be argued for making the precomplaint Isaac into the patriarch of the rabbinate. The rabbinate can, and perhaps should, be seen as a passive, conservative profession: Rabbis are to be the mediators between the various wisdoms of the Jews. Granted that a certain something is gained or lost in the translation from tradition to contemporary life; nevertheless it ought to be the rabbis' concern that the addition or subtraction be kept at a minimum. Indeed, were I a teacher of homiletics, I would want to stress that, when officiating at life-cycle events, the rabbi is to be only the instrument through which the tradition, the family, and the collectivity communicate. A rabbi who acts as though the deceased has died in order to give him an opportunity to display his erudition deserves to fail his course in homiletics.

I have noted for many years, through ongoing studies of Reform and traditional congregations, that the so-called cult of personality is much more dominant in Reform. I speculate that this is because Reform rabbis, having relatively little of the tradition to transmit, have instead presented themselves as though *they* were Judaism incarnate. I have noted this and have decried it, for I know that Judaism is too important to be made to suffer when the rabbi gets a better offer from a bigger temple.

Those who care about Judaism pray for rabbis who know and can transmit, rabbis who are Isaacs ready to be sacrificed, if only by subduing their egos, for the sake of the tradition and the future of Jewish learning.

However, as much as one might want to tell Isaac to quit complaining, and as much as one might want to congratulate the psychiatrist who can get Isaac to step passively back into his mythic role, conscience will not permit it. Cogent as it is, the argument for passive transitional figures does not ring true from the purely humanistic point of view, because to rob a person of his right to individuality for the sake of any institution, no matter how exalted, necessarily makes one feel guilty. While it may make no difference to history whether Neil Armstrong would really have rather been a poet, it would make a difference to Neil Armstrong, no matter how well he did his job as a nonpoet. Somehow one would feel bad to think of him risking his life, stuffed in a little capsule, simply because nature had seemingly endowed him with a perfect disposition for space travel. And one is equally disappointed in—and guilty about—the system that produced Neil Armstrong if, as a newspaper reported, it is true that he has never read a novel or a poem and is incapable of discussing an idea.

Something—if only a naïve belief in the right of each man to fulfill his potential or a more sophisticated but equally unprovable belief that each man ought to be free of the feeling that he dare not act on his own—makes me hope that Isaac did not experience his life the way I have imagined him articulating it to Eliezer. For just as I feel that something is wrong if there is too much of a discrepancy between a man's role and his identity, so I feel very sorry for the man who has so identified with his occupational role that he seems to have no other identity. Initially one is angry when one calls up an old classmate and his wife, also an old friend, says, "I'll see if the *rabbi* can talk to you now." Then one feels sad, suspecting that the man and his wife must feel that beneath the title there is no person. Such a man's sense of worth is so connected to what he thinks others value in him that he contracts himself, he diminishes himself, to fit inside the limits of his occupational role.

The apparent opposite happens to stigmatized individuals. If a person happens to be lame, he is often perceived as a limp with a man attached. Through achievement he may manage so to distinguish himself that his stigma is overlooked. Yet often the stigmatized individual finds a certain comfort in knowing that he has an identity, albeit a negative one. Hiding behind a role, or, worse, becoming the role to the exclusion of one's selfhood, is really a sort of self-stigmatization.

But it is not merely out of pity for the individual who loses his identity to his role that I address myself to the problem of overidentification with roles. Nor is it, as one might suspect, out of a fear that overidentification with symbols of rank and status might lead to a slavish submission to authority structure. This has already happened. What, then, is the ultimate objection to resolving dilemmas of identity through overidentification with roles? Not only does such a resolution rob the individual of his individuality; it deprives society of its only source of change—the person who is uncomfortable with himself or with his surroundings.

An overidentification with a role solves the tension between self and society in a way as detrimental to society as to the person. The reason is that freedom to act depends upon a human being's ability to trust the correctness of his own interpretation of his subjective response. Most individuals will not act on their impulses or intuitions in the social realm unless they are certain that they reflect some group consensus. Since occupational role behavior is, by definition, playing a part that has been written by others, a person who becomes inseparable from his role becomes totally separated, totally alienated, from his subjective experiences.

Organized religion is dependent upon two separate phenomena, a stable self-perpetuating role structure and individual religious experiences. Where the former is concerned, religion does not differ from any bureaucratic organization. It is only through the latter that religion distinguishes itself from any other institutional structure. At the present time, the main reason that Judaism seems to be in crisis is that its organizational aspect shows itself much stronger than the capacity of its members for deriving or recognizing religious experiences.

The problem facing Reform rabbis is not, as Charles Liebman claimed some years ago, that the Hebrew Union College has no notion of what the Jewish community is all about.[7] Thank God if that is true—who wants rabbis leaving the college programmed? The major problem is that somehow few rabbis are secure enough either as learned Jews or as adequate human beings to be open to their own personal insights into religious truths. Lacking the capacity to trust their own experiences and lacking the comprehensive knowledge to be efficient transmitters of the rabbinic tradition, they turn to the stale security of role-taking and over-learn a script for a tired play.

The rabbi needs to be able to ad-lib without fear of making a faux pas. He needs to know his part so well and himself so well that when he improvises, he improves the drama as much as he satisfies himself.

Once Judaism was surfeited with improvisations both good and bad, with prophets both true and false; then, somehow, it fell into the capable but throttling hands of efficient but uncreative directors. The time has come to free the actors or else the audience will drift away. Isaac must be allowed to weep and curse, to struggle, to fear, to laugh. The biblical text neglects to mention whether Abraham ever bothered to unbind Isaac. All we are told is that

"Abraham returned to his servants and they arose and went to Beersheba." Perhaps Isaac was left bound on the rock. Perhaps God meant him to untie himself. Or perhaps he waits for the unorthodox rabbi to set him free.

. . . . . . . . . . . . . . . . . . . . . . . . . . . . . . . . . . . . . . . . . . . . . . . . . . . . . . . . . . . . . .

# PART TWO

Out in the Field by Chance or by Choice

## Introductory Note

. . . . . . . . . . . . . . . . . . . . . . . . . . . . . . . . . . . . . . . . . . . . . . . . . . . . . . . . .

Of the following five essays, four are based on field studies conducted over a ten-year period; one bore witness to false expectations, thrusting a husband and father somewhat defensively back into the roles of sociologist and rabbi. I am referring here to my family's involvement in a Jewish day school, an experience that ultimately called up in me severe doubts about the stability of my own Jewish identity. As with all crises or near-crises, the experience was not without its educational value, even though the value of the education came not through the school's curriculum but rather through an encounter with *curricula vitarum* (that is, the runaround we were given when we found ourselves in the position of colliding with other people's ways of life).

The information obtained on the Jesus Jews is owed largely to the good fellowship that the group had to offer. The congregants whom I studied never asked me who I was or why I was there. They were glad to see me and shared with me their already shared intimacies—perhaps, as their slogan would have it, "to make another Jew smile." The study was done in "Key '73," a key that appears to have done little more than unlock a few coffers for Hillel foundations that were suddenly given the imperative to save the Jews from the Jewish Savior. The use I have made of deviant theory is clear; the reader, I trust, will recognize that I employed the methodology of transactional analysis as well. I began my research by asking myself what was in it for them, as well as what others associated with them had to gain (a drug addict who was saved from drugs) or lose (a Jew whose conversion into a Jesus Jew caused his parents grief). What my research uncovered—though, regrettably, I was unable to gather sufficient data about it—is the possibility that Jewish Jesus groups are a sort of halfway house for Gentiles seeking entry into "normative" Judaism, for non-Jewish widows or widowers of Jewish spouses, and for the hapless children of mixed marriages that were postulated on religious neutrality with the good intention of sparing their children conflict, but that resulted in unwittingly causing them religious deprivation.[1]

I did the original Birmingham Temple study as a graduate student (I was already a rabbi) at Brandeis University under the direction of my advisor and friend B. Z. Sobel, now of Haifa University. From the very beginning I found myself fully accepted by Rabbi Wine and his congregants. At the outset, a time of turmoil during which the Jewish authenticity of the congregation's children was made an issue by Jews hostile to the temple, I suspected that I owed all the cooperation and warmth I received to the fact that I was the first rabbi (other than Wine himself, of course) to set foot on whatever happened at the moment to be the temple's premises. Perhaps I was seen as lending them Jewish sanction. In the years since I have maintained close ties with Rabbi Wine, despite our different approaches to God, Israel, and Torah, as well as with members of the congregation.

The study of Makom was done under my direction by Earl Kaplan, then a Hebrew Union College student, with the full support of David Glazer, Makom's charismatic leader.

## chapter seven

# Flirting with Bankruptcy

Anyone who has given serious thought to the idea of Jewish day schools is aware of the many problems that such schools entail. Historically, since the mid-1800s the preponderance of Jews in America have achieved mobility through the public school system. Even today, with public schools under attack on every side—by educational experts, blacks and whites, liberals and conservatives—most Jewish children attend public schools. (To be sure, more often than not those schools are now located in suburbs, more or less safely segregated by social class and housing patterns, if not by law.) Because of their commitment to the benefits of public school education, many Jews have entertained reservations about day schools. Some argue that since nonpublic schools are difficult to support financially, they will inevitably have to seek government aid, thus inviting what liberals have professed to fear, an end to separation of church and state. Others contend that Jewish children isolated in day schools from contact with other Americans will be handicapped in their relationships with non-Jewish society (and even with the non–day school Jewish community).

On the other side, those who favor a day school education for their children contend that the United States offers no viable alternative to the day school if a parent wants to give his child a full appreciation of Jewish religion and culture. Where else will

Jewish children develop a definite attachment to the Hebrew language and to the festivals of the Jewish calendar? What but a day school can inspire them to see their lives in relation to the next holiday, to look forward to Purim and Pesach with the same eagerness that they anticipate their birthdays and with the same joyful anticipation that Christian children accord Christmas?[1]

To support a day school, one need not be an Orthodox Jew determined to keep one's children away from non-Jews and to make sure that they will see nothing attractive in the non-Jewish world. There are Jews who, though unorthodox, are nevertheless indifferent to the church-state issue and feel that the public school system offers a poor education. Occasionally such parents opt for a Jewish day school rather than one of the country day or experimental private schools.

Even so, despite several factors—the pressure on public schools, the parental fear that Jewish children are losing or are in danger of losing their Jewish identities, the tendency of American Jews to identify strongly with Israel, positive feelings about ethnicity and a decline in the sense of inferiority that Jewish immigrants often transmitted to their children—the Jewish day school movement has *not* caught on. With relatively few exceptions, Orthodox and ultra-Orthodox Jewish day schools—even those (and they are a majority) run by educators—face an almost daily fight for their continued existence. Orthodox leaders must constantly describe as "absolutely urgent" the need for a "massive infusion of funds" to keep alive their network of day schools in North America. Even "some of the most stable schools are . . . flirting with bankruptcy," they have been forced to admit.[2] The economic difficulties of the mid-1970s are of course responsible in large part for this dilemma, but even in earlier and more prosperous years, day schools were rarely able to achieve fiscal stability.

Why is this so? Why has the day school movement nearly always had to flirt with bankruptcy? It must be granted, after all, that, despite the fact that they tend to be hopelessly underpaid and often overworked, teachers at Jewish day schools are generally not inferior to those who are found in the public schools. In some important respects, of course, these teachers cannot be compared with their public school colleagues. The day school faculty is typified by an extreme reluctance to resist decisions made for them by the administration even when they disagree with those decisions. This, to be sure, is due in part to personality factors, but even more to the fact that the day school faculty is made up largely of part-time teachers. The day school is able to provide teachers with part-time employment because of its customary division between the Hebrew and general studies programs. To women who are married and must rear children and manage a home, a half-time job is a rare find. Furthermore, to retired teachers without enough stamina to survive a full day with a big public school class, the day school, with its half-day teaching load and its relatively small classes, is a blessing.

But day school teaching differs in other ways from public school teaching. Often enough it gives rise to a hierarchical arrangement that acknowledges that those who teach Hebrew subjects outrank in prestige and prerogatives those equipped "only" to teach English-language material.

Most day schools are found in large Jewish communities such as New York City; but even urban centers that have no pronounced Jewish character have seen the founding of such schools.[3] Consider, for instance, a midwestern city with an uncommonly large number of Reform Jews. Its day school history is worthy of study. The city had attracted a large German-Jewish population by the last decades of the nineteenth century, and although there was a significant influx of Eastern European Jews from the 1880s on, the Jewish population is not much larger now than it was when two of its oldest and most prestigious synagogues became Reform temples. Each of these two temples currently has a membership of well over a thousand families. Two smaller Reform temples together account for perhaps another thousand families. Thus, nearly three thousand families are Reform-affiliated. There is only one large Conservative synagogue. Of the two other Conservative synagogues, one is too minuscule and too poor to afford full-time rabbinical services, and the other is located in an area peripheral to the more affluent Jewish neighborhoods and, though rabbinically served, has a small membership. Perhaps there are, in all, two thousand families of Conservative affiliation. There are a number of Orthodox synagogues, but it is doubtful that their combined membership exceeds that of either of the two largest Reform temples. Community power has been, and continues to be, largely in the hands of Reform Jews much as in other cities a power elite of more traditional Jews has become wealthy and influential.[4] Thus the leadership of the Jewish Federation, which controls the community money needed to subsidize day school education, is predominantly Reform in affiliation. Despite the size and makeup of its Jewish population and the nontraditional sympathies of many of those who support the federation, the city has for at least twenty years supported two day schools in separate buildings, even though the two schools combined have rarely serviced as many as two hundred families. The newer of the day schools came into being about twenty years ago when some local activists, mostly Labor Zionists, determined to provide their children with an alternative to the existing day school, then under the complete domination of an antimodernist Orthodox rabbi.

The fervor of the Labor Zionists, after a great struggle, first to get the new school founded and financed, then to fight off a multitude of federation attempts to force it to merge with the Orthodox school, culminated in a day school belonging to, and dependent upon, no one denomination within Judaism. Its directors until recently tended to be men who, though personally observant, were recognized by the community as representing a sort of eclectic (*haskalah*-modernist) Judaism rather than any particular denominational commitment. Since such a director was not Orthodox and most of the school's founders were not Reform, its (always unofficial) ideological stance was by preference Zionist and by default Conservative. Traditional worship services were held at the school, holiday celebrations stressed traditional themes, and a nominal *kashrut* was maintained in the room where the children ate the lunches they brought from home. But the school made no serious attempt to persuade parents and teachers that halachic observance was a sine qua non for participation in the school's learning, teaching, or administrative activities. Furthermore, most of the school's founders and most of those active on its behalf were politically liberal and even took part in such efforts as were made in their conservatively Republican city, with its strong German and Southern tradition, to alleviate the plight of the blacks. Many lived in newly (if not, as events demonstrated, enduringly) integrated neighborhoods. Still, there was always a potential within the parent body for a swing to the right religiously, educationally, and politically.

In part this potential was linked to the fact that so many of those who elected to send their children to a Jewish day school were from Orthodox backgrounds. This was true not only of those whose discontent—generally *not* religious in character—with the older Orthodox school led them to the newer school; it was even true of some of the Reform-oriented academicians. Although often suspected by some of their fellow day school supporters of being "heretical" Jews, these academicians did not, for the most part, seek to influence the school to move religiously to the left. The most they could have been said to be guilty of was exercising their option to dispense with *kippot* at board meetings. In addition to the school's inner potential for a move to the right in the religious sphere, the changing political, economic, and racial scene at that time—plus two other variables discussed below—allowed the school's latent potential for educational and political conservatism to manifest itself in a most unpleasant way.

The last director of the *maskil* sort (he also directed the city's interdenominational Bureau of Jewish Education) retired in the late 1960s and was replaced by a man of pronounced and public Orthodox piety. Even had the new director been a strong leader, he would nonetheless have faced a formidable task. Holding his *s'michah* from an Orthodox *yeshivah,* a master's degree in education from an East Coast graduate school, and a doctorate from a midwestern university, he was engaged to serve as both the principal of the day school and the director of the city's geographically dispersed Talmud Torah system. The Talmud Torah system he administered had a different board of directors from the Bureau of Jewish Education and was housed, for the most part, on the premises of Orthodox synagogues whose rabbis much preferred the older Orthodox day school. Furthermore, there was competition, not only for the new administrator's time and energy, but for whatever funds were available to operate both the non-Orthodox day school and the Talmud Torah system. Thus, even a strong leader would have been torn asunder—although it is questionable whether a strong person would have agreed to attempt the dual role.

The new administrator was not a strong leader. He seemed to conceive of his role as one of mediation, drawing together the various factions that began to proliferate under his directorship. During his directorship adverse circumstances beyond his control continued developing. The day school was continually in debt, borrowing always on its future commitment from the federation. The director and some of the leadership saw in the city's troubled social scene sure signs that enrollment would increase, but notwithstanding their analysis, it did not rise until many years later, long after the departure of this director. At the same time, the Orthodox day school, although not growing enormously, began perceptibly to expand. The director's inability to achieve increased enrollment eventually cost him his job.

How did the director, guided by some rather strong personalities among his board members, analyze the situation? He and his advisors saw Jews abandoning the public school system of the central city because the once largely Jewish neighborhoods within the city now contained a large percentage of blacks, newcomers whose presence changed the composition and, in certain instances, the direction of the public schools. Furthermore, the suburb to which the most affluent Jews had moved lacked a public school system of its own; it depended on the systems of neighboring municipalities, so that its residents had to send their children out of the suburb, whether they attended public or private schools.

On the national scene, black anti-Semitism had become an issue, many influential Jewish spokesmen were arguing that the most secure position for Jews to occupy in the general society was squarely in the middle of the upper-middle classes where they could safely look out for their own interests.[5] In addition, the Nixon administration, after a few tentatives in the direction of "evenhandedness," appeared to have committed itself to endorsing the defense policies of Israel. At the same time, the White House was practicing "benign neglect" of the blacks and was allegedly rediscovering huge blocs of hitherto silent "middle Americans." While this was going on, however, inflation continued, and the wages of many middle-class people who had expected soon to be comfortable began buying less and less. Unemployment, for the first time in over three decades, began threatening middle-class Jews (those employees, for example, in the field of engineering).

All this occurred at the same time that numerous middle-class Jews had become convinced of the need to buy homes in neighborhoods away from the central city. The purchase of such homes cut deeply into any money they might otherwise have been in a position to spend for private education. If the intent of private education was basically to avoid contact with blacks, then the flight to the suburbs served this purpose very well.

During these years, too, new techniques in education were beginning to reach the public schools. More and more, people were taking seriously the criticism leveled at educational institutions. Parents began discounting the stress formerly given to the location of the school and even its ethnic or racial composition and instead began asking questions about open classrooms, ungraded classes, and the teaching methods employed by the teachers. The

Orthodox day school responded by introducing open classrooms and a Montessori kindergarten. One public school in a carefully integrated enclave within the city, a school with a student body that was 80 percent black, got a new black woman principal and, with her, ungraded classes with a heavy emphasis on individual student development.

But the non-Orthodox day school interpreted all these changes in a rather special way. The small group that controlled the school viewed with a degree of satisfaction the increasing conservatism of the national Jewish scene and the growing rift between Jews and blacks. In these developments they saw an opportunity for the day school to reverse the diminution of its student body and the concomitant financial crisis that had been getting more severe each year. The newly chosen president of the board even went so far as to tell one parent that the black situation was going "to save Judaism" because it would bring into the school a number of children whose parents otherwise would never have considered sending them to a day school.

The city has as part of its public school system a highly regarded—and educationally traditional—college preparatory secondary (that is, combined junior high and high) school. That school (a sort of "Latin school," a Bostonian would say) is located in what for a generation or so has been a predominantly black neighborhood. It has faced numerous onslaughts by blacks and others who object to its citywide character and its policy of imposing an entrance exam and limiting enrollment to students who are willing and able to take courses geared to a college preparatory level. As a result of the school's entrance policy and curricular emphasis, its student body is two-thirds white, including many Jews. The school has been fortunate in having a student and parent body largely free from incidents of racial strife. Alumni of the day school, which until recently had only six grades (it now has eight), usually attended this secondary school.

The leaders of the day school, notwithstanding its financial plight, sought to extend its program from six grades to seven. Did the director try to convince the parents of its sixth-grade children of the advantages of its small classes and the validity of building on the children's existent and reasonably extensive knowledge of Hebrew? One might have expected such an approach; but instead, at a meeting of parents, the director suggested that parents would be exposing their children to the danger of violence by enrolling them in the public prep school. This approach, it happens, was not

notably successful. In the fall only six out of a possible twelve
students enrolled in the new seventh grade. No recruits were
found for the seventh grade from outside the day school, despite
an attempt to project an image of the school as an elitist institution free from the tensions besetting public schools. The day
school, committed to having a seventh grade and promised funds
by the rabbi of the large Conservative synagogue whose son was
enrolled in the seventh grade, hired a full coterie of new teachers
in both the Hebrew and general studies departments. The school
had pledged itself to offer a program at least equal to that of the
public prep school, and so it had to hire six new part-time teachers
to teach the six students enrolled in the new seventh grade. Since
the rabbi was able ultimately to deliver less than half the amount
he had hoped to raise, and since enrollment was much below what
had been anticipated, the school's financial situation worsened.
The city's Jewish Federation had agreed to subsidize only the first
six grades of the day school. The school's already limited budget
was heavily burdened by the needs of the new grade, as were the
physical facilities of an already inadequate and unattractive
building.

Meanwhile, the members of the board found themselves less
and less frequently informed of policies crucial to the destiny of
the school. All during the year prior to the establishment of the
seventh grade, the chairman of the school's education committee
had refused to call a meeting, protesting that she was too busy.
When meetings were finally called late in the spring of the year,
their recommendations were never acted upon.

In the summer of that year, the board discovered that it had a
new president—a young, halachically scrupulous academician.
There had been no election. There was no attempt even to go
through the motions of informing the board. Only by noting that
the signature at the bottom of a letter identified him as president
did board members learn of his appointment. The new president
was not known for his liberal points of view, whether in religion,
racial matters, the rights of college students, or educational innovations, and he would hardly have been the choice of the more
liberal members either of the board or of the parents. This is not
to say, however, that he might not have been the choice of what
was by now a majority of those given policy-making power on the
governing board of the school.

In addition to the appointment (rather than election) of a quite
conservative new board president, it soon became apparent that

the body known as the executive committee had been abolished. Before long a teacher was fired by a group of board members claiming to act, it became evident, under the auspices of the abolished executive committee—although the president and the director did not indicate any discomfort with the sudden (and transient) reincarnation of a body they had so recently been content to bury.

The power group reached two other decisions: to force the resignation of the school's director and to relocate in the affluent suburb that had no public school system of its own. The day school was to abandon a middle-class neighborhood that housed the Jewish Center, was home to many elderly Jews, and was experiencing an increased degree of racial integration. The leadership had not previously asked the board or the parents whether or not they wished a relocation plan to be formulated.

Soon a number of events further testified to the unfortunate direction in which the school was heading. For example, the teachers were arbitrarily presented with a set of rules for good conduct. The rules included, among other strictures, the warning that teachers on the staff of the day school "must not openly desecrate the Sabbath"—a rule that presumably sanctioned private desecration and suggested that the halacha as interpreted by the clique was to be the new manual of discipline. (Rather amusingly—but how uncharacteristically?—a clique leader outspokenly in favor of the ruling was subsequently seen by a less halachically stringent board member shopping on the Sabbath at a local discount house.)

Next, a letter was sent to all parents stating that when day school children were invited to their homes, the laws of *kashrut* were to be observed. One parent, an Israeli, had served hamburgers from a fast-food restaurant at a birthday party. All the children, most of whom regularly go to nonkosher restaurants with their parents, had eaten the sandwiches. It was becoming apparent that the clique would no longer remain neutral on religious issues. Having gained control over the religious orientation of the school, the members of the clique were now extending their area of control into people's private lives. This was true even of those in the clique who were themselves not more than nominally observant. The school was being pushed to a more traditionalist stance and given to believe that it would soon be moved out of its home in an integrating middle-class neighborhood and relocated in an affluent suburb. Space was to be rented in, of all places, the religious school building of a huge Reform temple that had moved from the inner city a few years before and was now in need of cash with which to maintain its expensive suburban splendor. A clique leader (the very one seen shopping on the Sabbath) was heard to say that the move to the premises of a Reform congregation would make it even more necessary for the school to adopt a pietist style (lest the public confuse the school with its host congregation).

But those were not the only events taking place in the school. Over the years the school had advertised itself as willing to give special attention to children who entered the school beyond the first few grades and were, as a result, behind in Hebrew. In reality, however, what now took place was quite the opposite. Not only the child who entered late, but any student who had a learning problem in any area—and especially in Hebrew—was tormented by teachers and fellow students until he or she was withdrawn from the school. In the spring the son of a physician, a child who had been enrolled in the school in the second grade and was now in the fourth, became so unhappy that he refused to go to school. When his father asked to discuss the matter with the proper committee, he was informed that his son was a slow learner. The doctor withdrew all three of his children from the school. A check of the school's dropouts—rather a substantial percentage of the student body—revealed that their chief complaint about the school was its intolerance of any student who did not readily adapt to its tight program. The school simply would not deal with deviations of any kind.

A teacher of English in the new seventh grade began hearing rumors to the effect that she was under investigation for activities subversive of the school's purposes. It was true that she had been outspoken in her displeasure with the way a colleague was fired and did not permit her students to deride the unhappy teacher either before or after her dismissal; that she had criticized the relocation plan; that she had given expression to her fear that, in view of the investment the school had made in the seventh grade and the fact that one of the six seventh graders was the child of the leader of the clique and another was the Conservative rabbi's child, more than due heed was being given children of the seventh grade; and that she had spoken out against the policy that denied teachers representation on the school's board. What surprised her were the tactics subsequently employed, first to try to silence her, then to force her resignation.

First, she was asked to meet with an ad hoc teacher evaluation committee consisting of two clique personalities of predictably conservative bent in matters of educational policy and a third more liberal party, no doubt included to give the committee a more balanced appearance. Consistent with the clique's policy of secrecy, the teacher was called to the meeting ostensibly to give advice in planning the next year's curriculum. What happened at the meeting was that she was accused by the chairperson of "teaching values" rather than English and of actively expressing dissatisfaction with the school's policy, particularly in the area of teacher representation on the board and its committees.

Thereafter her classroom, which had had no visits from the director during the entire year, began to receive daily visitations. She was called to meeting after meeting. The leaders of the clique, however, were stymied, since the one outside educational specialist they consulted gave her a top rating as a teacher. Their setback was only temporary, though, because when she was offered a contract for the following year, it was for half the salary she had been receiving. Since this made it economically unfeasible for her to continue teaching there, she found it necessary to resign.

In the meantime there was a ground swell of parental unhappiness. It centered on the secrecy with which the clique operated and on the unwillingness of the school's leadership to accept any educational innovation or to deal sympathetically with students in need of a different approach. The meetings held to try to make sense of the board's decision came to naught because some of the discontented were suspicious of the Reform Jews in their midst. Husbands from Orthodox homes could not agree with their wives, who came from less observant backgrounds. The men tended to be less critical than their wives of the school, although all opposed the secrecy of the clique. Furthermore, it was difficult to sustain a prolonged assault on the school because things promised to be different the next year. A new director, young, vigorous, and innovative in day school education, was coming. The school would be housed in elegant surroundings in an affluent suburb. A wait-and-see attitude, coupled with the onset of summer, brought the year to an end.

During the summer board members and parents received a missive informing them that the relocation had to be abandoned, since the would-be host congregation had asked too high a rental; the old building, which the clique had decried as utterly unsuitable, was being remodeled; and a new president was at the reins. The previous president, it appeared, had resigned and had been succeeded by the vice-president. (Neither had ever been elected by the board.) The erstwhile vice-president, now president, had lent himself most willingly to the purposes of the clique. Would he continue under that influence? Or would he fall under the influence of the merger-minded federation and surrender the school to the Orthodox?

It is worthwhile reflecting on the problems facing our day school because they may be paradigmatic for other schools that attempt to be nondenominational and that rely on parents and the local federation to sustain them.

First, a day school without adequate financial backing is at the mercy of too many groups with conflicting interests. The men who allocate funds from the Jewish Federation are likely, whether Reform or Conservative in affiliation, to have a vested (if unconscious) interest in seeing the day school fail. Most of them belong to congregations that support afternoon or weekend Hebrew and religious schools, which in a way are competitive with a day school. For example, it was often rumored that even though his own children attended the day school, the powerful Conservative rabbi had an expensive new educational building to finance and fill and could not be expected to give his wholehearted support to the day school. A flourishing day school is bound to undercut enrollment in the educational activities of local congregations.

Second, a day school without adequate, broad financial support lacks proper administration. Because our school lacked the funds to hire a full administrative staff, a very small group of people who had the time—and, ultimately, an almost manic devotion to the school—came to insist on being rewarded for their efforts by being allowed to make virtually all the decisions affecting the school. Add to these a few more people with some money to give the school, and what emerged was a school run, not by professional educators, but by a clique of self-serving, self-styled executives dominating nearly every aspect of the school's activity.

Next, it is important to establish, clearly and distinctly, the school's ideological stance in matters of religion. It is not enough for a school to exist only as an alternative to Orthodox day schools. If it follows the pattern so well established by Conservative Jews—the pattern of demanding Orthodoxy in the institution while permitting personal nonobservance in public or at home—it is bound to fall into one of two traps. Either the more observant members of the parent body will, since they recognize no alternate type of Judaism, insist that the school adhere to the letter of Jewish law, or a glaring inconsistency will be allowed between what is taught in the school as correct behavior and what is practiced outside the school by many, perhaps even most, of the parents.

As it stands, a practicing, believing Reform or liberal Jew has no day school to which to send his children. The few Reform day schools that have been established are still at the very most embryonic. If a Reform parent wants traditional Judaism made available to his children, but only as one possible interpretation of Jewish life, there is simply no day school for him. Much of the blame for this state of affairs lies, of course, with Reform Jews themselves. Many are wary of traditional Judaism for reasons ranging from their own religious beliefs to snobbism to assimilationist tendencies. Thus far, few liberal or Reform Jews have been personally willing to fund a day school or even to provide the children necessary to maintain one. Furthermore, even if Reform Judaism as a movement were willing to support day schools, as seems from recent resolutions passed at intramovement conventions to be at least a possibility, it is doubtful whether these schools would present a traditional practice like *davening* to the children enrolled in them.

But all of these questions aside, there is a more serious issue, an issue of morality. It appears that some of the old fears that opponents of day schools have voiced over the years may not be groundless. If those willing to support day schools do so because they wish to isolate their children from Christians, white or black, or even from Jews who do not share their belief that they represent a Righteous Remnant of the Chosen People, the school must fall prey to parochialism in the worst sense of the word. In such a school the possibility of social strife is taken as good if it frightens people into sending their children to the school. Tolerance of others, even of children unable to fit into the tightly structured curriculum, is taken as an evil. Tolerance may lead to interaction with the tolerated and thereby erode the beliefs of the elite.

The flight to an affluent suburb was halted, not out of a sense of loyalty to the Jews who remained in an integrating neighborhood, but simply because the school could not afford the rent asked for the proposed new facility. There was a feeling that change in educational techniques would come about under a new, stronger director (also a man with an Orthodox commitment). Perhaps such change would have come about in any case because, in order to make the old building do, some flexibility as to class-

room use had to be built into the renovated structure. It is doubtful, even so, whether the school will veer away from the direction
in which it is now headed, i.e., into an eventual merger with the
Orthodox school. If a merger occurs it will be, as it always is,
according to the religious terms laid down by the Orthodox. The
present director, for all his educational verve and openness, will
certainly not oppose such a merger.

No matter how liberal Jews may change their stance with regard to state funding of day schools and no matter how urgently
they may come to recognize that a day school is the only alternative to a haphazard Jewish education, the price in terms of other
moral values remains too high to pay. What is the answer? How
are liberals to give their children a solid Jewish—and moral—
education without forcing them to discard the values of pluralism
and tolerance that promise them a good life in an open society?

· · · · · · · · · · · · · · · · · · · · · · · · · · · · · · · · · · · · · · · · · · · · · · · · · · · · · · · ·

## chapter eight

# The Jesus Hang-up

The traditional day school attempts to instill in children a kind of Jewish identity that unorthodox parents frequently find at odds with their own values. The school throws into relief deficiencies within the unorthodox community. In a more radical sense, the Jewish Jesus movement helps shape a form of Jewish identity held undesirable by virtually every segment within the normative Jewish community. Nevertheless, an encounter with Jesus Jews may well be as valuable as an encounter with a traditional day school for its illumination of what is likely to be lacking in all but ultra-Orthodox Judaism.

There are a number of ways to speak sociologically and psychologically about the Jewish Jesus people. One might, for instance try to examine them in demographic terms. How old are they? What is their educational level? What socioeconomic class are they from? Regrettably, however, little of this information is available. Or one might approach them from a purely psychological angle, seeking to determine what psychic needs are met through their acceptance of Jesus as the Messiah. Testimony about the problems from which Jesus has saved them offers a picture of a typical Jewish Jesus person who has been on drugs, has had problems with sex (either too much or too little), and feels a sense of extreme alienation from his nuclear family. But such a picture does not explain why these Jews solve their preconversion problems by becoming Jesus people. To dismiss them as freaks (in the traditional sense of the word) is to miss an opportunity to gain an insight, through them, into contemporary Jewish life.

What I propose to do here is to explore the Jewish Jesus phenomenon from the perspective of what is known in sociology as deviant theory[1]—to see the deviant as the person or group delineating for us what our norms are, thereby helping throw our values into relief so that we may either strengthen them or, if we find them inadequate, seek to change them. In other words, we can use deviants to tell us something about ourselves.

First of all, by what right do I label Jewish Jesus people deviant? I do so because I assume, perhaps erroneously, that despite their claims to the contrary, joining the Jesus movement and accepting Jesus as the Christ puts a Jew outside that ill-defined (but not at all utterly amorphous) entity known as the Jewish community. In general our willingness to tolerate Jewish Jesus people in our institutions and to accept them as our friends is not as great as it would be if they were "merely" transcendental meditators, atheists, Christians married to Jews, Jewish draft dodgers, Jews arrested for smoking pot, and—I suspect, but admittedly am not certain—black Jews or gay Jews. One of the conclusions this leads to is that the rank and file of the non-Orthodox Jewish community is growing increasingly tolerant of people formerly seen as ideologically or behaviorally deviant.

Let us assume that the American Jewish community does indeed regard the Jewish Jesus people as deviant and being somehow out of bounds. Conversely, let us assume that Jesus Jews consider themselves not only as still within the Jewish community but indeed as the only real Jews within it. What then can we learn about Jewish community values from those whom the Jewish community rejects and even fears?

First, at the risk of oversimplifying the Jewish Jesus movement, I want to attempt a characterization of it in terms of my own personal observations, interviews, and broad reading of "Jews for Jesus" literature.

1. Like other movements within the so-called Jesus revolution, the Jewish Jesus community is made up of people who have had a personal conversion experience in which Jesus entered their hearts and bodies and made them accept Jesus not only as the Messiah but as their personal Savior. Unlike other members of the Jesus movement, however, Jewish converts

did not come from a tradition that had already accepted
Jesus as the Messiah and Savior.

2. Jesus people—Jewish and non-Jewish—are radical fun-
   damentalists believing that every word in the Old and the
   New Testaments was revealed by God. They deny the validity of scientific approaches to Scripture and spurn any intel-
   lectualization that might impede their experiencing Jesus
   through his word.

3. Nearly universally, Jesus people feel that they had led
   meaningless, sinful lives prior to their finding Jesus. By
   their own testimony, the movement is made up of many
   people who were once on drugs or who in one way or another
   felt that they had reason to feel guilty about their sexuality.
   In fact, there is some evidence that Jesus people tend to
   exaggerate their former sinfulness in order to make more
   miraculous the extent of their salvation.

4. Jesus people feel superior to those who have not found Jesus.
   They feel good knowing that they are doing what God wants.
   If they are Jews, they feel superior to other Jews because
   they are "completed" Jews.

5. Jesus people feel intimately part of a group. They are a
   welcome part of a community of believers. They have a
   home.

6. Jesus people regard sex before marriage as sinful and therefore abstain from it.

Thus, middle-class American society—and middle-class Jewish
society in particular—does not satisfy any of the needs that are
met by the Jesus enthusiasts as a revolutionary movement. Protestants from staid, middle-class denominations who join the
Jesus movement can embarrass their church and their parents
by, in a sense, taking them at their word. This phenomenon is
well known to non- or lightly observant Conservative Jews who
send their children to Camp Ramah in order to deepen their children's commitment to Judaism. Catholic Jesus people, like the
Jews, are converts to what is essentially a Protestant evangelical
movement, but it is the Jews who, if they are not in revolt, stand
to gain the most from their affiliation with the Jesus movement.
Not only do they break with their families by becoming religious,
but they do so in a way that negates the validity of the entire
Jewish historical experience of the last two thousand years.

There is another payoff unique to Jews in the Jesus movement. Although they are in active revolt against their families and their heritage, they are also in a sense normalizing themselves within American society. Who is more American than Pat Boone or Johnny Cash? A Jewish Jesus person is an outsider by virtue of his alienation from the Jewish community through drugs or other socially unacceptable forms of behavior. By embracing Jesus, he not only gets revenge against the Jews but also gains entry into the most American of Americas—the America of Jesus Saves and Billy Graham. Still, it would be a serious mistake to see the Jewish Jesus movement solely as a negative phenomenon, a revolt against the Jewish community. The Jesus movement—with its emphasis on personal religious experience, its fundamentalism and anti-intellectualism, its ability to make its members feel that they possess a clean slate despite whatever sins they feel they have previously committed, its success in making its adherents feel religiously fulfilled, its substitution of a new group for the nuclear family, and its strongly puritanical sexual stance—points to true deficiencies within middle-class religious communities and especially within the non-Hasidic Jewish community.

In many instances middle-class religions, geared as they are to producing rational, reliable workers and consumers who accept the scientific, rational, logical, empirical explanation of how things are, have systematically stripped themselves of anything producing an individual or collective subjective mystical religious experience. Middle-class religions are more likely to be humanitarian in the grand sense of the word, supporting UNICEF, CARE, and the like, but they are far less likely to be accepting of individual deviants. Where would one expect to find an alcoholic or an ex-convict at prayer—in a Presbyterian church or at the Salvation Army? And where would one expect to find a Jewish addict at prayer—in a temple or at a Jesus meeting? For all its talk about concern for its lost souls, the Jewish community has been almost totally resistant to supporting and funding alternatives to the Jewish family. What do a Jewish runaway, a Jewish addict, and a down-and-out Jew have to turn to that is accepting and Jewish?

How can one be a *good* Jew? One can be Orthodox and observe the *mitzvot*. But Orthodoxy is based on study, intellectual attainment, a knowledge of Hebrew, a mastery of minutiae.[2] It is an in-group difficult to enter. Only the Lubavitcher Hasidim are willing to tolerate mistakes[3]—and they are gaining more Jewish followers than the Jesus movement. One can also be a good Jew by supporting Jewish causes and giving to Jewish charities. These options are available in the main to people with money who are able to derive meaning from affiliation with middle-class religious institutions. Thus, as much as certain people, particularly outcasts, seek to be good Jews, they have to struggle. By accepting Jesus, a young Jew who believes the teachings of the Hebrew Christians can consider himself a better Jew than anyone else who goes by that name.

There is also the matter of sexuality. We live in a culture, Jews and non-Jews alike, in which all of us are faced with several contradictory attitudes toward the attainment of sexual gratification. Our religious tradition (on this Judaism seems more lenient than Christianity)[4] warns us that sexual gratification outside of marriage is a grave sin. The American economy floods our senses with images designed to arouse us sexually while deluding us into believing that buying a certain toothpaste will give us an orgasm. Our liberal, scientific, psychologically sophisticated educated classes tell us that sex is good, that good sex is better, and that all of our sexual hang-ups are due to the repression inherent in the teaching of our traditional religions.

Where do modern Judaism and liberal Christianity stand? They stand outside the realm of human possibility. Either out of loyalty to tradition or out of Victorian prudery, they refuse to break with the traditional stand that sexual gratification outside of marriage is wrong. Their adherents are instead urged to accept the advice of experts such as scientists and psychologists, to stay in school for years and years, and to become self-supporting before marriage (early marriage, we are told, is neurotic).

What are the alternatives? One is: Damn the religion, full speed ahead—and hope that guilt doesn't catch up with us. The only other alternative is to put ourselves in situations where abstinence is given more importance and more group support than is sexual gratification. The Jesus movement, along with movements such as Hare Krishna and Hasidism, provides the latter alternative—a means of avoiding sexual guilt through group-supported abstinence. Modern religions, on the other hand, offer multiple clues that may produce guilt but that cannot protect people from feeling guilty.

The contemporary Jewish way of life has simply not developed an ideology capable of supporting premarital sexual exploration, nor has it been able to produce a cogent scientific argument against it. In a psychoreligious system that pities the neurotic aspect of sex-produced guilt and in a social climate that exults in the erotic and in the total pleasure the body can give, liberal Judaism has remained judiciously noncommittal on matters sexual. This attitude, or lack of one, has, for the most part, served progressive religious leaders well. Most non-Orthodox Jewish adolescents and postadolescents seem to find in this religious laissez-faire at best a manifestation of Judaism's progressive intent and at worst another instance of its unwillingness to take a positive stand on a positive good, i.e., premarital sex.

In the Jewish community, as in other sections of American life, many young people are unwilling or unable to surrender to the pull toward sexual excitation and its logical outcome, premarital sex. Although the traditional Jewish community once recognized the strength of the sex drive and demanded early marriage, today the middle classes see early marriage not only as a financial and educational impossibility but as a liability for creating a good marriage. Religious communities such as the Jesus people, Hare Krishna, and Lubavitchers provide environments that reinforce celibacy and make abstinence a virtue. Confession of past dalliance testifies to the newcomer's need for, and commitment to, the groups. Internalized restraint yields to external surveillance. In other words, a sanctified escape is provided from cultural and physical urges toward sexual gratification outside of holy matrimony. In exploring the appeal of the Jews for Jesus, it would be an error to underestimate this factor of sanctified celibacy.

Although it would be wrong to overemphasize the threat that Jews for Jesus offer Jewish survival, unorthodox and particularly non-Hasidic Jews will do well to look to this and other "deviant" communities for clues as to what may be missing in the normative Jewish community. For very valid historical reasons, Jewish communities have tended to deal with deviants in their midst by confining them to internal Jewish institutions (e.g., the pauper, the physically stigmatized, or the petty criminal) or by driving them out from under their aegis (e.g., the Jew who marries a non-Jew, the heretic, or the grand felon).[5]

At the present time, particularly for Jewish youths whom various social or psychological reasons deprive of a place within the normative Jewish community, some sort of exile seems necessary.[6] Unfortunately, the Jews for Jesus movement supplies such youths with a means of normalizing themselves within a community, makes them feel authentic both as Jews and as Americans, repudiates the Jewish community from which they feel alienated, and provides external protection from—and even a reward for denying—guilt-producing sexual impulses. Furthermore, it does so in a way that makes few intellectual demands.

It may well be that the established Jewish community should be grateful to the Jesus movement for siphoning off "undesirables," but it should also move Jews to reexamine their existing communal institutions to see how they might bring their deviants back under the wings of the Shekinah.

· · · · · · · · · · · · · · · · · · · · · · · · · · · · · · · · · · · · · · · · · · · · · · · · · ·

## chapter nine

# The Vision of Man Triumphant

It came as something of a shock when American Jews were apprised in the early 1960s of the existence in their midst of a self-confessed and outspokenly candid "atheist" rabbi at the head of a congregation of like-minded Jews in suburban Detroit.[1]

Most newsworthy events within the Jewish community in those years tended to come from the secular or quasi-secular segments of the institutional structure, such as the welfare and defense agencies, the charitable organizations, and the Zionist and pro- or anti-Israeli groupings. On the religious front life seemed to have stabilized around the typically American Jewish pattern of Orthodox, Conservative, and Reform, with a relatively quiescent Reconstructionist fringe and a large but amorphous category of those unconcerned, partially assimilated, or not formally affiliated with a synagogue.

With Rabbi Sherwin Wine and the Birmingham Temple, it became possible for the first time in many years to sense an impending event in the religious community that promised to go beyond situational and institutional adjustments and that foreshadowed major changes involving not just the religious professionals but an unknown (and possibly large) segment of the laity as well. Sociologists wondered if this was a self-generating event that could be explained (and, some hoped, contained) by the socioreligious peculiarities of a small suburban group in Michigan; or if it instead suggested the first rumblings of concern from an American Jewry moving beyond religious pliability, into the uncharted and threatening waters of radical religious innovation?

To some an avowedly atheist rabbi and an allegedly atheist congregation posed the threat of upsetting the delicately wrought structure of the American religious establishment, of which the Jews are a part. To others it represented a possible attempt to close the yawning abyss of cultural lag that separated contemporary religious institutions from the suspected nonbelief or attenuated beliefs of a vast number of Jews. The basic questions, however, were to what extent the birth of the Birmingham Temple adumbrated radical and far-reaching changes in American Jewish religious life, and what influence the event was likely to have on the community structure.

In the early spring of 1963, according to one of the founders of the Birmingham Temple, a group of eight families, four of which had belonged to the largest of the Detroit Reform temples (located at the time in a black neighborhood), asked the board of that synagogue whether it contemplated an imminent move to the suburbs. They were told that although such a move was under consideration, a building program was not expected in the immediate future. Dissatisfied with this answer, the group determined to form its own suburban Reform temple.

Crossing the Detroit River to Windsor, Ontario, they spoke with Rabbi Sherwin T. Wine of the Windsor Reform Temple, the first Reform synagogue in a town with a strong Orthodox community. The group approached Wine because they knew him from the past, when he had been assistant rabbi at Detroit's Temple Beth El. Subsequently he had served as a chaplain in Korea and had then returned to Beth El, where he had gained popularity as a preacher, youth group leader, teacher, and advisor to young couples. His preaching style, combining wit and whimsy with a large measure of subtle theatrics, attracted notice among Detroit Reform Jews. Wine had left Detroit, to serve the Windsor Reform Temple while he continued his work in philosophy at the University of Michigan, following a mutual agreement between him and Beth El's senior rabbi to terminate what had grown to be an unhappy senior-assistant relationship. At the time that the Birmingham group approached Wine, he had completed his course work for a doctorate at the University of Michigan and was thinking of entering academic life. Many of his professors and peers at the Hebrew Union College had predicted that Wine's intellectual gifts and personal eccentricities would find a more convivial climate in the academic environment.[2]

When the group, consisting of young professionals, came to Wine, he was excited by their proposal, and he in turn excited those who had come to ask for his advice. They included people who had been raised in Reform Judaism, some who had no Jewish training or former affiliations, and others whose commitment to Reform Judaism was high. Wine sensed in the group a strong discontent with existing temples and was quick to convert personal dissatisfaction into a dissatisfaction over ideology by questioning whether existing liberal temples promised a synthesis between science and religion but delivered instead a hodgepodge of infantile theology and quasi-scientific jargon; and whether, although Reform Judaism described itself as liberal, when confronted with the full results of reason it retreated into the clichés of Orthodoxy. If a new temple was to be formed in the northwest suburbs of Detroit, an area inhabited by the new breed of Jew, self-accepting but college-educated, had it no obligation to be a temple committed to the principle of free inquiry?

The Birmingham Temple was indeed founded on the principle of free inquiry. During its first months the Reform prayer book was used. Soon, however, it became obvious that many of the traditional prayers were inconsistent with the temple's philosophy. The ritual committee was instructed to produce a new liturgy for the temple. Within a short time mimeographed services were issued containing the rubrics of the Reform service— the Borchu, the Shema, the Mi Chomocho, a psalm or two, the Kaddish, and a standard Reform Torah service—but substituting for the body of some of these prayers and for the English sermonic prayers of the *Union Prayer Book* meditations on various themes such as tradition, individual potentiality, humanism, and love. Although the new liturgy was written by Wine and merely ratified by the committee, the feeling, nevertheless, was conveyed that this was the creation of the Birmingham Temple, and cohesion tightened while membership continued to grow. At this point in the temple's development, the word "God" was understood as the symbol for the "best in man." No congregant objected to the word being employed in such a manner.

The people who were joining the temple and espousing Wine's teachings and his new liturgy were, in the main, third-generation American Jews. They were young people who had attended col-

lege. Over 80 percent of the men and over 40 percent of the
women had B.A. degrees or their equivalent; of these, 60 percent
of the men and 25 percent of the women had advanced academic
degrees. Nearly 60 percent of the breadwinners were professionals. There were many educators, lawyers, and accountants, as
well as a few engineers, physicians, dentists, and psychiatrists.
To them Wine's teaching appeared reasonable. To those basically
unschooled in philosophy or theology, to those who had received
the rather minimal Jewish training available in American
synagogues during the late thirties and forties, Birmingham reinforced what they already believed. Psychoanalysis had said that
God was only your father projected onto the world; that to worship
your own needs was neurotic, to pray to a figment of your imagination, irrational. In Detroit, among the Jewish middle class,
psychiatry was and is regarded as unquestionably valid. The empirical method was assumed to be the only legitimate approach to
problem-solving. That the individual is sacred, that human
creativity is what deserves homage, that freedom from guilt is
desirable, that Judaism and humanism are compatible, that Reform Judaism permits liturgical innovations—these are all
teachings that were consonant with the educational training and
personal needs of the temple's members as well as with the doctrine of Reform Judaism. As for theology, the members of the congregation agreed with Rabbi Wine that "a God whose existence
had to be *saved* through mental gymnastics or anti-intellectual
leaps of faith was not worth having." They were convinced that to
have no God was the more honest position. God was a metaphor;
Moses, a teacher of morals and metaphors.

By September 1964, 148 families had affiliated with the Birmingham Temple. Over 50 percent of these families had never
belonged to a synagogue before. In addition a crowd of prospective
joiners and those who normally attended services on the high holy
days only came to witness the services. Together they filled the
auditorium of a public school. The readings from the new liturgy
still contained the Borchu, the Shema, the Kaddish, and other
traditional elements, but also included meditations based on
Fromm, Sartre, and Camus.

Unhampered by official links to an organized religious movement and emboldened by the continued zeal of the membership,
Rabbi Wine and his committee moved to what they believed to be
a more forthright position. In late October 1964 a directive was
issued to the faculty of the religious school stating that hereafter

the word "God" was no longer to be employed other than in a historical context. The teachers were told that if "ideal man" were meant, "ideal man" and not "God" should be used. Shortly after this the liturgy committee began issuing new services completely devoid of any mention of God. The Borchu, the Shema, and the Kaddish were dropped; in their place humanist Hebrew responses were sung to Israeli and Hasidic melodies. "*Baruch shalom ba'olam, baruch shalom ba'adam.* Blessed be peace in the world, blessed be peace in man. . . . *Baruch ha'or ba'olam, baruch ha'or ba'adam.* Blessed be the light in the world, blessed be the light in man." Instead of the Kaddish a memorial tribute was read, followed by the congregation singing "*Am Yisrael hai ad b'lee dai.* The people Israel lives eternally."

Certain psalms of a humanist nature were retained, such as "Behold how good it is for brothers to dwell together in unity," and segments of certain traditional prayers were kept when God was not the subject, such as Sim Shalom, a prayer for peace. An excerpt from a typical service illustrates the innovation.

CONGREGATION AND CHOIR

*Hin-nay ma tov oo-ma na-eem she-vet aheem gam ya-had*

READER

Religion is the act of worship. The wonder of sacred things excites our awesome tribute and leads us to adoration. Many men waste their reverence. They turn it to the lifeless world of mountains and stars where only dumb grandeur greets their conscious love; or with mythical charm they indulge it in an exotic realm of gods and angels in which children act out their fears and fantasies. How nice it would be to conjure up the strength and maturity and rescue religion for what is truly real and superbly worthy. In the tension between what man is and what he can become lies the invitation to worship. Against a mindless world that dispenses cruelty without malice and kindness without love, man stands to fulfill the destiny of his being. To tame the world in all its wildness to human need and to push back relentlessly the horizon of its mystery is an incredible mission. Yet human talent has it within its grasp if we but press the will of our determination. The vision of man triumphant is enough to seize the power of reverence and transform its energy into the pursuit of realistic ends. Each of us in all his possibility is an awesome being. Let us then adore the hero within us and pay rightful honor to what we must become.

SILENT MEDITATION

The radically new liturgy was ratified by the congregation, though not without some dissension. Virtually everyone agreed with the theological premises underlying the changes. Few, if any, were willing to speak up on God's behalf. All of them had agreed with the rabbi when he said that God was no more than a metaphor. How could they argue, then, for the retention of that metaphor? Furthermore, to retain the word "God" was, in reality, to contradict the premises on which the temple had been founded: truth based on the evidence of the senses and consistency of action and belief. When members requested the Kaddish, Wine charged them with harboring unresolved guilt feelings—unhealthy in persons seeking to realize their full potential. Some of the congregants felt that something was wrong, but due to their lack of Jewish knowledge and their admitted ignorance of theology, they could not identify what was troubling them. They were not troubled by the question of God's existence; they were, with Rabbi Wine, ignostic with regard to that problem. Furthermore, the nearly universal esteem in which they held Rabbi Wine kept them loyal to the temple, even if they shared some misgivings about its direction.

The issuance of a "God-less" service produced a change in the relationship between the temple and the larger Jewish community. Once the new service was introduced, the Detroit Reform rabbinate had the evidence necessary to launch a full-scale attack on the Birmingham Temple. Rabbi Wine was asked to appear before them to answer charges. Reporters were invited from the Detroit newspapers. Wine was charged with atheism. Rather than ignoring the accusation or explaining, as he does so carefully, the meaning of the word "ignostic" (one who to the question "Is there a God?" answers, "What does the word 'God' mean?"), which he used to refer to himself, Wine said, "If by atheist you mean a person who denies the existence of a Supreme Being existing in time and space and having the attributes of a human being, then I am an atheist." Although by such a definition every theologian from Philo to Tillich would be an atheist, the papers had their headline: "Rabbi Declares Himself Atheist." The wire services picked up the story, and within twenty-four hours the Birmingham Temple and its rabbi were national news. The Reform rabbis of Detroit also had what they wanted, for although Rabbi Wine was officially correct when he stated that there were no grounds on which a Reform rabbi could be unfrocked—a statement concurred in by the president of the CCAR—the Detroit rabbis were equally correct in assuming that the publicity could do the Birmingham Temple no good.[3]

Within a short time the *National Jewish Post and Opinion* submitted a question to Dr. Solomon Freehof, chairman of the

CCAR committee on responsa: May an atheist use the title "rabbi"?

Although the committee's responsa have technically only the status of recommendations, Rabbi Freehof, nevertheless, is a person highly respected in the Reform community, and his responsa have always been influential in forming opinions. Rabbi Freehof wrote:

> There is no question of his right to declare himself an atheist on the ground that his powers of reasoning cannot discover God in the universe. And it is also his right to organize an association of like believers. But he has no right to deceive the unwary. Using the word "rabbi" and using the word "congregation" constitute a deception. A rabbi means a teacher of Judaism. Even the most legalistic and non-mystic of the rabbis of the past, who were carefully logical in their decisions, felt that God was using them as an instrument and that their latest decision on the most practical matter was a continuation of the revelation at Mount Sinai. A rabbi, in his humbler way, feels that as much as it is in his power, he speaks for God and in God's name.
>
> So the congregation is always understood to mean an organization of religious purposes. The word "congregation" is a translation of *"Bes Ha-Knesses,"* which means the assemblies gathered for the worship of God. No one would object to Rabbi Wine and his group, if he had a Doctor's degree, to call himself Dr. Wine, and his group, The Rationalist Association of Detroit. But when he uses the title "Rabbi" and the term "synagogue" or "temple," he is luring in new members by false and heartless pretenses. He knows that people do not read philosophic manifestoes; they hear that a Rabbi has formed a Jewish congregation; they join it. When their children will be taught that God cannot be logically proved and therefore He is to be left out of the prayers, when their youth will be told that there is no religious foundation for ethics, these new members will have been cruelly deceived.
>
> What, then, is to be done with this man and this group? We do not have ways of unfrocking a rabbi. It is good that we do not. We must run the risk of freedom, but we must protect the Jewish community against the deception which will drag innocent children and unsuspecting elders into a group dedicated to the propaganda of atheism. This propaganda will be constant because the leader of the group will always feel called upon to defend his position.
>
> The Hebrew Union College has given him the title of rabbi. I do not know how they can withdraw it, but he, in candor, should refrain from using the title. I do not know whether his group is a member of the Union of American Hebrew Congregations. If it is, I do not know how it can be expelled. If it is not yet a member, it should not be admitted.

In the meantime, the Jewish congregations in Detroit, in order to protect their children and themselves from the teachings that God is not necessary in Jewish life, should not associate with it and should not acknowledge it as a Jewish congregation.[4]

*Time* magazine sent a reporter to interview Wine and his congregants, and its issue of 29 January 1965 contained a story called "The Atheist Rabbi." Wine was inundated by requests to explain his position. Even a notable like Mike Douglas asked him to appear for an interview on a nationally broadcast daytime television show.

Rabbis across the country began preaching and writing on the subject, using titles like "Atheism in Detroit: The Case of the Ignostic Rabbi and the Godless Congregation." The *Detroit Jewish News* refused to print the Birmingham Temple worship schedule under its list of "Detroit Jewish Religious Services," and the Masonic Temple of Birmingham, where the Birmingham Temple had moved its Friday night services in order to accommodate the four hundred or more people who were now attending, asked the temple to move, stating that the affirmation of a Supreme Being was the first principle of Masonry.[5] The publicity accompanying this eviction was sufficient to influence a public school in another suburb that had promised the temple a hall for services to request that the temple not use their school. The Unitarian Church of Birmingham offered its facilities, which the temple accepted reluctantly, not because they were ungrateful to the Unitarians, but because the most damaging charge that had been leveled against the temple was that it was assimilationist, leading its followers en masse out of Judaism. Thus, whether by plan or accident, the meeting that the Detroit rabbis called to investigate Rabbi Wine had the long-range effect of making the beliefs of the temple public knowledge and of linking to the congregation the stigmas of atheism and (even more damaging) assimilation and apostasy.

Although it cannot be denied that the Birmingham Temple was an embarrassment to the Reform movement, it had, until the meeting of the rabbis, remained in obscurity and had not affiliated with the Union of American Hebrew Congregations. Nor did it employ the word "Reform" in any part of its liturgy. Rabbi Wine is a member of the CCAR, but the general public is not aware that those initials denote a Reform agency. Although the first services were based on the Reform liturgy, the new format bore fewer similarities to a *Union Prayer Book* service than a Reform service did to an Orthodox one. Nevertheless, the members of the Birmingham Temple did consider themselves Reform, and this fact disturbed the Detroit rabbis for three reasons.

First, Reform had for years had to fight the charge of being more akin to Protestant or Unitarian Christianity than to traditional Judaism. In fact, a leading Detroit Conservative rabbi (who was himself assassinated), when asked to comment on the Birmingham Temple, said, "Why should I worry about the second assassin's bullet when the first [Reform] did the job?" Reform temples were called churches. Its music had been Protestantized, as had its style of worship. The charge of un-Jewishness had hurt Reform, not so much in the distant past when its members came mostly from the more assimilated German Jews, but more recently, in the competition with Conservative Judaism for the unaffiliated children of Eastern European immigrants. Especially at a time when Jewish ethnicity was valued by Americans as a whole, the charge of assimilationism hurt a Reform movement striving to prove its authenticity on the Jewish scene. The truth was, however, that as the Birmingham Temple conducted its services, there was less question about its Jewishness than in many Reform temples. Although hats were not worn, the visible symbols of the Jewish faith were stressed. Sabbath candles were lit, a *kiddush* was recited, the Torah was read, and Israeli and Hasidic music was played, leaving little doubt about the ethnic identity of the group. Wine, despite strong objections, continued to use the title "Rabbi"—which is, after all, very Jewish.

The second fear of the rabbis was that the atheism of the Birmingham Temple, located less than three miles from Father Coughlin's Church of the Little Flower, would arouse the hostility of the non-Jewish community, since tolerance by the rabbis of a place like the Birmingham Temple might seem to be a positive sanction and they thereby might find themselves guilty by association.

Third, it was feared that the combination of location, ideology, and a magnetic rabbi might prove attractive to young college-educated Jews in a new suburban area (where there was no other temple), whereas the established Reform temples would remain trapped within large buildings in the neighborhoods of tensions and would continue promulgating an unromantic ideology that quite possibly did not ring true to third- and fourth-generation American Jews.

Whatever the intentions of those who exposed the temple to publicity—and Rabbi Wine did not make their task difficult—the effects on the congregation were multiple. The flow of new members slowed to a trickle, while dropouts increased, torn by dissension and internal doubts, with the effect that Rabbi Wine became even more resolute in his stand and was moved finally to turn an experiment into a cause.

The dissension within the temple resulted from outside attacks on one issue alone: the question of Jewishness. Members said that they were not afraid of being called atheists. They did not like the appellation, but they did not consider it a charge worth denying. Many did not, in fact, consider themselves atheists, but agreed with Rabbi Wine that evidence was lacking for either an affirmation or a denial of any statement about the existence of God. But the charge of assimilation or un-Jewishness stung deeply. While it was true that a small percentage of temple members manifested a rather low degree of Jewish group attachment, the majority were reasonably high in their commitment to Jewish symbols and values. Reading books of Jewish interest, cooking and eating traditional Jewish food, working on behalf of the State of Israel—these were the activities that the group considered most meaningfully Jewish.

When asked why they should remain Jews, members responded: "Because I like it, because I was born a Jew and accept it as part of my identity as an individual." Only one out of a hundred found being Jewish a disturbing fact, whereas most described it as significant but not crucial in their lives. There was less than a 5 percent rate of intermarriage, lower than in the Jewish community as a whole. (One non-Jew joined and referred to herself as a Jew.)

Nevertheless, inasmuch as a denial of God and the elimination of the Shema are taken as a sign of defection from Judaism by American Jews, some members of the temple had grave doubts about the validity of their enterprise. (If the group had been comprised of avowed Jewish secularists, the absence of these affirmations would not have raised serious questions.) "Perhaps we've gone too far," some members of Rabbi Wine's congregation said. "Look at me, look at my husband, look at my kids, look at my house. How can you say I'm not Jewish? Yet people have been accusing my kids of not being Jewish. I don't know if it's worth it."

The leadership had now passed from those who thought of themselves as part of a universal movement to the moderates, those who believed that the future of the temple lay in its ability to stay well within the Jewish fold while clearly enunciating a doctrine of individuality that they called Jewish humanism. The moderates further believed that a cessation of publicity and conflict was desirable, and they wished to find a place for themselves in Reform Judaism. In any event, those involved declared that "for the first time in my life, religion has meaning," and their association with the Birmingham Temple was for them, on the whole, a positive experience.

Some observers tended to view the emergence of the Birmingham Temple as further proof of disintegrative tendencies in the Jewish community, but in fact it might have been appraised in quite the opposite fashion. It had long been recognized that a gap existed between the real beliefs of large numbers of American Jews and the institutional mechanism available for the expression of these beliefs. It could not be seriously argued that the low level of synagogue attendance or of religious observance among American Jews was adequately explained by the often repeated ploy that the synagogue and formal prayer occupied a very different place among Jews than the equivalent elements did among Christians. Prayer, after all, was no Christian invention, and the crowded synagogues of grandfather's generation were not nostalgic fictions. How many contemporary Jews could wholeheartedly subscribe to avowals that lay at the very center of the belief system of past generations—an interceding God responsive to prayer, a personal messiah, the chosenness of Israel, the extensive ritual safeguards and observances? The synagogues were empty, not because Judaism failed to provide them with an adequate role, but because increasingly large numbers of Jews no longer believed in what the synagogue traditionally represented. Many of these same Jews, however, refused the proferred choice of assimilation. They insisted that being Jewish was immutable, in large measure because of a belief in some vague law of sociological determinism that they assumed to be in force, but also because, however inarticulate and untutored they may have been, they sensed the existence of something precious and workable in the Jewish mode of life.

Thus, the Birmingham Temple could be viewed as a slow, awkward attempt by the congregation to bridge the gap that so often separated people from institutions they had inherited but had not experienced or created. It is clear that Rabbi Wine and his group had touched a sensitive spot in American Jewish life. The Birmingham Temple aroused much hostility, but it also won the attention of countless Jews whose interest in religious affairs had previously been minimal. Rabbis who in their entire ministry had never grappled publicly with the question of God's existence, with definitions of "Jew" and "Judaism," with the requirements for the rabbinate, or with the conflict between psychoanalysis and religion, had been forced to consider these subjects.

Almost every major Jewish publication had some opinion on the subject. The Reconstructionists regretted that the word "God" had to be dropped when Mordecai Kaplan apparently had already provided such an adequate meaning for the word. Hashomer Hatzair, a Marxist-Zionist youth movement, applauded Wine's honesty but told him that he was wasting his time in a religious movement; they advised him to drop the title "Rabbi" and come over to the side of the secularists.[6] Clearly, however, it was precisely because Wine refused to look for a new meaning for the word "God" yet clung to the title "Rabbi" with such insistence that he and his temple became a national phenomenon and aroused both intense hostility and support.

Some secularists agreed with religious Jews that Wine was abusing the title "Rabbi." Although truth may have been on their side, the sociology of America was against them. Even though, intellectually, American Jews know that they are not classifiable in purely religious terms, society has relegated them to the status of a religious group, and in accepting this status Jews have internalized the role that American society has defined for them. Although a rabbi may lack true power or authority, he is a necessary figure for legitimizing the Jew as a participant in the American way of life. He delivers an invocation at presidential inaugurations, is commissioned in the United States military chaplaincy, and provides an aura of religiosity to Kiwanis and other community fraternal groups. Although he is not, according to Jewish law, an indispensable figure at weddings and funerals, his presence is required according to the oral law of American Judaism. Indeed, even mixed marriages have become a rabbinic and not just a Jewish problem because despite the fact that secular alternatives exist for the performance of a marriage, Jews marrying Christians insist on religious wedding ceremonies—that is, weddings solemnized by rabbis. For Jews to fit properly into their place in American society as members of a religious grouping, they must have clergymen. Thus, for Wine to have shed the title "Rabbi" would have meant robbing his temple of the one feature that made it both legitimate and unique.

There are a number of Jewish secularist groups in the United States. In fact, the Birmingham Temple drew a substantial number of members from a local Detroit group, the Jewish Parents Institute. Until the establishment of the Birmingham Temple, these groups had lacked popular appeal despite their claim that large numbers of Jews shared their ideologies. They needed a representative, a leader recognized by the religious community as a legitimate officiant at life-cycle events.

In the past Jewish secularist groups had a specific raison d'être, Zionism, socialism, or non-Zionist nationalism; hence their appeal had been limited to those who shared their particular sympathies. The causes that they espoused were regarded by many third-generation middle-class American Jews as obsolete, though their effect—providing institutions in which Jewish culture could be taught and enjoyed—may have been appreciated.

What the Birmingham Temple and its rabbi did was translate one form of Jewish secularism into an American *religious* form—with Friday night and holy day services, with a Hebrew and a Sunday school, with adult study classes, with a pastor to visit the sick, comfort the bereaved, bury the dead, and name the newborn, but with a doctrine more American than Jewish.

To the extent that the Birmingham Temple succeeded in translating secularism into an American religion, it challenged nearly every nonreligious Jew in this country. To the nonaffiliated who said, "I delight in Jewish culture, but I don't believe in the theological commitments," it offered the alternative he or she claimed did not exist. It threatened both Reform and Conservative Judaism because, had it spread, it might have captured those people who would not have joined synagogues at all except for their desire to educate their children in the heritage of Judaism and their need to have a rabbi at life-cycle events. The precise extent of Jewish theological nonbelief is unknown, but if measured by attendance at services or responses to surveys of attitudes among Jewish college students, it is indeed considerable. The Birmingham Temple publicly illustrated that lack of belief and, what is more, endowed it with institutional legitimacy.

The past unpopularity of atheism in America needs no elaboration. But the stigma attached to the denial of God was, for the most part, merely a reflex from the pietistic past. Although many

Jews were embarrassed by the presence of a visible group of non-believers who had monopolized the headlines, the response of the Christian community was so slight as to allay any Jewish fears. Shortly after *Time* carried an article about Wine, it featured a story about Harvey Cox, a young Protestant seminary professor who asked for a moratorium on the word "God." It was at this time, too, that the Supreme Court of the United States ruled favorably on nonreligious conscientious objectors. The "Death of God" theologians subsequently received widespread publicity. Thus, even though atheism may have had unpopular connotations (as acknowledged by Wine, who called himself an ignostic, and by his congregants, who never once referred to themselves as atheists), the charge of atheism leveled against Jews did not appear to be an issue sufficient to arouse Gentile wrath or even a great amount of Gentile interest.

The Birmingham Temple and its rabbi laid themselves open to charges of atheism, and those Jewish institutional leaders who felt they had most to lose by the success of the temple, aided by Wine's willingness to be publicized, took full advantage of the opportunity. The antagonism of the Gentiles, however, never materialized sufficiently to frighten away potential affiliates with a group like the Birmingham Temple. Following the publicity Wine did have several speaking engagements canceled, allegedly at the instigation of some influential members of the Detroit Jewish community. Before long, however, he was subject to almost no harassment and was, in fact, a popular speaker at both Jewish and non-Jewish organizational meetings.

The Birmingham Temple presents a paradox that may be resolved either to the temple's detriment or to its growing success. If it is demonstrable that it is possible in America to sustain an institution that is atheistic but in all other respects religious (according to the current usage of the word), then it is not unlikely that the Birmingham Temple represents the first stage of what may become a larger movement. The possibility also exists, however, that an America willing openly to tolerate avowed atheists will, in the long run, no longer demand that a good American have a church affiliation. In that event people who now feel that they must join a synagogue, send their children to religious school, and have a clergyman at their celebrations will no longer feel so constrained; and the Birmingham Temple, which is the translation of Jewish secularism and religious skepticism into an acceptable religious form, will have lost its function.

## chapter ten

# Makom—Yiddish and Yoga

In 1969, when the youth of the United States and other developed countries seemed to have turned the culture of the middle classes inside out, the ever-perceptive social seer Margaret Mead wrote:

> Today, the central problem is commitment. To what past, present or future can the idealistic young commit themselves? Commitment in this sense would have been a meaningless question to primitive preliterate man. He was what he was: one of his own people, a people who very often used a special name for human beings to describe their own in contrast to all others. He might fail [in other ways]. But he could not change his commitment. He was who he was—inalienable, sheltered and fed with the cocoon of custom until his whole being expressed it.
>
> The idea of choice in commitment entered human history when competing styles of life were endowed with new kinds of sanctions of religious or political ideology. No longer a matter of minor comparisons between tribes, as civilization developed commitment became a matter of choice between entire systems of thought.[1]

The Jew is both the exception to and the very model of the type of person described by Dr. Mead. On the one hand, the Jew remains tribal, a factor enhanced by his reacquisition of a homeland and illustrated above by the desperate fear his institutions express toward exogamy. As we have seen, however, the American Jew is the classical example of the person with multiple options for commitment as well as options for multiple commitments. The limitations to these options are what we are attempting to define.

Just as the Birmingham Temple appeared as an option for the Jew of the precounterculture sixties, so the postcounterculture seventies have produced a new Jewish religious phenomenon that attempts both to expand and to contain the options of young adults. Such is the creation of Makom.

The Chicago Jewish community typifies the postcounterculture mood of the 1970s. A city with approximately twenty-five Reform temples and countless synagogues of other orientations, Chicago was swamped with young Jewish adults who less than a decade before had shown an outspoken hostility to Judaism, much like the young boy who declared, "I want everyone to know I don't belong only to *Jewish* things." In recent years these young adults had developed a life-style reflective both of their maturing and of their college idealism. Many who had jobs in the Loop and in other urban neighborhoods could not envision themselves commuting to a home in the suburbs. As a result they slowly began renting quarters in the apartment houses, brownstones, and high-rises of an area just north of the pseudocounterculture Old Town neighborhood. Soon enough the area had become so popular that rents were at a premium and places to live had become scarce. The migration back to urban living evolved into Chicago's first new neighborhood in many years. Whereas other Chicago neighborhoods had ethnic orientations, this one was an area for a generational group, an urban setting with a modern life-style for people in the twenty-one to forty-five years age bracket. Stores, restaurants, community theaters, pubs, cinemas, and bistros reflected the new type of consumer. This neighborhood of "swinging singles," young marrieds, and middle-class white-collar workers became known as New Town. The name was intended as a reaction to the garishness of Old Town and the out-of-date counterculture image that it tried to foster.

As one might have expected, the Jews of New Town felt a sense of religious identity but were unable to express it within the existing Jewish institutions of the city. In June 1973 an attempt to meet their spiritual and cultural needs took shape, for into the breach came Makom, the first Jewish "storefront synagogue" (patterned after the storefront churches abounding in the ghettos of urban blacks). Located in what had been a doctor's office, but with additional programs held in apartments, synagogues, and a Unitarian Church all situated in New Town, Makom developed as a Jewish spiritual community that operated on the principle of individual participation; that is, each person was expected to take responsibility for his actions—unlike the *chavurot* of the 1960s

where the group had come first and where people had been encouraged to live together in communes. Makom was, however, a
natural extension of the *chavurah* movement for people who had
experienced the upheavals of social activism.

Makom was envisioned as the new Jewish alternative for the
alienated, disaffected young adults of New Town. The concept
looked good on paper, but many doubted its practicability. That
was the gamble taken by Chicago's Jewish community. As it happened, that gamble became the most exciting Jewish happening
Chicago had ever witnessed.

The idea of Makom actually antedated the 1970s. It had begun
in the late 1960s when a Reform rabbi, Haskell Bernat (at the
time regional director for the Great Lakes Federation of the
Union of American Hebrew Congregations), noticed the various
Jewish communes springing up all over the country. Bernat
thought it would be worthwhile to give groups of young Jews the
financial support they needed to start new communes on campuses throughout the Midwest. He surmised that the new form of
Jewish community might even be able to take root in an urban
setting. "Just think," he said, "of young Jews organizing themselves with the financial backing of the Jewish Establishment.
We'd just give them the money and let them do their thing . . . no
strings attached."

In the winter of 1972, Bernat's idea began to take practical
shape. Aware of the influx of young, unaffiliated Jewish adults to
the New Town area, and sensing their desire for some new type of
Jewish community to meet their needs, Bernat made his move.
He met with leaders of both the Reform and Conservative Jewish
communities of Chicago to discuss the possibility of creating a
Jewish presence in New Town for the twenty-one to forty-five-
year-old target group. The goal was to establish four small groups
of fifteen members each who would form *chavurot*; these groups
would become the Jewish presence in the area.

Impressed with the idea, the leaders with whom Bernat spoke
created a steering panel called The Jewish Experience (TJE) to
underwrite the effort for a one-year experimental period. It took
only a matter of months for the money to be raised.

TJE's next task was to complete the details of the experiment.
They planned to ask a rabbinic student, either from the Hebrew
Union College or from the Jewish Theological Seminary, to take a
leave of absence and become TJE's intern. He would be provided
with an apartment and with a storefront location in New Town

where services, classes, programs, holiday celebrations, and meetings would be held. From that point on the intern would have total control of the experiment: everything from recruitment to program content to public relations would be subject to his authority; TJE would act only as an advisory panel.

A committee of TJE visited the seminary campuses to interview prospective candidates. The committee made known its criteria for the position and then discussed the experiment in detail. What TJE wanted was a man who felt comfortable within both Reform and Conservative Jewish patterns; he would have to be flexible enough to blend Jewish tradition with modern creativity in every dimension of the experiment. In addition, a qualified candidate would have to possess a sense of "street savvy" and be the type of outgoing personality with whom people in the New Town target group could identify.

After the final interviews had been completed in Chicago, TJE chose David Glazer, a Hebrew Union College student, to be the intern. Glazer had almost every quality for which they had been searching. A native Israeli, Glazer had developed a comfortable familiarity with Jewish practice as well as a fluency in Hebrew and Yiddish during his formative years. His adolescent days had been spent in a traditional home in Baltimore and had included study in a local high school *yeshiva*. After graduation he left home to attend Boston University; but finding liberal arts not to his liking, Glazer entered the School of Theater Arts and became interested in modern dance. Receiving his diploma from Boston University, he chose to enroll in the rabbinical program of the Hebrew Union College. By the end of the first semester, however, he felt the need to do something else. He left the college and returned to Israel, where he became a member of the prestigious Bat Dor dance troup of Tel Aviv. About a year later Glazer's interest in dance brought him back to America, this time to New York, where he appeared in the choruses of such shows as *To Live Another Summer*. All this time he was cultivating a taste for New York's fast-paced night life (which would prove to be a major asset in his efforts to recruit participants for Makom). By 1972 he tired of the artificiality of Broadway and reentered rabbinical school. But after another year of studies, he again began yearning for a new type of Jewish exposure. When Rabbi Bernat came to interview candidates for TJE, Glazer saw his opportunity.

Originally the New Town experiment was to have begun in the summer of 1973, but it suffered a serious setback when the

United Synagogue of America's central office withheld its share of the funding. The Chicago region had sent the donations to New York, earmarking them for the project, but the central office of the United Synagogue was skeptical of working in tandem with the Reform movement. In consequence, they resorted to a technicality to hold back the funds for Chicago. Bernat became quite disturbed about this move and vowed to initiate the experiment with or without Conservative help. Still, he realized that the Conservative members of TJE had not wavered in their support for the storefront synagogue, and he did not want to exclude those founding members of TJE who maintained a genuine interest. Through a combined effort of Reform and Conservative Jews in Chicago, the funds were released from New York, and the experiment was rescheduled for June 1974.

David Glazer moved to Chicago immediately after completing the second semester of the school year. Since his first objective was to acclimate himself to the city and its young adult community, he took to the streets, seeking out the people. In the daytime Glazer would roam the Lake Michigan beaches. Whether he joined a volleyball game, took a dip with new acquaintances, or stretched out in the sun, Glazer constantly talked up the idea of the alternative Jewish community. His evenings were spent promoting the storefront synagogue for any and all listeners in the bars, nightclubs, and restaurants. The word got around New Town.

Glazer's vision of the new-style community captured the fancy of a number of disaffected young Jews. He urged on them something totally different from typical houses of worship. A group of people would establish the kind of place (*makom*) where Jews from all walks of life could feel at home. Jewish interests could be pursued in a relaxed, loosely structured atmosphere. He told his listeners to watch for the opening of Makom; individuals who wanted more information gave Glazer their addresses and phone numbers. The seeds for a community had been planted.

More and more Jews were talking about Makom as the summer progressed. Here was David Glazer, a "mod," handsome young man *and a rabbi*, insisting that Judaism could thrive in a modern setting and still be authentic. Whether or not they believed that Glazer would succeed, their curiosity was aroused. They wanted a Jewish life-style that would meet their needs: the usual structure of an organized congregation was not for them. A number of people became attracted by Glazer's charismatic personality as well. The word-of-mouth publicity continued.

In late June Rabbi Bernat was elected to a large pulpit in Los Angeles. Glazer now had to serve as his own liaison to TJE, the role that had been Bernat's. One of his immediate tasks was to find a storefront for Makom. After weeks of searching he finally located a second-floor suite that formerly belonged to a doctor. The office location was ideal, only a block east of the corner of Clark and Diversey, one of the busiest corners in the entire New Town area. By late July 1974 Glazer was able to open the doors to Makom's headquarters. The first program was a creative Shabbat service and an *oneg*. Nine people attended; together with Glazer they comprised a *minyan*. Sensing a feeling of warmth despite the lack of numbers, Glazer invited them back for the next Shabbat service and asked them to bring friends. Again that week he was out on the streets talking about Makom.

For the second Shabbat, 18 people showed up; the following Shabbat, 40 were in attendance. To reinforce the developing good feelings, Glazer began holding a Havdalah ceremony on the lakefront: people would gather at the totem pole in Waveland Park and them move down to the beach. Weekdays found more and more people talking about Makom and "that mod Rabbi Glazer." On the Shabbat before Rosh Hashanah, 115 people came for services and the *oneg*.

Makom's High Holy Day services were conducted in the Second Unitarian Church, located about four blocks from the office. Glazer predicted a large turnout and began preparing for it. He arranged for fliers, posters, and a mailing. Guitarists, readers, and service writers volunteered their efforts. An old friend of Glazer's, Nancy Ginden, came north from Miami to help coordinate the proceedings. Michael Chase, a young man who had become captivated both by Glazer and by Makom's promise, offered to be the cantor. That evening, 17 September 1974, nearly 250 people packed themselves into the seats of the church to take part in a joyful Jewish worship experience. Those in attendance were singing, clapping their hands, and hugging one another by the end of the evening. It was, moreover, not only young adults from New Town who took part in the service; people came from the suburbs and the lakefront high-rises. Older adults with their children, wealthy socialites, and curious philanthropists also joined in the celebration. Apparently it appealed to them, for another large crowd returned the following morning.

During the days before Yom Kippur, Makom mobilized for action. On a set of file cards, Glazer had recorded the names, addresses, telephone numbers, and special interests of those who came for Rosh Hashanah. These cards—about three hundred in all—were alphabetized and added to the mailing list. Other volunteers began writing the services for Shabbat Shuvah and Yom Kippur. Glazer found himself glued to the telephone. The *Chicago Sun-Times* had published a two-page spread about the Rosh Hashanah service, as had the prestigious neighborhood tabloid, the *Lakeview Press*.[2] People kept calling to get information about future events and to offer assistance in the preparation of programs.

By this time Glazer had come to the conclusion that Makom was too large for one rabbinic intern. If he was to continue mingling with the people, another intern would have to handle administrative details and coordinate programs. Glazer prevailed on TJE to hire Neil Kraft, another Hebrew Union College student and a close friend of his, as Makom's second rabbi. Kraft satisfied both the need for an administrative intern and the sentiment for added programs of a traditional character. In addition, he had been raised in an Orthodox Jewish environment and knew how to develop programs expressive of *Yiddishkeit*.

Yom Kippur proved to be another important boost to the Makom community. The seats filled up so rapidly for Kol Nidre that Glazer had to come to the pulpit and urge those who could attend services at other congregations to do so. Even with that plea, over three hundred remained for the Makom service. An equally large crowd, by now usual, returned the following morning.

In the two months following Yom Kippur, Shabbat at Makom became a permanent part of the social life for many New Town Jews. Not only did TJE consider Makom to be a huge success in terms of these Shabbatot, but Jews from all over the city felt a vested interest in preserving this alternative community. In terms of both numbers of people and quality of programs, Makom had already surpassed its goal for the nine-month period. Glazer continued to promote Makom in the New Town gathering places, but he also spoke to temples, synagogues, and secular Jewish organizations around the city. Kraft, Ginden, and Chase coordinated the Makom activities, giving volunteers a variety of jobs and program tasks to do. Makom opened its doors every evening from 6:00 to 11:00. People came for classes, for program preparation, or simply to socialize.

Shabbat was still the high point of the week. A crowd of 150 or more filled all the rooms of the former doctor's office, and the

overflow spilled out into the hallways. Every Friday an anony-
mous person left a challah at the door. Thus, a *motzi* blessing was
added to the candle blessing and the *kiddush*. By November different individuals and small groups were writing the creative
services and conducting them. After services Makom people set
up refreshment tables for others to enjoy while listening to Israeli
music, chatting with friends, and meeting new people. At 11:00
P.M. Makom would close its doors, but the *oneg* would continue at
someone's apartment until the wee hours of the morning.

With larger numbers of people taking part in Makom activities,
Glazer and Kraft chose to broaden the base of Makom's
decision-making power. They created a steering committee, a
group of about ten people, to help shape the future direction of the
community. As in any group this committee suffered a variety of
personality conflicts that often led to temporary frictions. All of
the committee members, however, shared two overriding goals.
First, they believed in the importance of maintaining Makom's
vitality. Second, they agreed that, despite any personality conflicts, the community was better for having several people participate in the significant decision making.

By mid-December Makom had grown so large that a number of
new realities had to be faced. Shabbat services had undergone
such expansion that Makom's facilities were unable to accommodate the crowds. Arrangements were made with Temple Sholom,
a large congregation on Lake Shore Drive near New Town, to hold
Shabbat services in the temple's basement. (Many wondered if
Makom people would feel uncomfortable about coming to an established temple, but the initial gatherings dispelled these fears.)
Also, the large number of participants had put a strain on the
budget. In addition to accepting speaking engagements, oversee-
ing the entire project, and meeting with people informally, Glazer
began soliciting funds from the Jewish community. Michael
Chase, too, devoted a great deal of his energy to the fund-raising
task. Meanwhile, Nancy Ginden became the administrator, taking full responsibility for the organizational needs of Makom;
Neil Kraft concentrated on the program, worship, and the educational projects. In effect, Makom developed a natural structure in
order to serve the needs of its rapidly growing constituency. The
Chicago Jewish community proved quite supportive of Makom.
Various civic groups donated time and money to underwrite the
experiment. TJE continued to be a valuable source of advice and
information. In many instances the committee acted as a helpful

liaison to the rest of the Jewish community. The prestigious Chicago Board of Rabbis not only extended full membership to Glazer and Kraft, but also promoted Makom among its congregations, thereby adding to Makom's moral and financial support.

Makom took two steps to ensure that its size and small bureaucracy would not negate its warmth and personal touch. Michael Chase and others assumed responsibility for the creation, distribution, and analysis of a Makom community questionnaire, whose purpose was to allow for a broad range of views in any future plans. Also, the celebration of Hanukkah reinforced the *haimish* atmosphere of Makom. On the first evening of the holiday, 350 people came to the Unitarian Church for Makom's creative service and a latke party. The *Chicago Tribune* covered the festivities and published a lengthy article along with a number of pictures.[3] For the rest of the holiday, smaller parties, complete with menorah lighting and chanted blessings, were held in various apartments, much like the *oneg Shabbat*.

By January Makom could claim a fantastic achievement. Six months before, the experiment had begun with a "hip" rabbi talking to people on the beaches and in the bistros, and with nine people attending the inaugural Shabbat service. Since then Makom had evolved into a loosely tied community of some four hundred diverse people. A small organizing committee effectively channeled the special interests and talents within this community. The Jewish community had taken Makom to its heart both in word and in deed. They recognized its innovative flair, its authentic Jewish life-style amidst modern settings, its dynamic presence in New Town, and its ability to attract participants from the entire metropolitan area. Most important, they had fallen in love with Makom's charismatic rabbi, David Glazer.

Notwithstanding the initial expectation of a community of disaffected young New Town Jews, Makom's people actually came to include a wide range of personality types from a diversity of backgrounds. Both the card file and personal contacts made it evident that young and old Jews alike from Evanston, Mount Prospect, the Gold Coast, Rogers Park, Olympia Fields, Old Town, Hyde Park, Glencoe, the University of Chicago, and elsewhere—literally a fifty-mile radius—comprised the amorphous group. Some Makom people participated frequently in the activities (once a week and sometimes more often); most others attended programs on a less regular basis. On Shabbat, the high point of Makom's week, hipsters mixed with lonely hearts, male

chauvinists argued with Women's Libbers, posh socialites hob-
nobbed with homosexuals. Most boundaries of social stratification
went ignored at a Makom function.

The special interest of Makom participants reflected Jewish,
secular, and fad cultures. The card file listed mixtures of all three.
One person's hobbies included Hebrew, hatha-yoga, Jewish history, and meditation; another enjoyed "administration, teaching
elementary Hebrew, meditation, philosophy, comparative religion, music, and developing a street theater." A third mentioned
needlepoint, tennis, Yiddish, Jewish cooking, and arts and crafts.
Other cards asked for everything from Yiddish and Yoga to folk
dancing and self-development lectures. The questionnaire sought
to uncover why these people came to Makom. The steering committee understood that any combination of factors influenced an
individual. Some came to meet a person of the opposite sex. Some
came to study Torah. Some needed a place to belong. Some
wanted an informal synagogue for celebrating the Jewish holidays. Some merely wanted to rebel against organized Judaism.

When the community's size began to diminish the feeling of
closeness, Glazer tried to organize small *chavurot*, which would
hold their own services, study sessions, and holiday celebrations.
Mentioning this idea at a Shabbat service, he was surprised to
encounter a strong measure of opposition. At this point, apparently, people enjoyed mingling in the larger community and saw
nothing attractive in the exclusivity of the smaller *chavurah*.
Thus, the original concept of small groups within a large community had to be abandoned.

Makom regulars reflected the size and diversity of the community. Nancy Ginden, for example, had developed a livelihood as an
artist. Michael Chase had spent years as part of the New York
City rock music scene. He had played an important part in promoting the George Harrison Bangladesh concert. Later he studied
in India with Guru Maharji. Even Bart Collier, the pastor of the
Unitarian Church, became a Makom regular. Enamored of the
Makom community, he was an important fixture at both social
and worship events. The list goes on and on. A heavily made-up
girl would spend Shabbat looking for the right pickup. A former
Conservative rabbi, now a hospital administrator, found a meaningful role for himself teaching classes and conducting services. A
former actor in local Chicago theater productions came to Makom
to relieve the depression of a pending divorce. An advertising
executive just wanted to meet some Jewish people. A

psychoanalyst enjoyed being able to dance and sing in traditional Jewish patterns. A secretary satisfied certain needs by organizing party and *oneg* refreshments. Two Orthodox rabbis taught Talmud and arranged small *ferbrangen*s. Makom's people truly came from all walks of life to satisfy all kinds of needs. In this light one person aptly described Makom as a Jewish spiritual community operating on the principle of individual participation within a setting of social interaction, cultural programs, classes, worship, and Jewish life-cycle events.

The first programs that David Glazer created in his new role as Makom's rabbi were the life-cycle celebrations, and these continued to be the most successful in terms of both quantity and quality of participation. People seemed to come out of the woodwork for these events. The creative Shabbat services and *oneg Shabbat* instilled in people a positive feeling for Judaism and Jewish identity. For many this marked their first interest in the religion since the alienation that had manifested itself in adolescent or undergraduate days.

A spillover effect resulted for other life-cycle programs. Rosh Hashanah and Yom Kippur created positive attitudes toward Makom, attitudes reinforced by the other holiday celebrations. People converged on a local Orthodox synagogue to celebrate Sukkot and Simhat Torah. Amazed neighbors saw an assortment of "freaks and straights" dancing in the streets. People gathered at the lakefront (before the weather grew too cold) for Havdalah and then dispersed to continue the socializing at smaller parties. Hanukkah's massive crowd and good time gave the community an infusion of new people with new ideas. Many, it was clear, came to these events more for social contact than from a desire to observe a Jewish holiday, but a certain sensitivity to life-cycle events began growing even in the most socially oriented individuals. By the end of December, those who had originally come mainly for social reasons now also consciously attended to take part in a Jewish celebration.

Makom initiated a twofold educational program immediately after Yom Kippur. The program followed the model of the free university, the alternative form of education that had developed in radical subcultures during the late 1960s. For adults a broad spectrum of classes was offered. Topics included Yiddish, Orthodox-Conservative-Reform philosophy, history, Orthodox law, Jewish cooking, the Bible, Judaism and women's rights, and a weekly *ferbrangen*. For families Makom held a religious school on Sunday mornings. Unlike the more traditional forms of religious school, Makom's school taught whole families, adults and children together. Using the techniques of the open classroom and student-centered curriculum, Glazer and Kraft created an ongoing program of family activities founded on Jewish holidays and values.

Depending on the perspective, one could call these classes a success or a failure. If one analyzes the quality of content, then the program met its objective. Courses were well prepared, teachers showed great interest in the students, students came with a desire to learn, and the intellectual level was high. On the other hand, if one analyzes community-wide consciousness-raising, then the program fell short of its initial projections. Only a small percentage of the 350 people listed on the file cards attended the sessions, and those who did attend did so only irregularly. The *ferbrangen* had to be discontinued for lack of interest.

By January the steering committee had reevaluated the program and had made recommendations to improve it. Classes would be promoted with the same kind of intensity as the holiday celebrations. Small fees would be charged to induce regular attendance. The idea was to establish peer reinforcements for the idea that education was as important to the community as the life-cycle events were. The suggestions worked: Makom now had over one hundred people enrolled in its adult classes, and the religious school had increased in size each week. A Shabbat Torah brunch was begun and met with initial success. Education had arrived for the Makom community.

Although the overt purpose of every Makom event falls into the area of either education or life cycle, the social element remains a covert, all-pervasive influence. Many people take advantage of the opportunity to meet with friends or to make new friends at Makom functions. For many a sense of belonging and identification exists that cannot be found with any other group. Makom activities facilitate the chance to contact other Jews with similar interests.

One of the goals of the questionnaire was to determine if the social factor was the key element in the growth of Makom. Although no analysis had been attempted, the feeling was that New Town residents and other young adults had tired of bars and nightclubs as meeting places. Singles needed a less artificial environment to meet other singles. Couples wanted to add a Jewish dimension to their relationship, but not within a stereotypical religious institution. Thus, much like the synagogues in ancient Judea,[4] Makom became the social center for its diverse community.

By almost any standard Makom had become a success story in contemporary American Jewish religious life. A strong Jewish presence now exists in the New Town area, an alternative to organized religious institutions. Also, through media coverage and public-speaking engagements by its interns, Makom has created a broad base of support throughout the Chicago Jewish community. Participants, it bears repeating, come not only from New Town, but from all over the city. Only halfway through its experimental year, Makom had reached nearly six times as many people (350) as it had hoped to reach by the end of that year. Most important, Makom provided a social outlet for young Jewish adults and employed that outlet to foster positive Jewish identities, ritual practice, and new levels of religious awareness. The only drawbacks were that, for a time, the educational programs failed to capture the imagination of the community; the size of the group and the need for adequate programs strained the budget; and the community resisted developing small *chavurot* that might have enhanced the sense of a more personal Judaism.

A variety of social forces operate continuously within Makom. The two main elements are the evolution and maintenance of the community and David Glazer's role as the Makom director. Makom, it is evident, is no *chavurah*, but instead is a broad-based community with a diverse membership. Still, Makom does have the potential to develop *chavurot* within its large membership. Many of the reasons for the vitality of the community stem from the foresight of TJE, which had the insight to realize that disaffected Jews did not need another temple or synagogue, but rather a clear-cut alternative to organized institutions. TJE endeavors to support Makom but at the same time to avoid interfering with its natural evolution. To a large degree it has been successful. Then, too, David Glazer and the steering committee had the sense to eschew the group exclusivity that eventually had stifled the *chavurah* movement of the 1960s. (The failure of the earlier *chavurot* may account for the community's resistance to breaking into smaller groups.)

Although the Makom community is authentically Jewish, it reflects a typical American religious viewpoint that places primary importance on the individual. What Niebuhr said of the Protestant Denominationalists of the nineteenth century is equally true of these Jews of New Town—they have no unitary composition as a group. Within their shared activist attitudes toward life, they preserve a large measure of individual self-consciousness. The people have a general level of education and culture, they have their financial security and physical comfort (despite the recession), and they have promoted a sense of Jewish peer identity. When it comes to belief and practice, the New Town Jews manifest a highly personal religion, like their Protestant counterparts. Righteousness is seen as a matter of right actions carried out in obedience to a series of divinely inspired *mitzvot*. The ethical good is the moral welfare of the individual. Despite the positive orientation of Makom and its community-wide support, one cannot ignore the existing tension between disaffected young Jews and present religious institutions. As Lewis Coser wrote, the distinction between an in-group and the outside world is established through modes of conflict where the outside elements are both the target of hostility and the positive reference.[5] It is clear that American temples and synagogues are disdained for their rigid structure but appreciated for their positive aspects—promoting community pride, being conducive to social intercourse, and providing educational and worship opportunities.

In addition, it appears that the evolution of Makom closely follows Smelser's model of collective behavior, a series of five sequential actions that band a number of individuals into a collectivity.[6] First, a *structural conduciveness* in the social system allowed for the beginning of Makom. Bernat's ability to translate his idea into reality, and TJE's full support of the experiment, reflected the desire for an alternative Jewish community for young Jewish adults. Second, the *structural strain* in the Jewish community could be felt. Members of the community feared the loss of their youth, while the youth had no idea how to create a Jewish communal identity of their own. Third, the *growth and spread of a general belief* pervaded Chicago Jewry. A storefront synagogue in New Town could become a viable addition to the city's other Jewish organizations. Fourth, the *precipitating factor* of word-of-mouth information about a hip rabbi aroused the curiosity of the target group. Finally, *mobilization for action* was needed. David Glazer did this almost single-handedly through his power of persuasion and his ability to inspire a positive feeling in those who came to Makom functions.

Collectivities are known to disintegrate rapidly. If Makom programs evolve into an acceptable pattern of regularity (i.e., weekly attendance of Shabbat services), the process will change the group from a collectivity into an ongoing community. Makom's community will need continual high quality in programming and periodic reinforcement of positive Jewish attitudes in order to ensure its existence and viability.

It is doubtful that Makom would have achieved its level of success under any other rabbinic intern than David Glazer. Glazer displayed an understanding of the New Town Jews that was essential to the building of the community. He shared a life-style with the residents. His Judaic background gave him the empathy to develop the kind of contemporary Jewish programs that people wanted and needed. Opportunities for social contact occurred in modern Jewish settings of education, celebration, and worship. At the same time, Glazer radiated a good feeling for Judaism as a religion. This positive identity was the primary shared value of the community.

Glazer had one other quality that heightened both his pro-gramming skills and his human sensitivity: he had charisma. Naturally endowed with dynamism, he attracted people to him-self. Males and females alike were stimulated by his intellect, his empathy, his love for Judaism, his contemporary attire, his "street savvy," his physical appearance, and all the other traits of a charismatic leader. Establishing himself as the "Mod Rabbi of New Town" through both media coverage and word of mouth, Glazer brought the people to Makom in the manner of a Jewish Pied Piper. Makom's high-quality programs then ensured that the people would return on their own.

Equally important, Glazer shared his authority and decision-making power with the community at large. The steering com-mittee and the questionnaire convinced people that he was con-cerned about their feelings and opinions. Not only did this en-hance his charismatic strength; it also gave the community the feeling that Makom belonged to everyone. No clique, no in-group, no individual owned Makom.

Some wondered if Makom had become a David Glazer personal-ity cult. At the present time there exists no means of determining this, nor is there any need to do so. Makom has survived as a successful modern Jewish community. If Makom survives Glazer's return to his studies at the Hebrew Union College it certainly will deserve to be deemed something far greater than a cult. Whether a cult or a community at present, Makom, under his influence, has brought Jewish meaning to the lives of hun-dreds of disaffected young Jewish adults. The lesson for American

Jewry seems quite clear. Normative Judaism has often enough in the past encouraged the blending of innovation with tradition. Positive change does not threaten an end to the Jewish way of life. On the contrary, such change offers hope of bringing the disaffected back into the mainstream of American Judaism.

## chapter eleven

# Unorthodox Alternatives

It is worthwhile comparing the emergence of the Birmingham
Temple in the mid-1960s and the development of Makom in the
mid-1970s. In the mid-sixties, before the development of the counterculture, the Birmingham Temple was founded by eight couples
who felt no strong or particular alienation from the Jewish community. These couples had the help of a handsome, single, rather
young (thirty-five), articulate rabbi who had moved religiously
from the right-wing Conservative Judaism of his youth through
the philosophy department of the University of Michigan and on
to Hebrew Union College. Then, after his ordination, he returned
to Detroit as assistant rabbi in a classical Reform temple. After a
stint as a chaplain, a return engagement as assistant at the classical Reform temple, and a stay in Windsor as its only Reform
rabbi, Wine was eager, when guaranteed a living wage, to cross
the river back to Detroit to become founding rabbi of a new temple (called Birmingham after the swanky northwest Detroit suburb, where, ironically, it has never been located). Since the temple depended on Wine's charisma, it was willing to be formed in
his image—aloof, intellectual, sophisticated, and coolly casual
toward the existence of God.

The mid-1960s were a time of luxury, both economic and intellectual. The Free Speech movement at Berkeley was breaking
into the news. Detroit was changing: whites were leaving the city,

but the auto and construction industries were booming. There were distant rumblings from the nonwhite minorities who had become part of the Great Society, but militant civil rights advocates had not yet turned Negroes into blacks. There were also echoes from M-2s in Indochina, but Israel was at peace; ethnicity had not become a life-style; and the media had time and space to devote to Bishop Robinson's *Honest to God* and Fletcher's *Situation Ethics*. The "Death of God" movement seemed to go hand in hand with the civil rights movement. Rationalism was triumphant. Hair was just beginning to grow on the counter-culture.[2]

The issue for the Birmingham Temple was really whether or not its publicized atheism would provoke sufficient negative reactions in the non-Jewish community to warrant denying the temple and its members a comfortable place within the Jewish community. For the Reform establishment, the issue was whether the movement was permissive enough to permit atheists a place within it. But the issue was never pressed. Sherwin Wine's right to use the title "rabbi" was never officially challenged by the CCAR, and the Birmingham Temple never needed to develop the militancy of today's Jewish gays. Unlike the gays, the straight ignostics saw no need to press for membership within the Union of American Hebrew Congregations.[3]

Ten years later, in the mid-1970s, the Birmingham Temple is housed in an adequate building in Farmington, Michigan, less than a mile from the Labor Zionist Alliance, but miles further from Birmingham than the huge classical Reform temple that Wine had assisted as a newly ordained rabbi. The Birmingham Temple survived the Detroit riots of 1967; it reflected quietly on the Six-Day War; it stood rationally steadfast against American involvement in Vietnam. Ironically, its biggest disappointment came from the generation it claimed it would be saving for Judaism.

The counterculture, with its mysticism, its fascination with the occult, its disgust with technology, its embracing of ethnic costumery, its active involvement in rather than passive contemplation of sexuality, posed the greatest threat to the survival of the Birmingham Temple. While Rabbi Wine's congregation was devoting itself to rational discussions and worshipping the "best in man," the young generation was either "tuning in or dropping out" and becoming the Frankenstein monster created by "cool McNamaran logicians." The counterculture, even in its modified form, avoided the Birmingham Temple, whose membership is now drawn primarily from vestigial humanists wishing their sons and daughters to have bar or bat mitzvahs or to be confirmed (the latter a ceremony that need have no Hebrew content). The Birmingham Temple is rented by establishmentarian Jewish organizations for meetings and socials. Its Friday night service is no longer a phenomenon. It has disappeared from the eye of the media, and information about it is generally obtainable only through subscription to *Humanistic Judaism* (a periodical published by three congregations close in belief to Rabbi Wine) or through scrutiny of the synagogue section of the *Detroit Jewish News*. In size its membership now is equal to or somewhat greater than its membership when it was a phenomenon; but as an attempt to meet the needs of the next generation, it is no more successful nor was it any more foresighted than were "the best and the brightest" in whose image it had sought to create itself.

In apparent contrast to the creation of the Birmingham Temple, which was initiated by unaffiliated laymen seeking a rabbi who were in fact led into religious radicalism by a charismatic leader, stands the birth of Makom in Chicago. Makom, we have seen, was the brainchild of a rabbinic representative of a national Reform Jewish organization, the Union of American Hebrew Congregations, and was eventually cosponsored by a national Conservative body, the United Synagogue of America. Makom was not created in a suburb, but rather in a part of the central city that had become a magnet for the avant-garde, former members of the counterculture, those who had moved back from the suburbs, those who had never married and those who were divorced, those who were creative and those who aspired to creativity. In Makom, paradoxically, one sees what seems to be a successful attempt by organized religion to appeal to those assumed to be disillusioned by organized religion or shunned by existent Jewish institutional forms. Makom is a perfect example of the co-option of the counterculture person, the anti-institutionalist, and the deviant—a co-option by the very institutions that may, in fact, have had a role in propelling persons into the counterculture, forcing them out of religious institutions and making them deviant. It is precisely to the divorced, the homosexual, the anticlerical, the mixed married, and other deviants that Makom makes its strongest appeal.

Makom went so far as to secure two young men, neither as yet ordained and one as far removed from the rabbinic stereotype as is conceivable, and to grant them the use of the title "rabbi" to demonstrate to potential affiliators the noninstitutionalized nature of the place. In fact, when Makom calls itself a synagogue, which it rarely does, the word is prefixed by the term "storefront." In short, Makom might be regarded as a very well intentioned, highly successful fraud—although it is certainly unfair to impute subterfuge to either its conceiver, its leaders, or those who avail themselves of its offerings.

With the Birmingham Temple, one has the advantage of some ten years' hindsight. It began as a novelty. It appeared to offer the possibility that it would be the starting place of a new movement designed to appeal to a new generation of Jews enlightened about God through empiricism and not bound to the past by guilt. It was to be the true and logical fulfillment of the eighteenth-century enlightenment and its nineteenth-century Reform extension. However, it failed to anticipate a host of events that rendered it less appealing to most Jews than Lubavitcher Hasidism; its members (possibly Rabbi Wine and a few others are to be excepted) settled for a position of respectability within the Jewish mainstream in a modest but quite solid suburban temple.

Makom shares with the Birmingham Temple a wish to cater to the needs of the modern Jew. It is crucial to note, however, that in America, among Jews as among others, such terms as "contemporary" quickly dissolve into "establishment" or "faddist." Makom is definitely God-accepting, though theologically amorphous. It is ideological, rational, and physical (in contrast to previous manifestations of westernized Judaism); and it accepts the current belief that today's and, it is hoped, tomorrow's Jews do not wish to pursue individualism if individualism means loneliness. They are willing to surrender their ego to what Freud calls the "oceanic feeling"—that is, they are willing to abandon empiricism for community (no matter how unenlightened this may appear).

It is essential to bear in mind that, no matter what the apparent differences between Makom and Jewish humanism are, they have a great deal in common. Both are centered on a charismatic personality. Although Wine and Glazer could not be more dissimilar in their "presentation of self," they and their institutions are as one in attempting to meet Jews where they are today. Neither the Birmingham Temple nor Makom is willing to surrender its claims to Jewish authenticity, and both are examples of methods whereby Jews are offered unorthodox Judaism in order to preserve for the sake of Jewish survival the scattered remnants of the household of Israel.

. . . . . . . . . . . . . . . . . . . . . . . . . . . . . . . . . . . . . . . . . . . . . . . . . . . . . . . .

# PART THREE

Children, Women, and Men—The Use and Misuse of
Myth in the Formation of American Jewish Identity

## Introductory Note

. . . . . . . . . . . . . . . . . . . . . . . . . . . . . . . . . . . . . . . . . . . . . . .

The final three essays of this book explore the existence of certain Jewish myths, past and present, in the face of current knowledge. The first focuses on the importance of legends, fantasies, and myths in the shaping of Jewish identity. I have taken two ancient legends (each grounded in some historical reality)—the story of the founding of a rabbinical academy at Yavneh and that of the last-ditch military stand of Jewish zealots at the fortress of Masada. These two events date back to the same historical moment within the geographical confines of ancient postbiblical Israel but traditionally are the outgrowths of two antagonistic Jewish values. One maintains that passivity in the face of external authority is to be encouraged among Jews, as long as Jews are left the freedom to study Torah—a principle that, with the support of external authority, was excellently suited to the maintenance of rabbinic authority over the Jewish masses. The other is exemplified by the Jewish zealots who preferred to commit suicide rather than surrender to external authority. What I am attempting to demonstrate is the sociological and psychological importance of these two legends in the mythos of Jewish identity, but I think it equally significant to note how American unorthodox Judaism has tried to weave the two legends into a single myth supporting both the centrality of religious authority and the need to fight to the death for Jewish survival. This is a noble ideal—there can be no disputing it—but it seems unlikely to have the psychosocial effects of a true myth.

The second essay seeks to explain historically, sociologically, and psychologically why the stereotype of the Jewish woman, a stereotype made mythic through the creative enterprises of Jews of both sexes, is perpetuated, even among Jewish women who should know better but whose internalization of the myth has reinforced their self-doubt. I venture to predict, however, that, in the face of heightened female consciousness and the well-educated Jewish women of today, a revolution is in the offing.

Finally, the essay on which I rest my case deals, appropriately enough, with the Sabbath in American Jewish life. For many Jewish men work is not drudgery but a freely chosen vocation. Work freely chosen, emotionally and economically rewarding, is at odds with the need for a day of rest from labor. Nevertheless, the myth of the Sabbath as a foretaste of the messianic world to come, or as a return to Eden, remains desperately needed in a civilization that operates through "surplus repression" and teaches its members to forget how to play. The Sabbath is no dead myth, nor does it need to be secularized or profaned. It can become, if allowed to adapt itself to current reality, a day set apart, holy in the truly—perhaps truest—Jewish sense of the word.

· · · · · · · · · · · · · · · · · · · · · · · · · · · · · · · · · · · · · · · · · · · · · · · · · · · · · · ·

## chapter twelve

## Yavneh versus Masada

Of all the rallying cries shouted in the ears of American Jews, hardly any have become less subject to challenge or more cliché-ridden than the call to give our children a "Jewish identity." Some people adept in the jargon of individual psychology glibly describe someone as having an "identity crisis," a term usually applied to what one might call the inability of an individual to find either a satisfactory relationship between the various factors that make up his self or much of a reward in the roles that his society asks him to play. Anyone attempting to understand American Jews is struck by the astonishing lack of overlap in conceptualization among the people who speak of Jewish identity as a group concern while describing individuals as falling unfortunate prey to identity crises. This is to say that the word "identity" used in one context is not seen to bear a relationship to the same term used in another context.

The lack of overlap is unfortunate, because while one group of scientists, the ego psychologists, has gathered extensive case-study data and, building on psychoanalytic theory, has begun to fill in the missing links between individuals and collectivities, another group of scientists is attempting to determine whether a person has or lacks a positive Jewish identity by studying him to see whether or not he meets preestablished criteria.

The ego psychologists have developed for those concerned with identity theories and case histories that seek to demonstrate the inseparability of psyche, body, and cultural complexes in the process we call identity. It is evident to the ego psychologists, but has apparently been lost on those who measure Jewish identity by commitment to Jewish institutions, that between the individual and the institutions there are the needs of his drives, his body, his ego defense system, his family, his country, his culture—all of which must somehow be integrated before it is possible to speak of a person's identity.[1]

The noted psychoanalyst Jacob Arlow provided the insights that sparked the idea for my speculations. Arlow argued, in an unpublished lecture given in the spring of 1969 at a meeting of the Cincinnati Psychoanalytic Society, that if a society is to give meaning to the values it wants its members to acknowledge, it must provide its members with some solutions to their interpsychic conflicts. This it does, if at all, through the process of renunciation and identification, i.e., through the formation of the superego, a process that is never completely successful. Nevertheless, the process is more likely to succeed if a mythos is operative, one replete with a hero, identification with whom gives the child, the youth, and the adult a feeling that what he is doing is good for him and for his collectivity.[2]

It is noteworthy that in his lecture Arlow illustrated the dynamics of the search for proper heroes (i.e., proper for the collectives) by contrasting the figures of Rabbi Yochanan ben Zaccai and the Maccabees. He pointed out that, historically, when the Jewish situation called for a rather compliant, passive hero to be replaced by more active, more iconoclastic heroes, greater emphasis was laid on the Maccabees than on Rabbi Yochanan.[3]

What follows, then, is an attempt to gain a better understanding of the importance of mythmaking in identity formation, particularly for those concerned with Jewish identity. I want to explore in some detail the impact of the Yavneh legend and the recent effort by American Jewish educators to replace it with a Masada myth, incorporating the achievements of Yavneh with the seemingly antithetical personalities and events that constitute the Masada episode. In this way, perhaps, some light will be shed on the viability of Jewish life in America and especially on what has been overlooked in other studies of the formation of Jewish identity.[4]

When I was a small boy just beginning Sunday school and weekday Hebrew lessons, my teacher told me a story. Shortly before the destruction of the Second Temple, Jerusalem was under a heavy siege. The situation was hopeless. The Jewish nation was doomed. Judaism was going to die out. Suddenly, out of desperation, the wise Rabbi Yochanan ben Zaccai seized upon a plan. He would feign death. He would be put in a coffin and his students would carry him out of Jerusalem, whereupon he would go straight to the Roman general who was laying siege to the city. Yochanan would ask him a small favor—permission to establish a school in a forgotten village. The preparations were exciting. First the coffin had to be carefully weighted to ensure the authentic feel of a dead man. Next, Yochanan had to get into the box and have it sealed. Then came the most suspenseful part: the Roman guards had to allow the cortege to pass. "Make them open the coffin," yelled a centurion. "No, it's against our religion," replied the students. "Then let's make sure he's really dead. Pierce the coffin with your spears, men," the tough centurion commanded. "Please," the students pleaded, "it's bad enough that we have lost our beloved rabbi. Must we suffer further by having his body mutilated?" For some reason that escaped me then, given the reputed cruelty of the Romans, the soldiers desisted from stabbing the coffin. The cortege was permitted to leave the city. Yochanan then went to the Roman general and greeted him by hailing him as emperor. The general was about to chastise the rabbi for his apparent error when a messenger suddenly appeared with the news that the emperor had died and that the general had been named his successor. The general was pleased with Yochanan's prophetic qualities. He decreed that Yochanan was entitled to a favor. "I'm not asking you for much, O Caesar. Simply allow me and my few students to establish a little school in a small town named Yavneh." It seemed to the new ruler to be a reasonably insignificant wish, so he granted the old rabbi's request. My Sunday school teacher then went on to tell us what a fool the emperor had been, since because of that little school, the light of Torah was kept burning. Yavneh became the seat of an illustrious rabbinical academy. The Roman empire is now dead. But the Jews have survived because they have always known that there is more strength in learning than in force. That is why they are alive, despite all of the persecutions that they have had to endure.

I was impressed with that legend and its clear meaning. When I heard it for the first time at the age of nine, World War II had recently ended. Tales of the Holocaust were beginning to enter the consciousness of American Jewish youth. Remnants of destroyed Jewish communities were struggling to reassemble in

Palestine and elsewhere. American Jews were beginning to return to the synagogue in the wake of the Jewish agony. The story of Yavneh's founding seemed appropriate to the year in which I first heard it. It was not difficult to picture Yavneh as an ancient prototype of the Hebrew school I was attending. The classrooms were musty. The teacher was known in my city as a scholar. It was rumored that he had received *s'michah* in some Polish *yeshiva* now laid waste by the Nazis.

The legend of Yavneh's founding that my teacher told and that was presented as history in the textbooks of my childhood differs in some important details from the version in the Talmud. According to the talmudic account, it is not Yochanan but his nephew who devises the escape plan. Most significantly, however, it is not the cruel Romans who seek to spear the casket; it is the rabbi's fellow Jews, the Biryonim (usually thought to be zealots), who present the final obstacle to Yochanan's exit from the city. It is they and not the Romans who must be persuaded that it would be a political error to mutilate the corpse of a great rabbi. The talmudic account makes the Jewish zealots into the true enemies of Torah. Furthermore, the Talmud elaborates on the method of prophecy employed by Yochanan. The rabbi recites biblical proof texts through which he has come to know in advance of the Roman general's grand promotion.[5]

It is easy to explain the differences between the Sunday school version and its talmudic source. Children would find it difficult to accept the fact that Jewish soldiers were a greater hindrance to the rabbi's plan than were the hated Roman enemy. It would be thought pedagogically unsound to admit that Jewish factionalism was rampant when the survival of the people was at stake. As for the deletion of the rabbi's use of proof texts, pure prophecy is more wondrous to an American child than predictions based on the interpretation of Scripture. The use of proof texts as the heart of Torah study would bear an unwholesome resemblance to the rantings of Christian revivalist preachers. The clever twist of a text is lost on a youth ignorant of its place in Jewish tradition.

Both versions of the story, but especially the Sunday school derivative, served an important function. The story operated as a rescue fantasy, offering an alternative to those tales of rescue that predominated in an America at war. Freud and others have written extensively on the importance of rescue fantasies in the development of the human personality.[6] Such fantasies provide children with a safe outlet from the parental oppression that is part of the oedipal struggle. A male child who unconsciously desires to rid himself of his father so that he might take his place at the side of his mother needs release from the anxiety that this wish may cause. He finds the release in a story like "Jack and the Beanstalk," a fantasy in which a young boy slays a devouring giant and returns to his mother with a goose that lays golden eggs; the boy and his mother are thus provided with the potential for living together happily ever after. Girls who unconsciously see their mothers as rivals for fatherly love find a release in tales such as "Cinderella" and "Snow White," fantasies in which "some day her prince will come" and remove her forever from the tyranny of wicked stepmothers who keep her sweeping cinders or, worse, try to kill her with poisoned apples. The displacement of murderous thoughts onto a fairy tale enables the child to live within the structure of the family.

But there is another utility to rescue fantasies, for they function not only on a psychological level but on a sociological level as well. Since we are living at a time when women are exploring and reassessing their traditional roles within the family and society, perhaps it is now easier to see the sociological ramifications of rescue fantasies such as "Cinderella" and "Snow White" than to move directly into their role in the shaping of male and group identities. Even without our new awareness of the place of women within our culture, it is relatively easy to grasp the psychological value of the Cinderella, Snow White, Rapunsel, and Sleeping Beauty stories. In each of these stories, the young girl is at the mercy of a witch or a wicked stepmother until at some distant time—up to a hundred years in the case of poor Sleeping Beauty—a handsome prince comes along and rescues the girl from her wicked female captors. Well-schooled as we now are in the ways of psychoanalytic interpretation, we do not find it difficult to accept the explanation that suggests that wicked stepmothers or evil witches are replacements for real mothers, thoughts about whose removal are dangerous or even treasonous. We do not find it hard to believe that the prince is a replacement for a father because to admit consciously a desire to marry one's father would be to acknowledge a wish for an incestuous relationship and thus would cause intolerable guilt or anxiety.

We have, however, been socialized into overlooking other functions of these tales—the fact, for instance, that beyond their psychological uses they also serve sociological ends. They all portray females as being passive recipients of male benevolence. The girls cannot help themselves. They must sweep cinders, be locked in towers, or lie in a comatose state until a male rescuer chances by. These are not stories in which a Jack climbs a beanstalk and rids himself of his oppressor, or a Saint George slays a dragon to prevent the devouring of virgins. The woodsman rescues Red Riding Hood and her grandmother; without him, Red Riding Hood would be a wolf's dessert. Thus, these stories serve not only to relieve young girls from oedipal anxiety but also to reinforce social norms about what roles women are to have—not controlling their destinies, taking matters into their own hands, or becoming active shapers of their own futures.[7]

A culture that desires passivity in its women and valor in its men is likely to provide rescue fantasies appropriate not only to its members' psychological needs but also to the roles it wishes its members to play in the larger society. Myths, legends, folktales, and fairy tales are thus agencies of socialization; but it must be remembered that in order for them to have a social value, they must be firmly rooted in the realities of the individual psyche.

It is safe to say that the emphasis in American rescue fantasies has been, for males, on physical action and even violence, when necessary. American folktales tell of men heroically confronting the enemy. Superman fights crime by beating up criminals. Batman and Robin, with some help from technology, punch their way to justice. Enough has been written on the role of the Western to make my point. In the Horatio Alger epics, it may have been diligence and clean living that got the hero his reward—but not until he did something physically heroic such as saving the millionaire's daughter from drowning did he get the recognition that we know he deserved. Military exploits have made men president of the United States: where would John F. Kennedy have been without PT 109?

Seen in this light, the story of Rabbi Yochanan ben Zaccai runs counter to the American grain. It elucidates what had heretofore been a conflict between the American and Jewish identities; for if we reexamine the tale as a group rescue fantasy, we find in it elements that seem odd and strangely foreign to the American mentality. It is a legend that is passive in its activity; for while it is true that its outcome was the founding of a school, the method of achieving this goal depended upon passivity. The rabbi had to pretend to be dead. His students had to be mourners. His meeting with the general had to take into account the fact that he recognized the Roman as having complete control over his and Jewish destiny. As a result, he had to demonstrate that he was submissive to alien authority. In the talmudic account it is not even the rabbi himself who devises the scheme. When the rabbi makes his prophecy, it is through a method that not only demonstrates his skill at interpreting Scripture but also betrays a certain helplessness in the face of inevitability. Passivity, etiquette, acknowledgment of authority, and skill in ascertaining an already predetermined event through mental acumen—these are what assure the Jewish future.

To be sure, the method worked. Yavneh became the center of Jewish learning long after the Jewish state was destroyed.[8] And it was precisely Yochanan's success, as recorded in the legend, that allowed Yavneh to become woven into the fabric of Jewish identity from that time until the rebirth of active Jewish nationalism within the last hundred years. This is not to say that, within the vast web of life and legend that is the record of Jewish history, other myths have not gained sway over the identity of the Jew. It is to argue, however, that for people living *semper et ubique* within the borders of alien and often hostile peoples, the Yavneh story could and did serve as a socializing model for Jewish survival. Furthermore, for a people whose leaders were often the heads of academies and as such were skilled at interpreting sacred texts, the legend served as a reinforcement of religious authority as well as a reminder of the power of alien secular authority.

It is possible to find within the legend a paradigm for certain aspects of Jewish identity, for indeed it must be granted that, by identifying with Yochanan and his small band of scholars, a Jewish youth could meet his psychological rescue needs as well as develop a relationship to his people, his religion, and external (i.e., non-Jewish) authority. On a psychological level, the legend provides a child with the fantasy of rescuing Torah and Shekinah (two "feminine" aspects of Judaism) while doing no violence to the male authority figures represented by the rabbi-leader and emperor-leader. And, of course, since the Torah and Israel both came into being by divine sanction, saving them means that one is serving the Ultimate Father, the One in Heaven. Anyone who labors in Torah pleases God. How much more pleasing is one who rescues as well as studies Torah.

As a socializing myth, too, the story has validity. It teaches that cleverness, learning, and the proper recognition of reality are in the end more fruitful than hopeless, violent revolt. This has been a well-honored Jewish attitude throughout the two millennia since Rabbi Yochanan ben Zaccai was allowed to settle at Yavneh.

There have, however, been periods in which Yochanan's solution seems particularly inappropriate. Ours appears to be such a time. There are a number of reasons why this is true. One is that when Jews are given access to the culture of the general society, invariably its values become part of their identity. Thus, when a culture extols as heroes those who are activists rather than passive students, a tension develops between two equally compelling sets of cultural values. American culture, we have already noted, has traditionally chosen as role models men such as those who said, "Damn the torpedoes, full speed ahead." Even the scholarly achievements of such founding fathers as Franklin and Jefferson are de-emphasized in favor of their inventions and their willingness to challenge and confront what they regarded as illicit authority. Americans place a stress on deed rather than word. It is rather pitiful to read textbooks on American Jewish history whose authors seek almost in vain to discover colonial Jews fitting the American image of fighter and activist.[9]

A second and more compelling reason for the need to replace the Yavneh legend with a different type of rescue fantasy lies in the events of World War II. Bruno Bettelheim, Hannah Arendt, and others have examined the remains of the European Jewish communities and found them sadly lacking in the will to gain mastery over their own fates. No matter how much is inspired by *kiddush ha-shem*, no matter how valiant the defenders of the Warsaw ghetto were, no matter how we detest the attack on European Jewry's few survivors by their critics, we are forced to suspect a certain glimmer of truth in their conclusions. And when we read of the attempt of certain European Jewish communal leaders and even some rabbis to reach a compromise with brutal and merciless authority, we have to find something lacking in the Yavneh solution. Sometimes passivity in the face of villainous authority is of no use. How can we offer Yavneh to those reared in the shadow of the Holocaust?[10]

Then, of course, there is the State of Israel. It is impossible to deny that, were it not for the military stance assumed by the Israelis, there would be no Jewish state today. No matter how much land was redeemed through money, no matter how the genius of the Jews made the desert bloom, there is one fact that seems irrefutable: without armed might and the willingness to employ it, Israel would not be available today to the Torah students who gather there to study and expound the Holy Books. In the second-century case of Rabbi Akiva and Bar Kochba, where rabbis and soldiers are joined, it appears that Akiva falls prey to the error of thinking that he was living at the time of the Messiah. Believing that one has found the Messiah is a mistake that activist rabbinic Jews make frequently enough.[11] So we search our history for legends seemingly more appropriate to our needs. Rabbinical literature fails us, for it is mostly the work of the men of Yavneh. The Bible is more helpful, but it has too much to do with God—to a skeptical, secular generation, it presents too many theological problems. Where, then, do we turn for a new myth? We go to Jewish writings that do not have rabbinical authorship. We find in the apocryphal Books of Maccabees and the volumes of Flavius Josephus some possible alternative legends.

Perhaps it is not too well known that the association of Hanukkah with the military victories of the Hasmoneans has not always been central to the festival's celebration. The Talmud makes little of the Hasmoneans in general and contains only a brief statement about Hanukkah. The primary emphasis of the talmudic account is on the miracle of the oil that burned beyond its natural capacity.[12] To the extent that the later rabbis made use of the narrative found in the Books of Maccabees, it was to emphasize Mattathias's faithfulness to Jewish law and to extol the bravery of Hannah and her seven sons who preferred to be martyred rather than violate God's commandments.[13] For the Jews of the premodern period, Hanukkah was never more than a rather minor observance. It became an important festival only for modern Jews.

Living in a secular culture, modern Jews have needed the Maccabees as culture heroes; they have needed Hanukkah as a rival to Christmas; they have needed a modern concept like freedom of religious choice to tie the exploits of the Maccabees and the winter solstice festival together in a package with which both Jews and non-Jews could live. It is unnecessary to dwell on the emphasis given the Maccabees in our lifetime, though it is worth noting that, in the actual accounts of the sons of Mattathias, only Judah was called Maccabee (probably "hammer"). In modern versions, those connected with the Hasmonean victory are almost always called Maccabees. Maccabiads (athletic events similar to the Olympics) are held in Israel, and the story of how Judah fought for religious liberty is well known to Jewish children (as well as to non-Jewish children in areas of heavy Jewish population).

Although Hanukkah enjoys great popularity, the story of the Maccabees and their descendants, the later Hasmoneans, offers some obstacles to those in search of a heroic myth. The first, and least important, is that the victory of the Maccabees was short-lived and that the Hasmonean dynasts subsequently proved to be tyrannical protégés of Rome.[14] A greater difficulty with the heroism of the Maccabees may be that, in being locked into Hanukkah as it is, that military force holds certain cultural conflicts for American Jews. If there is any time of year in America when it is inappropriate to speak of war and rebellion, it is in that season of paying homage to the Prince of Peace. One might call it Jewish *mazel* to need to build a festival around military success while the rest of the culture makes a nearly total effort to forget the world as it really is. The Maccabees and their nationalistic revolt fit well into the mythos of the State of Israel, but are not of equal service to American Jews.

There is another place to turn for a suitable myth—the story of Masada. Although its original version makes it questionable as a rescue fantasy, its modern retelling has that possibility, a possibility that has already been exploited by both Israelis and American Jews. At first glance the account of the defense and destruction of the fortress of Masada presents special barriers for the weaving of the episode into Jewish legendry and fantasy. One obstacle is, of course, the fact that the story of Masada is contained in the works of Flavius Josephus.[15] Although Josephus is a friend to those trying to decipher Jewish history, his own personal behavior is not exemplary to those seeking new heroes.

Flavius Josephus (or Joseph, the son of Matthias, the name he bore for the first three decades of his life) is known to us nearly exclusively through his own writings. Through these writings he seems to bear much in common with other fabulous characters of the ancient world. At the age of fourteen, he was able to engage the rabbis in discussion so intelligently that they asked his advice—a feat allegedly accomplished by another precocious youth, the adolescent Jesus of Nazareth.[16] At the age of sixteen, "on hearing of one [Essene] named Bannus who dwelt in the wilderness, wearing only such clothing as trees provide, feeding on such things as grew themselves, and using frequent ablutions of cold water, by day and night, for purity's sake I became his devoted disciple"—in what we would now call a psychosocial moratorium. With the mythic hero's penchant for the number three, he leaves the Essenes after a three-year stay, only to join the Pharisees, a group not known for its love for the Hasmonean family, from which his mother was descended.[17] Seven or eight years after leaving the Essenes and joining the Pharisees, Joseph is sent on his first rescue mission. He goes to Rome for the purpose of saving certain Jewish priests whom the brutal procurator Felix had dispatched to Rome to be tried before Nero for some undetermined offense. In Rome he becomes friends with a Jewish actor who helps him procure an audience with the empress Poppaea Sabina. She takes a liking to Josephus, and he returns to Judea after having saved the lives of the priests.[18]

He then undertakes an even more heroic task. He goes to the Galilee as a commanding general to lead a rebellion against Rome. Josephus leaves two contradictory accounts of his military mission in the Galilee: in one he claims to have attempted to lead his people to military victory; in the other he states that his purpose was to convince the Galileans of the futility of challenging Rome. In either case it is clear that a bloody battle exacts heavy tolls in dead and wounded on both sides. Finally the Jews are vanquished, but Josephus survives. Not only does he survive, but he goes over to the Romans—again, he claims, with a rescue mission. This time it is to try to convince any Jews contemplating rebellion against Rome of the foolhardiness of such plans.[19]

It would be interesting to speculate on the psychological factors involved in Josephus's radical shift of loyalties. Earlier in his life he had abandoned his upper-class origins for a sect renouncing material goods. Then he became a member of a party antagonistic to his family. Next he employed his high-born status to save his father's priestly colleagues. Then he attempted to rescue the rebels of the Galilee. At the age of thirty, he went over to the Romans, substituting for his own family's name that of the Roman general under whose onslaught he had nearly lost his life (interestingly enough, the same general to whom Yochanan ben Zaccai fled from Jerusalem—and this is not all that Yochanan and Josephus have in common).[20] Yet, under his new name and under the protection of his new family, somewhat like his biblical namesake Joseph—indeed, in his precociousness, his narrow escape from death, his ability to charm, his ease in the face of a foreign power, and his view of himself as a Deliverer, he seems to identify himself closely with the biblical Joseph (whether by design or chance, we do not know)—he sets out to redeem his people, first by warning them not to resist Rome, and finally by writing a history of the Jews whose purpose is to redeem their dignity in the eyes of the Greco-Roman world.[21]

Yet for all his heroic qualities, Josephus is not the stuff of which Jewish heroes are made. He stood with the Romans while the Holy Temple was being razed and while his people were being slaughtered in its defense. In fact, his name and his work would have perished forever among the Jews were it not for the irony that someone had forged into his writings what was for centuries thought to be the only historical reference to Jesus of Nazareth.[22] To the Jews, from the time of the fall of Galilee virtually to the present, Josephus's name, when recalled at all, evoked a set of reactions reserved by Christians for Judas Iscariot.[23] Still, and also ironic, modern weavers of Jewish myth, including the non-Jew James Michener in *The Source,* cannot do without Josephus, for without his writings there could be no Masada for a new myth and a new generation of Jews.

The fortress of Masada was built by the Hasmoneans and subsequently enlarged by Herod the Great.[24] Later, at the close of the war with Rome that destroyed the Jewish state and with it the temple in Jerusalem, Masada enabled about one thousand men, women, and children to hold off the furious attacks of Flavius Silva, the Roman governor of Judea, and the additional legions that he summoned to crush this last citadel of the Jewish zealots. Finally, after seven months of incredible valor and privation, it became certain that on the morrow Masada would be taken, the men killed, the women raped and, along with the children, sold into slavery. Josephus writes that he learned of the last hours of Masada from two women and five children who had somehow escaped the fate of the others.[25] Their report inspired him—in proper Hellenistic historiographical fashion—to compose a speech for Eleazar ben Yair, the leader of the defenders of Masada. The speech went, in part, as follows:

> Our fate at break of day is certain capture, but there is still the free choice of a noble death with those we hold most dear. For our enemies, fervently though they pray to take us alive, can no more prevent this than we can now hope to defeat them in battle. Maybe, indeed, we ought from the very first . . . to have read God's purpose and to have recognized that the Jewish race, once beloved of Him, had been doomed to perdition. . . . For not even the impregnable nature of this fortress has availed to save us; nay, though ample provisions are ours, piles of arms and a superabundance of every other requisite, yet we have been deprived, manifestly by God Him-

self, of all hope of deliverance. For it was not of their own accord that those flames which were driving against the enemy turned back upon the [defense] wall constructed by us; no, all this betokens wrath at the many wrongs which we madly dared to inflict upon our countrymen. The penalty for those crimes let us pay not to our bitterest foes, the Romans, but to God through the act of our own hands. It will be more tolerable than the other. Let our wives thus die undishonoured, our children unacquainted with slavery; and, when they are gone, let us render a generous service to each other, preserving our liberty as a noble winding-sheet. But first let us destroy our chattels and the fortress by fire; for the Romans, well I know, will be grieved to lose at once our persons and the lucre. Our provisions only let us spare; for they will testify, when we are dead, that it was not want which subdued us, but that, in keeping with our initial resolve, we preferred death to slavery.

Since Ben Yair's speech proved less convincing than he had hoped, he spoke again.

Let us have pity on ourselves, our children and our wives, while it is still in our power to find pity from ourselves. For we were born for death, we and those whom we have begotten; and this even the fortunate cannot escape. But outrage and servitude and the sight of our wives being led to shame with their children—these are no necessary evils imposed by nature on mankind, but befall, through their own cowardice, those who, having the chance of forestalling them by death, refuse to take it. . . . No, while [our] hands are free and grasp the sword, let them render an honourable service. Unenslaved by the foe let us die, as free men with our children and wives let us quit this life together! This our laws enjoin, this our wives and children implore of us. The need for this is of God's sending, the reverse of this is the Romans' desire, and their fear is lest a single one of us should die before capture. Haste we then to leave them, instead of their hoped-for enjoyment at securing us, amazement at our death and admiration of our fortitude.[26]

Josephus then informs us that Ben Yair's words were heeded. First the men quickly killed their wives and children, then each other, and finally the last man fell on his sword and perished. When the Romans entered the bastion they found a scene that threw them into terror. All were dead except for Josephus's surviving witnesses. All property had been burned except some provisions indicating that none had died but for freedom.[27]

The story is attractive, but it clearly violates certain rules necessary for a rescue myth that might help strengthen Jewish identity in America. First, it was recorded by Josephus, whom Jews have traditionally regarded as a traitor.[28] Next, and more crucial, is the tragic outcome of the story. The American mentality is able to assimilate stories of defeat (after all, Texas remembers the Alamo, and the American South the Civil War), but it is hardly capable of dealing with a struggle that is not a fight to the finish and that, worst of all, culminates in the mass suicide of the heroes. "Give me liberty or give me death" might be an American rallying cry, and "Better dead than Red" might have inspired some Americans in the 1950s and early 1960s, but neither of these slogans was ever meant to imply suicide. They were taken to mean that the tyrants would have to kill every last freedom-loving patriot. Thus, the Masada story would seem to fail as a replacement for the Yavneh story given us by the Talmud and rabbinical tradition.

However, the story of the Masada myth is not finished. In an ingenious way it has become part of modern Jewish mythology. This has happened largely as a result of the rebirth of the Jewish state. Jewry's survival after the war that ended with Masada, the Roman empire's failure to survive, and the fact that there are today Jewish zealots willing to die rather than lose their homeland—these circumstances are not in themselves enough to make Masada the psychological substitute for Yavneh. What has happened is that a conscious effort on the part of American Jewish institutions has made Masada into a myth compatible with American Jewish identity needs and institutional values. This has been accomplished by combining elements of the past, the present, and rabbinic tradition. Not surprisingly, much of the work has been done under the auspices of the Conservative movement in Judaism, a movement that might be called, not-withstanding its ties to tradition, the most American of the Jewish religious movements.[29]

Mythic use has been made of a number of factors, chief among them the linking of Masada to the career of a contemporary Jewish military hero victorious in all his attempts to deliver Israel from its genocidal enemies. That man is Yigael Yadin, a figure particularly adaptable to the building of a myth. He is described by one American Jewish writer as

"one of the heroes of modern Israel. Born in Jerusalem in 1917, he got his first taste of soldiering at the age of 14, when he became a member of the Haganah, the underground resistance army fighting against the British occupation of Palestine." Then Yadin "rose to become chief of planning and operations for the Haganah."

General Yadin played a major part in Israel's victory in 1948. In one famous incident, he won a crucial battle by using his knowledge of an ancient, forgotten Roman road across the desert.

This knowledge came from Yigael's first great interest in life—
the science of archeology. His father [E. L. Sukenik] was a world-
famous archeologist, and young Yigael had determined to be an
archeologist himself, before necessity turned him into a soldier.
After the war was over he went back to his studies. In 1952, General Yadin left the army and joined the Hebrew University in
Jerusalem. There he became Professor of Archology.

Professor Yadin was soon as renowned an archeologist and
scholar as he had been a general. He conducted a number of important expeditions to ancient sites in Israel, where he made some
historic discoveries. He was awarded prizes for his work and won
many honors throughout the world.

In 1963 Yigael Yadin led the Masada Archeological Expedition to
the mighty citadel near the Dead Sea which every archeologist in
Israel had longed to excavate. The expedition dug at Masada until
1965. Its finds amazed the world.[30]

Thus, in the person of Yadin we have an ideal figure to bridge
the gap between the ancient and modern world—a hero. As both
general and archeologist, he embodies military prowess, modern
science, and a Jewish scholarly love for Israel, its history, and its
antisuicidal laws. In addition to Yadin's vital connection with
Masada, there are other factors that make the excavated fortress
a convenient answer to the American Jewish quest for a new
myth.

A book entitled *The Heroes of Masada,* by Geraldine Rosenfield,
has been issued by the Conservative movement. In the opening
chapter, called "Heroes of Today," Mrs. Rosenfield introduces us
to Reuven:

Reuven is nineteen years old. He is tall and sunburned, is a hard-
kicking soccer expert, and plays a very tricky *halil.* (This is a
wooden flute which you may know as a recorder.) . . . If you happened to meet Reuven you might think, "This fellow is great fun.
He's a great ball player. He's pretty handy with a *halil* and with a
tractor." You would probably never come up with the thought, "He
is a hero."

But Reuven turned out to be one hero among many, among two
and a quarter million, in fact, during the historic six days, that
started on June 5, 1967.

. . . When it came his turn to serve in the Army he was assigned
to duty with a tank unit. So Reuven found himself behind the wheel
of a tank instead of a tractor.

. . . One day the Company commander announced that all soldiers
must put on clean dress uniforms. They had been invited to join a
ceremony on the rock fortress of Masada.

. . . On the day Reuven and his fellow students climbed up the
steep side of Masada they joined in a graduation exercise for men
and women who had just become officers in the Israeli Army. The

soldiers stood at attention in V-shaped formation while the band played cheerily and rousing speeches were made. A huge bonfire was lit in the center and smaller fires glowed in a half-circle. Every new soldier was presented with a Bible to remind him above all of his God, his people and his history. Reuven repeated with his comrades "Masada shall not fall again!"[31]

The author's purpose is patent. She wishes her young reader to identify with the farmer-soldier. She also desires her reader to see in Masada the reminder, not of a terrible defeat, but rather of another time of glory that, like our own, offered an opportunity to save the Jewish people, its Torah, and its tradition from threats to their freedom and survival.

By paying little heed to the historical past and laying much emphasis on the present and future, we have once again given Masada a new place in the Jewish mythos. Yadin and Reuven are not losers; they are winners who excel at everything they undertake. They are not passive schoolmasters; they are warrior-scientist-scholars or soccer-kicking, tractor-driving good fellows. And they—more than the eloquent Eleazar ben Yair or the traitorous Josephus—*belong* at Masada.

Masada has other uses, too, as the focal point of a myth. For example, the existence of Masada, unlike that of the temple or the academy at Yavneh, does not have to be imagined. It is there to visit and, even more, to visit us, as it has done in a traveling exhibit under the auspices of the Conservative-sponsored Jewish Museum of New York.[32] It is tangible and real and made palpable to us through a knowledge of the Jewish past, the heroics of daring archeologists, and the mastery of modern scientific tools and concepts. It is no burning bush for whose existence we must take the word of God and Moses on faith.

And there is one final use that it has served. To those who argue that Jewish physical survival and observance of the law are incompatible, Masada seems to offer refutation. Masada's ruins contain what have been designated ritual baths, a classroom, sacred scrolls, and a synagogue. One of the mythmaking books referred to above puts the matter this way:

> To the Zealots, their religious faith was the most important thing in life. Even while they were besieged on Masada, fighting for existence, they still devoutly observed the laws of their religion.
>
> Some of these laws dealt with ritual bathing. On certain occasions, pious Jews were required to dip themselves in a special bathing pool of pure water. This pool had to be of certain size and shape. And when one day, digging and probing atop Masada, the archeologists came upon an unusual structure that the Zealots had

added to the casemate wall, they realized almost at once that they had found an ancient ritual bathing pool.

After excavating the pool, they discovered that it had been built in exact obedience to the ancient rules. It was divided into separate chambers. One chamber caught rain water and stored it. A pipe led from this chamber to the main part of the pool. Before bathing, the Jews would unplug this pipe and let some of the rain water flow into the main part of the pool. According to the ancient rules, the rain water purified the other water there. The devout Zealots could then enter the pool and bathe.

Later, digging elsewhere within the fortress, the members of the expedition uncovered a second ritual bathing pool. It had been built in exactly the same way as the first one. Both structures can be seen at Masada today. Standing on the dry mountaintop under the scorching Judean sun, they show how strong was the Zealots' faith—how fervently they clung to their religion, even under conditions of the most incredible difficulty. But, we are told, "amid all the hardship and danger of life on Masada, the Zealots also kept up their study of the Bible," for the archaeologists also "uncovered a religious schoolroom in which Zealot children used to sit—when they were not needed for other tasks, such as helping to defend the fortress." And there is more:

The most exciting discovery of all, among the religious structures of the Zealots, was made early in the expedition's stay at Masada. "At the very beginning of our first season of excavations, while digging in the northwestern section of the wall of Masada, we came upon a strange structure," says the expedition leader. "It was unlike any of the buildings we had excavated up to then in the casemate wall. Early in the dig we noticed what looked like benches plastered with clay protruding from the debris inside the building, next to the walls. Gradually, pillars began to appear, made in sections. When we had finished excavating, what appeared before us was a rectangular structure with benches all round the walls, tier upon tier, all plastered with clay."

The benches, the archeologists soon learned, had been built by the Zealots. Some of them were made of pieces of stone columns taken from the remains of Herod's palaces. The strange rectangular structure with its many benches had obviously been used for public meetings. But meetings of what sort? Why had the Zealots gathered together there?

The archeologists continued their digging, and finally they had their answer. The Zealots had gathered there to pray. The building was a synagogue.

The archeologists were not really sure at first. But as they dug the evidence mounted. The building faced in the proper direction for a synagogue—toward Jerusalem—and within it they found things that may have been used in religious ceremonies. The diggers' excitement grew.

"If what we had just unearthed was indeed a synagogue," says the expedition leader, "then this was a discovery of front-ranked importance in the field of Jewish archeology and certainly one of the most important finds in Masada. For up to then the very earliest synagogues discovered in Israel belonged to the end of the second or beginning of the third century A.D."

In other words, if this building on Masada turned out to be a synagogue, it would be the oldest one in the world. One last discovery finally convinced the [archeologists] that the mysterious structure was a synagogue. They found that below the floor, in two carefully dug pits, the Zealots had buried scrolls.[33]

The construction of the modern Masada myth is now virtually complete. The suggestion that there was a classroom in the fortress and that a certain room was used for a synagogue (although there is no way of verifying that fact) makes that clear. The possibility that there were *mikvehs*, a school, and a synagogue, and the certainty that Masada contained sacred scrolls are central to the building of the new myth. Although the scrolls found there included no complete copy of the most sacred Five Books of Moses—in fact, they included excerpts from the Book of Psalms, the noncanonical Book of Jubilees, and the Book of Ecclesiasticus[34]—the mythmakers could hail the information that the psalm fragments were identical with the official Masoretic text of the Bible used today. Masada thus could be used to validate the traditional belief, i.e., the reliability of the traditional rendition of Hebrew Scripture. The Ben Sirah (Ecclesiasticus) and Jubilee scrolls (found in Hebrew editions) allowed the claim that the books' original language was Hebrew, rather than the Greek of all other ancient editions.[35]

The mythmakers chose to ignore another possible conclusion—namely, that the zealots had followed a religion that deviated in significant and even radical ways from what is now accepted as normative Judaism. It would be as though archeologists would at some future date discover the ruins of a synagogue of today—only a meeting hall, classrooms, and some fragmented copies of the New Testament (which most synagogues have in their libraries)—and conclude that they had found a Christian church.

But myths are not built on hard fact, even though today's myths undoubtedly must contain at least shreds of scientific material in order to be credible to a modern Westerner. The Masada myth has such shreds. It has action. It has physical existence. It has a new happy ending and a new hero in the person of Yadin. And, most important to those who seek to place Masada among their Jewish myths, it contains the elements of existing American institutional Judaism—a classroom, a synagogue, the sacred writings (i.e., elements from the tradition that Jews are dependent on scholarship no matter what). So these essentials are now in place. What remains to be seen is whether that element most crucial to a myth is also there, its ability to meet the individual psychic needs of enough members of a group so that it is usable as an effective socializing agent.

From a psychological standpoint, the new Masada myth has both strengths and weaknesses. One strength is that, unlike the Yavneh legend, Masada includes among its defenders whole families, with women and children fighting and dying alongside the men. Masada was a family affair. Josephus tells us that, after Eleazar ben Yair delivered his oration, he expected he would have to convince them further to accept his fatal plan, "but was cut short by his hearers, who . . . were all in haste to do the deed."[36] Josephus tells of the devotion of the men, not only to their own families, but to their comrades.

> While they caressed and embraced their wives and took their children in their arms, clinging in tears to those parting kisses, at the same instant, as though served by hands other than their own, they accomplished their purpose, having the thought of the ills they would endure under the enemy's hands to console them for their constraint in killing them. And in the end not one was found a truant in so daring a deed; all carried through their task with their dearest ones. Wretched victims of necessity, to whom to slay with their own hands their own wives and children seemed the lightest of evils! Unable, indeed, any longer to endure their anguish at what they had done, and feeling that they wronged the slain by surviving them if it were but for a moment, they quickly piled together all the stores and set them on fire; then [they chose] by lot ten of their number to dispatch the rest.[37]

Psychologically this part of the story is potent. External authority is ultimately defied. The Roman loses all control over the faithful Jew; at the same time the Jew finds in death a full commitment to family and community and, perhaps above all, wins through his martyrdom the favor of God the Father. If the tragic episode appears unappealing to children, it can be argued that it may prove to be gratifying as well. The fear of being mutilated by one's father, so much a part of the oedipal struggle, is indeed enacted; but the fact that the father does not survive the child, and that when the story is told today the child is not only alive but physically able and called upon, like Yadin and his confrères, to prevent another Masada (i.e., to rescue fathers, mothers, and other children as well as the community), might suffice to turn the unhappy defeat of the original Masada into a sort of oedipal triumph. Such a triumph would be similar to the psychological satisfaction the believer gets from dying in Christ, only to share in his resurrection and join the army of the redeemed whose mission it is to save those who do not share his standing with God.

The modern Masada myth now has all the psychological glory of Yavneh. Now the people of Masada may be seen to have preserved Judaism, not only by keeping the faith, but especially by leaving for posterity a synagogue, a school, and sacred scrolls that help contemporary Jews heighten *their* faith in the continuity of tradition. Torah was saved by Masada. The Shekinah was rescued by the zealots—but this rescue is only successful if Jews today are willing to study and to fight for God, Israel, and Torah. Masada has these psychological possibilities plus an additional advantage over Yavneh: it does not place the Jewish mythos in conflict with American values. The defenders of Masada, either of old or in the person of Yadin, did not passively trick and cajole their way past the enemy. They did not beg the enemy for a small favor. They fought him, finally overcame him, and took back from him not a wretched musty little *yeshiva* but the entire land of Israel. No American could have done more.

Still, there are several flaws in the efficacy of the Masada myth. The most obvious for a person concerned with the building of Jewish identity in America is true of both Yavneh and Masada. In order for either legend to achieve its goal as a myth, i.e., to meet both psychological and group needs, it must be transmitted by believing adults to children who are ready to believe. If the chain of belief is broken and the matrix within which the myth has preserved its psychological and social reality has been shattered, the myth will fail in its function. If the community no longer believes the myth but merely feels that it is good for children, the children know that what they are hearing is at best a good story and at worst a package of foolishness. It is doubtful that Jews bereft of belief in their own myths, a condition common among second- and third-generation Americans, can utilize Masada, even though Masada conflicts less than Yavneh with the American ethos. It is significant that, though Masada is popular with Jewish youth, it is most appealing to leaders and members of the Jewish Defense League (JDL), an organization that draws its membership from those closest in generation to Europe, young people who are not well entrenched in the middle classes, retain a strong attachment to Orthodoxy, and see their future not in

America but in Israel. For them the slogan "Never again" is equivalent to the Israeli soldiers' oath—"Masada shall not fall again." It is ironic that, consciously or not, the JDL, with its open rejection of American society, has come to replicate most closely one American way of life: given to racism, relying on jingoism, instructed to achieve their aims through violence, they seem, externals aside, to emulate John Wayne more than the sage Hillel.[38]

Herein lies the final paradox in the Yavneh-Masada saga. At a time when more and more American youth, both Jews and non-Jews, are coming to distrust institutions, to seek to escape from a society that seems to demand individual submission to national societal causes and aggression and violence in the name of freedom, neither myth is satisfying, and yet both are. At Yavneh one could turn one's back on the world, as long as one could place ideology and methodology above self, and as long as one was willing never to challenge proper authority. At Masada one could live in a community, cherish one's ties to family and group, and challenge authority to the end, as long as one was willing to accept violence as a code of conduct.

What are called for now are not Yavneh and Masada, but new and better myths that will show themselves able to transform social reality without denying its psychological underpinnings.

. . . . . . . . . . . . . . . . . . . . . . . . . . . . . . . . . . . . . . . . . . . . . . . . . . . .

## chapter thirteen

## What Ever Happened to Lilith?

She is, of course, fat, noisy, spoiled and anxious to the point of near-hysteria. She rules her husband and her children with the vigor of a marine drill-sergeant tempered only by enough malignant over-protective hovering to lull her victims into thinking that her bossing is benevolent and that her formidable presence is the family's sole shelter from the evils of the non-Jewish (and therefore hostile) world. . . .

She is also, by and large, a fraud. For the popular conception of the Jewish wife and mother, sketched above and firmly imbedded in the public consciousness is no more authentic than a caricature drawn with something less than good taste. . . .

Part folklore, part ancient ghetto history, part fiction fostered by puckish and imaginative Jewish novelists and comedians, the Jewish wife is, as we will document in these pages, the world's most libeled female. The fact is that 30 years ago the caricature that still makes people chuckle today contained more than a kernel of truth. Today it is absurdly obsolete.[1]

"Where are you from?"
"New York."
"I mean your ancestors." . . .
"Polish Jews on one side, Russian on the other—"
"I thought so. You *look* Jewish."
"And you look like an English anti-Semite."
"Oh come on—I *like* Jews."
"Some of your best friends . . ."
"It's just that Jewish girls are so bloody good in bed." . . .

"You're the only person I've ever met who thought I looked Jewish." . . . (Enough of sex—Let's get back to bigotry.) His thinking I looked Jewish actually excited me. God only knows why.

"Look—I'm not an anti-Semite, but *you* are. Why do you think you don't look Jewish?"

"Because people always think I'm German—and I've spent half my life listening to anti-Semitic stories told by people who assumed I wasn't—"[2]

These two passages—the first from *The Jewish Wife,* by Gwen Gibson Schwartz and Barbara Wyden, two non-Jews married to Jews, and the second from Erica Jong's autobiographical novel *Fear of Flying* (a conversation between the heroine, Isadora Wing, a Jewish woman married to a Chinese psychoanalyst, and Adrian Goodlove, a British Langian analyst with whom she is about to fly away)—reflect, I believe, popular stereotypes of Jewish women in America. But it will not suffice to say, as Schwartz and Wyden do, that "the Jewish wife is . . . the world's most libeled female," nor is the fictive Ms. Wing's horniness to be adequately explained by the description she offers of her own mother.

Of course it all began with my mother: Judith Stoloff White, also known as Jude. Not obscure. But hard to get down on paper. My love for her and my hate for her are so bafflingly intertwined that I can hardly *see* her. I never know who is who. She is me and I am she and we are all together. The umbilical cord which connects us has never been cut so it has sickened and rotted and turned black. The very intensity of our need has made us denounce each other. We want to eat each other up. We want to strangle each other with love. We want to run screaming from each other in panic before either of these things can happen.

When I think of my mother I envy Alexander Portnoy. If only I had a *real* Jewish mother—easily pigeonholed and filed away—a real literary property. (I am always envying writers and their relatives. Nabokov and Lowell and Tucci with their closets full of elegant aristocratic skeletons, Roth and Bellow and Friedman with their pop parents, sticky as Passover wine, greasy as matzoh-ball soup.)

My mother smelled of *Joy* or *Diorissimo,* and she didn't cook much. When I try to distill down the basics of what she taught me about life I am left with this:

1. Above all, never be *ordinary.*

2. The world is a predatory place: Eat faster!

"Ordinary" was the worst insult she could find for anything. I remember her taking me shopping and the look of disdain with which she would freeze the salesladies in Saks when they suggested that some dress or pair of shoes was "very popular—we've sold fifty already this week." That was all she needed to hear. . . .

How all this clogged up every avenue of creative and rebellious expression for me is clear:

1. I couldn't be a hippy because my mother already dressed like a hippy (while believing in territoriality and the universality of war).
2. I couldn't rebel against Judaism because I hadn't any to rebel against.
3. I couldn't rail at my Jewish mother because the problem was deeper than Jewishness or mothers.
4. I couldn't be an artist on pain of being painted over.
5. I couldn't be a poet on pain of being crossed out.
6. I couldn't be anything else because that was *ordinary*.
7. I couldn't be a communist because my mother had been there.
8. I couldn't be a rebel (or, at very least, a pariah) by marrying Bennett because my mother would think that was "at any rate, *not* ordinary."

What possibilities remained open to me? In what cramped corner could I act out what I so presumptuously called my life? I felt rather like those children of pot-smoking parents who become raging squares. I could, perhaps, take off across Europe with Adrian Goodlove, and never come home to New York at all.

And yet . . . I also have another mother. She is tall and thin, but her cheeks are softer than willow tips, and when I nuzzle into her fur coat on the ride home, I feel that no harm can come to me ever. She teaches me the names of flowers. She hugs and kisses me after some bully in the playground (a psychiatrist's son) grabs my new English tricycle and rolls it down a hill into the playground fence. She sits up nights with me listening to the compositions I have written for school and she thinks I am the greatest writer in history even though I am only eight. She laughs at my jokes as if I were Milton Berle and Groucho Marx and Irwin Corey rolled into one. She takes me and Randy and Lalah and Chloe ice-skating on Central Park Lake with ten of our friends, and while all the other mothers sit home and play bridge and send maids to call for their children, she laces up all our skates (with freezing fingers) and then puts on her own skates and glides around the lake with us, pointing out danger spots (thin ice), teaching us figure eights, and laughing and talking and glowing pink with the cold. I am so proud of her!

Randy and I boast to our friends that our mother (with her long flowing hair and huge brown eyes) is so young that she never has to wear makeup. She's no old fuddy-duddy like the other mothers. She wears turtlenecks and ski pants just like us. She wears her long hair in a velvet ribbon just like us. And we don't even call her Mother because she's so much fun. She isn't like anyone else.[3]

Both mothers—the one in *The Jewish Wife* and the one depicted in *Fear of Flying*—still persist as stereotypes presented in the media. The Jewish wife appears in motion pictures like *The Heartbreak Kid,* on television as characters like Rhoda and her mother, and in the monologues of Joan Rivers, for example. Erica

Jong's stereotype of both Wing and her mother can be seen in the images of television's Maude and Hollywood products like Barbra Streisand's role in *The Way We Were* and the physician mother in *The Gambler*. In brief, the Jewish woman as presented in the media is either a female who controls through guilt, is overly concerned with food (either by stuffing others or by weight-watching), exalts her son while enduring her husband and ignoring her daughter until she becomes of marriageable age, or is an exotic, seductive, creative neurotic torn between devotion to family and pursuit of individual romantic goals, be they sexual (as in Norman Mailer's *Time of Her Time*), creative and sexual (as in *Fear of Flying*), or ideological and sexual (as in *The Way We Were*, "Maude" [before she joined the Community Church], or John Updike's *Couples*). Immigrant apparitions such as Gertrude Berg's Molly Goldberg and Fred Allen's Mrs. Nusbaum have vanished, but otherwise it is a most intriguing fact that stereotypes of Jewish women in the media have altered very little over the past thirty years. Why in the face of a rapidly changing social climate do the stereotypes of the Jewish woman persist in the media—and, it might be added, at the expense of the Jewish woman's self-image? There is, to be sure, a related question: Is the stereotype presented in the pop culture really a bad one, or is it in fact geared to Jewish writers' accurate perception of the wish-fantasies of the mass (and mostly non-Jewish) audience?

For the sake of brevity, I am going to limit myself to the Eastern European *shtetl* and the United States. I want to make distinctions between fact and fancy and between wish and reality, distinctions that may be artifical, for wish often leads to reality, which is magnified and simplified into stereotype, which, in turn is reacted against or acted out.

In the *shtetl*, for example, religious laws, not easily broken because of the high visibility that results from small-town living, entitled women to some sexual gratification. It is also to be kept in mind that the rules of ritual purity made their right to sexual gratification roughly commensurate with their likelihood of conception—a reverse rhythm system. Jewish women were recognized as creatures with strong libidos, as were Jewish men, who protected their wives from their neighbors and vice versa by imposing upon the women laws of modesty in dress and virtual unsightliness in male eyes (though there are certain features that even a nun would have had difficulty hiding in an age that knew nothing of bras or sunglasses). Jewish women from wealthy families presented their fathers, whether voluntarily or not, with bright sons-in-law who could spend their days in prayer and study; it was presumed that this would increase for both fathers and husbands the possibility of winning appointments to positions in the Academy on High and would ensure for the women more frequent sexual gratification (since scholars did not have to leave home on long journeys to earn a living). On the other hand, the *shtetl* being essentially a culture of poverty, the labor of most women and men was needed to sustain a household. The women had small gardens, bargained in the marketplace, and often managed the family economy, and the men often stayed away for long periods of time peddling. Women, though suffering low status, were not without practical skills—especially in a society where Torah study was exalted and where pragmatics further mired one in the slime of this world.[4]

History reminds us of the frequency of pogroms that left Jewish men unable to defend their wives from rape. As Richard Rubenstein has speculated in *Power Struggle*, there must have been no greater humiliation that a Jewish male could be forced to endure than to stand helplessly by while his wife, daughter, or sister was being raped by Gentiles.[5] Powerlessness led to projection, which led to the defense mechanism of "Jewish humor," a species of *Galgenhumor* that thinly masks the blame incurred by the victim while at the same time eroticizing her. "Let my mother go," the child pleaded with the Cossack. "Shut up," said the mother, "A pogrom is a pogrom!" Schooled in piety and pragmatism but not robbed of her sexuality, the Jewish woman left the *shtetl* for the ghettos of America where her scholar husband lost his status or her worker husband struggled to earn a living while learning a new language. Before marriage she often found herself in a sweat shop where, unprotected by the watchful eye of a small community, she could be made to serve her employers as a lowly plaything.[6] The exotic, the foreign, the strange, no matter how lowly, becomes the object of the insider's lust. Vulnerable, free from oedipal taint, the female outsider becomes an erotic fantasy. Occasionally, if the insider is powerful enough, his fantasy translates into reality. Meanwhile, two seemingly opposing forces work in collusion. The oppressed, degraded male and the oppressor work together to create a stereotype, the first in order to de-eroticize his woman while he himself conforms to the degraded image provided by the oppressor, the second in order to dehumanize the object of his oppression and his lust and to render himself thereby free from guilt.

As the Jew rose economically, he often did so at the expense of his and his woman's self-esteem.[7] He frequently used the stereotype as a mask that permitted him to keep his opponent off guard. He belittled himself, he laughed at himself, while subtly outwitting his non-Jewish or assimilated adversary. He remained on the outside, a middleman between lower- and upper-class Gentiles. Humor became both his defense and his offense. Reading the fantasy of his customer, he was able, with the emergence of movies, radio, and television, to exploit the repressed wishes of the masses, whether upper, middle, or lower class. As a Jew on stage, he allowed the masses to laugh at him. As a Jew backstage, he laughed at the masses and served them up sex objects and the stuff of which fantasies are made. As the occasion offered itself, no doubt he tested the quality of the fantasy on the casting couch. At the same time, he was assigning Jewish females to another couch, that of the analyst. For while all this was going on, the Jewish woman, liberated from religious law, from the sweat shop, and even from the family business, found herself the brunt of Jewish humor. She was treated like, and became, a sort of princess. The apple of her father's eye, she was shielded, educated, and beautified (even surgically). Her enormous talents and her exotic sexuality had to be contained. But how to contain them? Hold before her mirror the "horrible Jewish mother"? Make her the object of her own derision? Allow her education free and full expression only in the company of other Jewish women? Organize her into Hadassahs, Sisterhoods, Councils of Jewish Women? Marry her off as quickly and as well as possible, but keep her constantly off guard, fearful of her homeliness, frightened of her unfeminine brightness? Make her uncertain of how well she is raising her children? Keep her thinking she is too fat, too aggressive, too threatening to make her tolerable to anyone but a benign Jewish husband? In fact the Jewish woman has been a queen among women, but in fantasy projected into stereotype she has been a witch stuffing her children with food and devouring them with guilt. And all this is functional to the Jewish male, able through these means to keep his woman safely at home or in the company of Jewish women and children, no threat to his already threatened masculinity.[8]

True, the Jewish woman is at the forefront of the Women's Liberation movement. She sits on the House Judiciary Committee. She edits *Ms.* She writes the *Feminine Mystique* and *Fear of Flying*. She becomes psychoanalyst (mainly of children). She founds Weight Watchers. She anchors a major television news show. But in the media, in the pop culture, she remains that fantasy, Portnoy's mother. Or she is Joan Rivers or Rhoda. Or she continues to be the castrating Brenda Patimkin or the heartbroken kid. And whom are we kidding? She is in the media what she was in the *shtetl* and even earlier, the feared goddess Lilith, the sexual bomb that must be defused, first by Jewish law, and then by Jewish stereotype, a task made no less difficult by the media's willingness to accept the stereotype because it is funny and because it is safe. The stereotyped Jewish woman is a salable image, but why and for whom? The question becomes more urgent, more potent, in this age of raised consciousness. There will soon come a time when she will shatter the mirror handed her by Jewish and non-Jewish society—and it is the Jewish male and the non-Jewish female who are in for bad luck.

. . . . . . . . . . . . . . . . . . . . . . . . . . . . . . . . . . . . . . . . . . . . . . . .

## chapter fourteen

# I Think I'd Rather Work!

We have speculated in some depth about the Jewish woman and the stereotypes with which she is forced to struggle. But the Jewish male, too, has his own peculiar set of stereotypes to confront in the industrialized West, and the Sabbath may help him see this more clearly.

Many dimensions are involved in a sociological evaluation of the contemporary American Shabbat. The dimension thus far best explored in the literature has been that of observance. The findings of this exploration have been more or less uniform. Briefly summarized, they reveal that a minority of Jews observe the traditional Shabbat "thou shalt and shalt nots." Only 10 percent go to synagogue more than once a month, for example. The Friday night family meal remains the most popular Sabbath observance, but even in the child-centered suburban culture of Marshall Sklare's Lakeville, no more than 30 percent of the families surveyed had one regularly. Viewed statistically (the way it has most often been viewed in American sociology) the Shabbat offers little consolation to those who pray, "just as Israel shall keep the Sabbath so shall the Sabbath keep Israel."[1]

What I intend to explore here, however, is a dimension of the Shabbat that has been neglected because it appears to be the very antithesis of the Shabbat concept. It is my contention that no discussion of the Shabbat, no prescription for its restoration to primacy among Jewish holy days, can take place without an examination of what the Shabbat is supposed to contrast with, namely, work. For just as the Shabbat is more than the sum total of the rituals performed on the seventh day, work is more than the time spent on a job.

Reform and Conservative rabbis minister to few hewers of wood and drawers of water. They are more likely to have on their congregational boards buyers of veneer and shareholders in the waterworks. Therefore, when I talk about work I mean the jobs from which middle-class people draw the major portion of their incomes. With rare exceptions this work involves more the tongue and the tail than the torment of the heavy load. The workers are more likely to suffer from strained eyes than strained muscles. What can "rest" mean, when work does not consist of "toting barges and lifting bales"?

Other problems still need to be probed. Is work still a curse, or in this era of relative middle-class plenty is it the culmination of a student career that presents the Jewish youth with the widest range of job possibilities? Harvey Swados has written about the "myth of the Happy Worker" and has shown that nearly every working class employee dreams of leaving the factory or mill; and a plethora of studies indicate that the professions, managerial work, and self-employment are those occupations from which the smallest percentage of workers would depart, offered any alternative.[2]

In short, the "terror of work" is absent among North American Jews. Most of them are doing what they want to do. Far from being a curse, their work is their salvation. A divine command to desist from what one most enjoys is hardly a blessing.

This seems to me to be the crux of the contemporary problem of the Shabbat, for American Jewish males, at least. Work does not mean what it used to mean. Therefore, rest does not mean what it used to mean. Thus, Shabbat continues to endure at present primarily as an opportunity to testify to one's Jewishness. That is to say, "I observe the Shabbat because I wish publicly to demonstrate that I am a committed Jew rather than because of the intrinsic value of the Shabbat." This makes the Shabbat into a Jewish "pseudo-event," to borrow Daniel Boorstin's term.[3] As long as the Shabbat is not rooted in the modern Jew's relation to work and play, it must remain artificial.

Let me briefly review "work" in the Jewish world view of the past seventy-five years; relate attitudes toward the Shabbat to this view; and, finally, propose a Shabbat relative to the place of work in our own day.

The *shtetl* Jew lived for the Shabbat. His weekly life was dominated by two concerns: having enough work to sustain his family and having enough strength to sustain the enormous psychological and physical burden imposed upon him by the work he did. Most Jews were poor. Their incomes were tenuous. The pursuit of *parnoseh* put them into contact with the unpredictable, unstable socioeconomic world of the Eastern European Christian peasant. The *shtetl* Jew as scholar-craftsman is a pious myth, though certainly not a figment of the imagination. Most Jews were tailors and wagonmasters and shoemakers, barkeepers and middlemen—though they longed to be scholars. Most work was semiskilled, societally scorned, and scarce. A rest from cursed labor, the worry of uncertain *parnoseh,* even an enforced rest, was indeed a blessing. Work itself was not a *mitzvah.* In general, the Jews who immigrated to America from Eastern Europe were people whose occupations had given them financial insecurity and a very low position in the status hierarchy of the *shtetl* or ghetto. As Norman Mailer writes, "the poor are the great voyagers."[4] When they came to America, however, they found themselves exposed to two ideologies that, though contrasting in many ways, agreed on one fundamental fact—the importance of work. Both socialism, with its exaltation of the worker, and the Protestant and capitalist ethic, with its elevation of hard work to *mitzvah* status, made involvement in the pursuit of one's livelihood more than merely a means to an end. It was a way of proving one's virility. Sloth was the prime sin of the American ethos. Not overwork, but unrewarded, unrecognized, uninspiring, alienating work was the arch enemy of the proletariat. Both ideologies place the traditional Sabbath as a day of rest on shaky ground. The American ethos makes the day of rest into a day of recuperation. The Sabbath's only justification is that in the long run it enables an exhausted worker to regain his energy; through the teachings of the church one learns the virtues of deferred gratification. For the successful it is a day to show God how wise was His choice for good fortune.

To the Jewish socialists, the Sabbath was a product of the old order designed to keep workers poor by preventing them from working an extra day. It was one more symbol of the devaluation of the worker, because implicit in the sanctification of rest is a judgment about the profane quality of work.

Thus when they entered the portals of the new world, the bulk of American Jewry gained a new world view in which work, not Shabbat, was the prime value. If the older immigrants themselves did not learn, their public school–educated children soon learned that all rewards in this world come through work. Jews learned quickly. This lesson was part of being an American. For the first time keeping the Sabbath became contradictory to the dominant ideology and not just an added burden on the economic needs of the Jews. The problem of Saturday versus Sunday was never the fundamental Sabbath problem for the majority of Jews. Instead, the question of the Shabbat was whether to keep it on Saturday or not at all.

If work is holy, why rest? Fresh air or card games both provide more of a change from the work week than that ritually difficult Old World institution, the Shabbat. America is the land of work. Weiss, Harwood, and Riesman offer this observation:

> Except for a few science fiction writers and other Utopians, no Americans have ever proposed as an eventual aim of national policy the elimination of work. There are people who work harder than we, such as the Germans and Swiss, but it is doubtful if there are any people on earth to whom work is as important to a man's self. Our problems arise when we must do work that has too little meaning, or when work invades other areas of our lives, or when there is too little work for us or when the rewards of work are insufficient, or its conditions oppressive.[5]

This is the world into which the Shabbat, the foretaste of heaven, fell. In America the contrast has never been between work and Shabbat; it has been, until recently, between work and sloth. The Great Depression was more depressing in America than nearly anywhere else except Germany. The American worker regarded no work not only as a physical disaster, but as a psychologically castrating catastrophe.

After World War II still another blow was dealt to the Shabbat-work relationship. For the first time in modern Jewish history, Jews were permitted not only to work in occupations determined by the external Gentile community and the prejudices of the internal Jewish community, but to enter careers of their own choice. Jews could be engineers or college professors. They had that freedom to select work that comes with financially secure parents, higher education, and an ever-expanding economy. In a culture that placed a premium on work, the Jewish male in World War II America was in the enviable position of not only having a job, but having a job that he *liked*. *Children of the Gilded Ghetto* makes the point that rather few third-generation Jews in Minneapolis went into their father's business, even though doing so ensured financial success.[6]

Here I want to pause in order to refute a notion that Americans observe but that their traditional attitude toward work keeps them from perceiving. Far from being merely a burdensome source of money to spend in one's leisure time, work itself is the objective of working. It is the organizing principle in a man's life. In *Who Was Who* obituaries, a man's occupation is almost always listed immediately after his name and long before the names of his survivors. Men dread retirement, even when they have no financial worries, because work is life. As the tightrope walker Karl Wallenda said, after his family perished in a fall from the wire and as he was about to resume his career, "Life is on the wire. The rest is waiting."[7] So work is life. To work and to love are the goals of a healthy man, according to Freud, and to love one's work is the closest to sublimation one comes in western culture. This is the era in which Jews, Orthodox or unorthodox, find themselves and the Shabbat, an era in which the only certain escape from the terror of finitude is prolonged submergence in work. When for some reason a man and his work are not a good fit, or no fit at all, an American man gets sick. Impotence and unemployment correllate significantly. Matriarchy emerges in America when men work hours that are not too long but too short or too degrading. The Moynihan report on the Negro family documents this point.[8] But this is an era that may be ending.

What, then, of the Shabbat in a country in which work is king and Jews can bask in the reflected glory of its sovereignty? Several trends, in both American and American Jewish life, lend promise to what has heretofore been only the hope of concerned Jews that Saturday will again be Shabbat, something special, something sanctified and sanctifying.

One trend is the willingness of a small but significant group of Jews to observe the Shabbat in a way clearly different from an ordinary day off. In large cities there are Jews, intellectual and professional, who, due to a stay in Israel, a personal commitment to Judaism, or even a belief in God, search for a means to make the Shabbat a new day. They do not regard the halacha pertaining to the Shabbat as binding, but neither do they feel the need of deliberately violating it, if in some of it they can find whatever they are looking for.[9] Rabbis must look at what they do for suggestions and be suggestive in their own right. They must resign themselves to the circumstance that for the majority of American Jews, the Shabbat is a dead symbol, but so is nearly every other traditional Jewish symbol at least part of the time. This does not mean that Judaism is dead, nor does it mean that one can, through reason, replace the old symbols with those of one's own design. That is not the way symbols become symbols. Symbols emerge from the depth of feeling and historical experience. Symbols happen. More importantly, however, rabbis cannot claim to be leaders of the Jews merely because they share with the majority the feeling that for them, too, these old symbols are dead. Religious leadership is not granted to those who can only say: "You don't find the Shabbat meaningful; well, neither do I. That means you and I have something in common." There is a miniscule but important group of those who want the Shabbat. That is positive trend number one.

The second positive trend is more problematical, but more interesting in its possibilities. The American attitude toward work is under attack from several sides. America is a society that has for the first time in history reached a stage in which too much work, rather than too little, is a danger to the economic progress of the ruling elite. Automation can produce goods more quickly and more cheaply than men can. But men are needed to buy the goods. Furthermore, it is clear, men want to work; they need to work. So at the present time a stalemate has emerged between the work ethic and the usually irreversible force of technological progress. This stalemate manifests itself in the outcropping of phenomena like the "hippies" and counterculture people, who both attract and repulse most Americans: on the one hand, they do what virtually all Americans at one time or another would like to do, namely, play all day; and on the other hand, they seem so miserable doing it. It is possible that this apparent misery is what the golden age of abundance holds in store for Americans. The important fact is, however, that the concept of play is returning to the realm of adult human possibility for the first time since civilization took Adam from the garden.

Herbert Marcuse theorizes, and the hippies demonstrate for us, another meaning for play. "In a genuinely humane civilization," Marcuse writes, "the human existence will be play rather than toil and man will live in display rather than need." And he goes on: "These ideas represent one of the most advanced positions of thought. It must be understood that the liberation from the reality which is here envisaged is not transcendental, 'inner,' or merely intellectual freedom . . . but freedom *in* the reality. The reality that 'loses its seriousness' is the inhumane reality of want and need, and it loses its seriousness when wants and needs can be satisfied without alienated labor. Then, man is free to 'play' with his faculties and potentialities and with those of nature, and only by 'playing' with them is he free. His world is then display . . . , and its order is that of beauty. Because it is the realization of freedom, play is *more* than the constraining physical and moral reality: '. . . man is only *serious* with the agreeable, the good, the perfect; but with beauty he plays.'"

True freedom is the freedom to play, to invest one's libidinal energy, not in what has to be done, but in what ought to be, will be: freedom itself, the freedom to play. "The mental faculty exercising this freedom is that of *imagination*," says Marcuse.[10]

Those who have carefully studied the hippies have noted that one of the outstanding characteristics of their way of life is their disavowal of expertise—they even play music badly. In a world in which playing baseball means joining the little league, playing tennis means making the team, and being a musician means performing publicly, doing something badly is revolutionary. Most social critics agree, too, that the one major contribution of the hippies to our lives is their music, the first truly indigenous music produced by American whites.[11]

Marcuse summarizes his vision of the possibilities for the affluent society as follows:

(1) The transformation of toil (labor) into play, and of repressive productivity into "display"—a transformation that must be preceded by the conquest of want (scarcity) as the determining factor of civilization.

(2) The self-sublimation of sensuousness . . . and the de-sublimation of reason . . . in order to reconcile the basic antagonistic impulses.

(3) The conquest of time in so far as time is destructive of lasting gratification.

These elements are practically identical with those of a reconciliation between pleasure principle and reality principle.[12]

One can note the similarities between Marcuse's vision and the traditional conception of the Shabbat as a foretaste of the Messiah. Right now synagogues and Shabbat reflect the present. Services and Shabbat programs are most often slavishly worshipful of form and as devoid of fantasy and fancy as sisterhood teas.

A future for mankind that is an era when repression no longer rules, where play is returned, where time is decathected is, for Marcuse and others, not a luxury but man's only hope. If others dare not desist from dreaming of this Shabbat of Shabbats, dare rabbis desist from "remembering the Seventh Day to keep it holy"?

# Conclusion

Writing of Jews in his classic *Childhood and Society,* Erik H. Erikson first examined traditional psychoanalytical thought on anti-Semitism, but then went on to offer a most interesting interpretation of the theory of psychosocial identity.

The universal concept of defensive rigidity and of adaptive flexibility, of conservatism and progressivism, in the Jews of the Diaspora expresses itself in the opposition of two trends: dogmatic orthodoxy, and opportunistic adaptability. These trends, of course, were favored by centuries of dispersion. We may think here of types such as the religiously dogmatic, culturally reactionary Jew, to whom change and time mean absolutely nothing: the Letter is his reality. And we may think of his opposite, the Jew to whom geographic dispersion and cultural multiplicity have become "second nature": relativism becomes for him the absolute, exchange value his tool.

There are extreme types which can be seen as living caricatures: the bearded Jew in his kaftan, and Sammy Glick. The psychoanalyst, however, knows that this same set of opposites, this conflict between the adherence to the Letter, and the surrender to the changing price of things pervades the unconscious conflicts of men and women of Jewish extraction who do not consider themselves, nor are considered by others, as "Jewish" in a denominational or racial sense. Here that Letter may have become political or scientific dogma (socialism, Zionism, psychoanalysis) quite removed from the dogma of the Talmud, yet quoted and argued in a way not unlike the disputation of passages from the Talmud and the tradition of their ancestors; and exchange value may have become obsessive preoccupation with the comparative value—of values. Economically and professionally, later stages of history have exploited what earlier history initiated: the Jews were confined to what they did best, while they, of course, learned to perfect what they were permitted to do. Thus they have become not only the traditional traders of goods, but also the mediators in cultural change, the interpreters in the arts and sciences, the healers of disease and of inner conflict. Their strength, in these fields, lies in a responsible sense of relativity. But this defines Jewish weakness as well: for where the sense of relativity loses its responsibility it can become cynical relativism.

Jewish genius, in turn, quietly possessed of the courage of the ages, lifts the matter of relative values to a plane on which known reality becomes relative to more inclusive orders. In the religious sphere we have observed that Christian ethics is based on a radical subordination of this world to "the other world," of earthly empires to the Kingdom of God: when Hitler called conscience a Jewish blemish, he included Christianity and its doctrine of sin and salvation.

In modern times, man's freedom of will, of the conscious choice of his values, and of his power of judgment have been questioned by the theories of three Jews. The Marxian theory of historical determinism established the fact that our values unconsciously depend on the means by which we make a living. (As a psychological fact this is not entirely identical with the political doctrine of Marxism, which in a variety of countries has led to a variety of socialisms.) In psychology, Freud's theory of the unconscious showed abundantly that we are unaware of the worst and of the best in our motivations. Finally, it was Einstein's theory of relativity which gave modern reorientation the broad basis of changing physical theory. He showed that, indeed, our measuring sticks are relative to the relationships which we measure.

It is clear that the theories of these men can each be shown to have emerged at the "logical" moment in the history of their respective fields; and that these thinkers climaxed the cultural and scientific crisis of Europe not because they were Jews, but because they were Jews *and* Germans *and* Europeans. Yet the ingredients which go into radical innovations at the crossroads of any field have hardly been studied; and we may well ask whether it is altogether mere historical accident that Marx, Freud, and Einstein, all men of German-Jewish ancestry, have come to formulate and, moreover, to *personify* radical redefinitions on the very ground man thought he stood on.

Strong eras and strong countries assimilate the contribution of strong Jews because their sense of identity is enhanced by progressive redefinitions. In times of collective anxiety, however, the very suggestion of relativity is resented, and this especially by those classes which are about to lose status and self-esteem. In their effort to find a platform of conservation, they cling with grim single-mindedness to the few absolutes which they hope will save them. It is at this point that paranoid anti-Semitism is aroused by agitators of many descriptions and purposes, who exploit mass cowardice and mass cruelty.[1]

In his book *Boundaries* the social scientist Robert Jay Lifton observes:

> One response to the crisis of boundaries is a desperate attempt to hold fast to all existing categories, to keep all definitions pure. This, is, unfortunately, the impulse of a great deal of political, military, and cultural thought throughout the world, including that of classical Marxism and classical psychoanalysis. More than being merely conservative, this response is a *reaction* to a perceived threat of chaos; it all too readily lends itself to nostalgic visions of restoring a golden age of exact boundaries, an age in which men allegedly knew exactly where they stood. The approach is self-defeating and, moreover, impossible to maintain.
>
> The opposite response is to destroy, or seek to destroy, all boundaries, in the name of an all-encompassing oneness. Norman O. Brown, for instance, holds up the model of Dionysus, "the mad god [who] breaks down the boundaries; releases the prisoners; abolishes repression; and abolishes the *principium individuationis* substituting for the unity of man and the unity of man with nature." Quite simply, according to Brown, "The conclusion of the whole matter is, break down the boundaries, the walls." But this impulse to eliminate all boundaries confuses a great mythological vision (embodying a basic component of the imagination) with a "solution" for man's problems of living. The approach all too readily collapses into a pseudo-instinctualism in which the only heroes are the infant, the pre-human animal, and the schizophrenic.
>
> Though seemingly antagonistic to one another, these two absolute responses share a schematic disdain for history, and for man's symbol-forming connection with history. Were they our only approaches to the question of boundaries, they would, if anything, escalate our present spiritual warfare with ourselves, and at the same time render it more static.
>
> There is, however, an alternative. Boundaries can be viewed as neither permanent nor by definition false, but rather as essential and yet subject to the fundamental forces for change characterizing our age. We require images of limit and restraint, if only to help us grasp what we are transcending. We need distinctions between our biology and our history, all the more so as we seek to bring these together in a sense of ourselves that is unprecedentedly fluid and tenuous. In speaking of boundaries of destruction, of death and life, of the self, or revolution, and of the New History, I bring together various strands of my work . . . woven around, and specifically addressed to one overall issue: the breakdown and re-creation of the boundaries of our existence. I end up with no definitive conclusions, no permanent "walls," but only with a series of specters, directions, and possibilities.[2]

Both of these statements may be taken to summarize the hopes and dangers that face American Jews in their attempt to seek solutions to problems of identity. Ways need to be worked out to maintain the flexibility that can only loosely be called the "Jewish essence." I have attempted in this book to examine some of the stresses placed on Jews working at this task—a task that involves a continuous reevaluation of the acceptable boundaries in the quest for a secure American Jewish identity. There is no question in my mind that this is a healthy process, one that has historically led to Jewish survival. The real question is whether American Jews are willing to wrestle with this problem. My own feeling is that it is worth everything to maintain a Jewish people capable of preserving those values that make for not only a wholesome Jew but a humanity that is humane. It may not be for American Jews to complete this mission, but neither are they free to abandon it.

# Notes

························································

INTRODUCTION

1. Florence M. Fitch, *One God: The Ways We Worship Him* (New York: Lothrop, Lee & Shepard Co., 1944).

2. See Charles J. Tull, *Father Coughlin and the New Deal* (Syracuse, N.Y.: Syracuse University Press, 1965); and Julian Morgenstern to Bishop Francis C. Kelly, *American Jewish Archives* 26 (1974): 190–93.

3. Acts 8:1; 9:1–30.

4. See Yitzhak Baer, *A History of the Jews in Christian Spain*, 2 vols. (Philadelphia: Jewish Publication Society of America, 1971), 2:141–50.

5. Sigmund Freud, *Moses and Monotheism* (New York: Vintage, 1955). Much of the German original first appeared in *Imago* in 1937.

6. I noticed in the late fall and early winter of 1976 that the exclusive shopping district of Beverly Hills, California, featured palm trees and street lights decorated alternately in Christmas red and green and Jewish blue and white (with tinsel snowflakes that, on closer inspection, turned out to be six-pointed stars!). Thus, "the season to be jolly" has been expanded and the distinction between Jews and Gentiles simultaneously emphasized and reduced.

The same effect was produced by Franco Zeffirelli's six-hour television movie *Jesus of Nazareth*. Broadcast during Holy Week of 1977 (which coincided with Passover), the film had received the "recommendation of at least one rabbi, Marc H. Tanenbaum of the American Jewish Committee" (*New York Times*, 3 April 1977, p. D–33).

In fiction no one has handled the question of Jewish feelings toward Christian symbols more deftly than Grace Paley in her short story "The Loudest Voice," in *The Little Disturbances of Man* (Garden City: Doubleday, 1959).

7. On Jewish attitudes toward Jesus, see Hyman G. Enelow, *A Jewish View of Jesus* (New York: Macmillan, 1920); Morris Goldstein, *Jesus in the Jewish Tradition* (New York: Macmillan, 1950); and Emil G. Hirsch, *The Jews and Jesus*

(Chicago: Bloch & Newman, 1893). See also Samuel Sandmel, "Isaac Mayer Wise's 'Jesus Himself,'" in *Essays in American Jewish History,* American Jewish Archives Festschrift (Cincinnati: American Jewish Archives, 1958), pp. 325ff.

8. See Freud, *Moses and Monotheism,* pp. 9–10; and idem, "The Poet and Day-Dreaming," *Collected Papers,* 24 vols. (London: Hogarth Press, 1953), 4:173–75.

9. See Luke 2:42–50. See also Philip Roth's short story "The Conversion of the Jews" in *Goodbye, Columbus, and Five Short Stories* (Boston: Houghton Mifflin, 1959).

10. See Matt. 22:21, 26:39–42, 64. See also Erik H. Erikson, *Childhood and Society,* 2d ed., rev. and enl. (New York: Norton, 1963), chap. 7.

## CHAPTER ONE

1. See Philip Birnbaum, ed., *Daily Prayer Book* (New York: Hebrew Publishing Co., 1949), pp. 774–78; Jerome R. Mintz, *Legends of the Hasidim* (Chicago: University of Chicago Press, 1968), p. 126; and Solomon Ganzfried, *Code of Jewish Law: Kitzur Shulhan Aruh,* trans. H. E. Goldin, rev. ed. (New York: Hebrew Publishing Co., 1961), pp. 39–40.

2. John 3:3, 5, 7; Gal. 2:20.

3. See, for example, the preliminary morning service in Birnbaum, p. 14. The Reform movement's new *Gates of Prayer: The New Union Prayer Book* (New York: Central Conference of American Rabbis, 1975), p. 51, reflects a retreat from the conventional Reform scarcity of references to the human body.

4. See David Philipson, *The Reform Movement in Judaism* (New York: Macmillan, 1931), pp. 2–3; and John M. Cuddihy, *The Ordeal of Civility* (New York: Delta, 1976), pp. 4–14.

5. Sigmund Freud, *The Future of an Illusion,* trans. W. D. Robson-Scott (New York: Liveright, 1955).

6. Philip Slater, *The Pursuit of Loneliness* (Boston: Beacon Press, 1971); Edward Hall, *The Silent Language* (New York: Doubleday, 1959); idem, *The Hidden Dimension* (New York: Doubleday, 1966); and Erving Goffman, *Behavior in Public Places* (New York: Free Press, 1963).

7. Jakob Josef Petuchowski, *Prayerbook Reform in Europe* (New York: World Union for Progressive Judaism, 1968), p. 105.

8. Ibid., p. 108.

9. Ibid., pp. 113–14.

10. Report of Committee on Guide for Synagogue Decorum, Joel Y. Zion, chairman, *Central Conference of American Rabbis Yearbook* 74 (1964): 60–63 (hereafter cited as *CCAR Yearbook*).

11. Goffman, *Behavior in Public Places,* p. 199.

12. See Joseph Gutmann, "How Traditional Are Our Traditions?", in his *Beauty in Holiness* (New York: Ktav, 1970), pp. 418–19.

13. See Freud, "The Excretory Functions in Psycho-Analysis and Folklore," *Collected Papers,* 5:90.

14. See *Gates of Prayer,* p. 633.

## CHAPTER TWO

1. See Philipson, p. 150.

2. See "Report of the *Ad Hoc* Committee on Mixed Marriage," Herman E. Schaalman, chairman, and Roland Gittelsohn's remarks to the committee, *CCAR Yearbook* 83 (1973): 59–64, 79–81.

3. See Norman Mirsky, "Mixed Marriage and the Reform Rabbinate," *Midstream* 16 (January 1970): 40–46.

4. See Andrew F. Key, *The Theology of Isaac Mayer Wise* (Cincinnati: American Jewish Archives, 1962), pp. 45, 51; and Stanley F. Chyet, "Isaac Mayer Wise: Portraits by David Philipson," in B. W. Korn, ed., *A Bicentennial Festschrift for Jacob Rader Marcus* (New York: Ktav, 1976), p. 78.

5. See Jacob R. Marcus, *Studies in American Jewish History* (Cincinnati: Hebrew Union College Press, 1969), pp. 33, 203–5; and Daniel J. Elazar, *Community and Polity* (Philadelphia: Jewish Publication Society, 1976), p. 149.

6. Elazar, pp. 270–71.

7. See Lawrence Siegel, "Reflections on Neo-Reform in the Central Conference of American Rabbis," *American Jewish Archives* 20 (1968): 63–84; Nathan Glazer, *American Judaism* (Chicago: University of Chicago Press, 1957), p. 84; and Elazar, pp. 104, 123–24.

8. See Fred Massarik and Alvin Chenkin, "United States National Jewish Population Study: A First Report," *American Jewish Year Book* 74 (1973): 295; and Albert Ehrman and C. Abraham Fenster, "Conversion and American Orthodox Judaism," *Jewish Journal of Sociology* 10 (June 1968): 47–53.

9. See Louis A. Berman, *Jews and Intermarriage* (New York: Thomas Yoseloff, 1968), pp. 140–41, 149–50, 152–53, 306–9.

10. See Albert M. Lewis, "Conversion as a Process of Adult Socialization" (M.A.H.L. ordination thesis, Hebrew Union College, Cincinnati, 1969).

11. *New York Times,* 15 September 1974, p. 58.

12. See Richard L. Rubenstein, "Intermarriage and Conversion on the American College Campus," in Werner J. Cahnman, ed., *Intermarriage and Jewish Life* (New York: Herzl Press, 1963), pp. 140–41; and idem, "Communications: On Intermarriage," *Midstream* 16 (April 1970): 65–68.

13. Report of Recording Secretary, Isaac E. Marcuson, *CCAR Yearbook* 53 (1943): 32; and Report of Administrative Secretary, Isaac E. Marcuson, *CCAR Yearbook* 54 (1944): 28–29.

14. See Terry Zintl, "A Supermarket of Options," *Detroit Free Press,* 24 March 1977; and the discussion of Rabbi Sherwin Wine's views in chap. 9 below.

**CHAPTER THREE**

1. Report of Committee on Mixed Marriage, Herman E. Schaalman, chairman, *CCAR Yearbook* 83 (1973): 63–64 (italics added). See also Resolution of Committee on Mixed Marriage, ibid., p. 97.

2. *Proceedings of the Rabbinical Assembly* 28 (1964): 238–52.

3. Ibid. See also Albert I. Gordon, *Intermarriage* (Boston: Beacon Press, 1964), pp. 163–65.

4. See Massarik and Chenkin, pp. 292–306.

5. Ibid., p. 292.

6. Ibid., p. 293. Passages from "U.S. National Jewish Population Study: A First Report," by Fred Massarik and Alvin Chenkin, *American Jewish Year Book,* vol. 74, are reprinted with permission.

7. Ibid.

8. See Berman, p. 564; and Albert I. Gordon, p. 1.

9. Massarik and Chenkin, pp. 292–93.

10. Ibid., p. 295.

11. Ibid.

12. See Ronald Millstein's statement, *CCAR Yearbook* 83 (1973): 78.

13. See Mintz, pp. 142–43, and Charles S. Liebman, *The Ambivalent American Jew* (Philadelphia: Jewish Publication Society, 1973), pp. 178–87.

14. On the *chavurah* movement, see Stephen C. Lerner, "The Havurot," *Conservative Judaism* 24 (September 1970): 2–15; and David H. Roskes, "A Look Back at the Beginnings of the Havurah Movement" (in Yiddish), *Yugntruf,* March 1977, pp. 6–8, 18–19.

15. Massarik and Chenkin, p. 295.

16. See Gwen G. Schwartz and Barbara Wyden, *The Jewish Wife* (New York: Peter H. Wyden, 1969), chap. 17. See also Jessie Bernard, *The Future of Marriage* (New York: Bantam, 1973), pp. 37–38. Women in the twenty-five to forty-four age group from Providence, Rhode Island's Jewish community averaged by 1963 a total of 13.6 years of education (see Sidney Goldstein, "American Jewry, 1970: A Demographic Profile," *American Jewish Year Book* 72 [1971]: 64).

17. Well over one-third of Providence Jewry's daughters below the age of twenty were living outside of Rhode Island by 1963 (see S. Goldstein, p. 52).

18. See Dayton D. McKean, "The State, the Church, and the Lobby," in J. W. Smith and A. L. Jamison, eds., *Religion in American Life,* 4 vols. (Princeton: Princeton University Press, 1961), 2:122; and Sydney E. Ahlstrom, *A Religious History of the American People* (New Haven: Yale University Press, 1972), pp. 642–44, 867–72.

19. Two pertinent essays—Thomas F. O'Dea's "The Crisis of the Contemporary Religious Consciousness" and Daniel Callahan's "The Quest for Social Relevance"—appeared in *Daedalus,* Winter 1967, which was devoted to "Religion in America."

20. See, for example, Rubinstein, pp. 130–33. For a Christian's view of the Jewish family, see Herbert W. Schneider, *Religion in Twentieth Century America,* rev. ed. (New York: Atheneum, 1964), pp. 185–86.

21. Theodore I. Lenn et al., *Rabbi and Synagogue in Reform Judaism* (New York: Central Conference of American Rabbis, 1972), p. 124.

CHAPTER FOUR

1. See my study "The Making of a Reform Rabbi" (Ph.D. diss., Brandeis University, 1971); Charles S. Liebman, "The Training of American Rabbis," *American Jewish Year Book* 69 (1968): 3–112; and Lenn, chap. 6.

2. See Mintz, p. 89.

3. See Liebman, "Training of American Rabbis," pp. 7–9.

4. See Philipson, p. 357.

5. See Leonard J. Mervis, "The Social Justice Movement and the American Reform Rabbi," *American Jewish Archives* 7 (1955): 171–230; and Steven E. Foster, "The Development of the Social Action Program of Reform Judaism, 1878–1969" (M.A.H.L. ordination thesis, Hebrew Union College, Cincinnati, 1970).

6. Elazar, p. 270.

7. On competition between Reform and Conservatism, especially in post–World War II suburbia, see Marshall Sklare, *Conservative Judaism: An American Religious Movement* (New York: Schocken, 1972), pp. 256–57; Marshall Sklare and Joseph Greenblum, *Jewish Identity on the Suburban Frontier* (New York: Basic Books, 1967), p. 121; Jacob Sodden, "The Impact of Suburbanization on the

Synagogue" (Ph.D. diss., New York University, 1962), pp. 88, 392, 404, 409; and Joseph Rudavsky, "Growing Pains of a Suburban Jewish Community," *Jewish Digest* 12 (November 1966): 21–26.

8. See Siegel, pp. 65 ff.

9. See Lenn, chap. 16, and Leonard J. Fein et al., *Reform is a Verb* (New York: Union of American Hebrew Congregations, 1972), pp. 75, 89.

10. See Isaac M. Wise, "The World of My Books," *American Jewish Archives* 6 (1954): 141–44; Chyet, "Isaac Mayer Wise," p. 78; and Michael A. Meyer, "A Centennial History," in Samuel E. Karff, ed., *Hebrew Union College–Jewish Institute of Religion at One Hundred Years* (Cincinnati: Hebrew Union College Press, 1976), p. 22.

11. Mirsky, "Making of a Reform Rabbi," p. 266.

12. Ibid., pp. 252–61 (italics added).

13. *Rabbi's Manual*, rev. ed. (New York: Central Conference of American Rabbis, 1961).

14. On Freehof, see Walter Jacob et al., eds., *Essays in Honor of Solomon B. Freehof* (Pittsburgh: Rodef Shalom Congregation, 1964).

15. See Solomon B. Freehof, *Current Reform Responsa* (Cincinnati: Hebrew Union College Press, 1969), pp. 161–62.

## CHAPTER FIVE

1. See Priscilla and William Proctor, *Women in the Pulpit* (Garden City: Doubleday, 1976), chap. 8. Reform Judaism acquired its first woman cantor, Barbara Herman, in 1975 (*New York Times,* 9 June 1975, p. 35).

2. For a cogent discussion of women's rabbinic eligibility, see Jordan Ofseyer, "Why Not Women as Conservative Rabbis?", *United Synagogue Review* 29 (Fall 1976): 6–7, 28, 30. See also sentiments by Conservative rabbinical leaders in favor of the ordination of women in the *New York Times,* 7 May 1974, p. 23, and 21 April 1975, p. 32.

3. See, for example, the Mishnaic tractate Avot 1:5, in which one sage, Yose ben Yochanan of Jerusalem, urges, "Don't have much conversation with women," and cites earlier sages who were sure that whoever spoke much with women would injure himself and ultimately might even "inherit hell."

4. See Joshua Trachtenberg, *Jewish Magic and Superstition* (New York: Atheneum, 1975). Again, see Avot 2:8, where Hillel, the sage par excellence, is recorded as saying, "The more women, the more witchcraft; the more maidservants, the more lewdness."

5. See *CCAR Yearbook* 32 (1922): 156–77; and Jacob R. Marcus, "Rabbi Sally—The First Woman Rabbi, 1972," *American Jewish Archives* 26 (1974): 236–37.

6. See Guiding Principles of Reform Judaism, Samuel S. Cohon, chairman, *CCAR Yearbook* 47 (1937): 94–114; and Report of Committee on Resolutions, ibid. 32 (1922): 81–82.

7. See, for example, Report of Committee on Mixed Marriage, ibid. 83 (1973): 75–84, 89–97.

8. Leon I. Feuer, "A Note to My Colleagues," *Central Conference of American Rabbis Journal,* October 1971, pp. 21–27.

9. See Proctor and Proctor, pp. 131–33, 135, 137; and Anne L. Lerner, "Who Hast Not Made Me a Man," *American Jewish Year Book* 77 (1977): 17, 24.

10. See S. Goldstein, pp. 15–19; and Gerhard Lenski, *The Religious Factor* (Garden City: Doubleday, 1961), pp. 213–14.

11. See Schwartz and Wyden, pp. 177–93; Massarik and Chenkin, pp. 280–81; and *The World Almanac and Book of Facts: 1977* (New York: Newspaper Enterprise Association, 1976), p. 224.

12. See A. L. Lerner, p. 34.

13. See Proctor and Proctor, pp. 141, 143–44; and Marcus, "Rabbi Sally—The First Woman Rabbi, 1972," pp. 236–38.

14. Rabbi Priesand has, in fact, adopted a more militantly feminist stance in recent years (see her *Judaism and the New Woman* [New York: Behrman House, 1975]). In her years as a rabbinical student, however, I saw in her, as she sat in my classes, someone far more devoted to the rabbinate than to feminism; on more than a few occasions she made it clear that she was no devotee of Women's Lib.

15. See Mirsky, "Making of a Reform Rabbi," pp. 64–65.

CHAPTER SIX

1. The text of the Akedah, the binding of Isaac, is Gen. 22:1–19, read not only on Rosh Hashanah but also daily as part of the preliminary morning service in Orthodox congregations. The Tachanun petition, recited on Mondays and Thursdays, days on which the Pentateuch is read in traditionalist synagogues, reads: ". . . Let the binding of [Abraham's] only son appear before you [God] for Israel's sake"—i.e., let Isaac's sacrificial binding serve as a vicarious atonement for the sins of the Jewish people.

2. See Gen. 24; 27:15–29.

3. See ibid. 15:2; 24:2–4, 34–66.

4. See ibid. 16:11–16; 21:8–21.

5. See ibid. 32:24–29.

6. See the text of the Amidah in Birnbaum, pp. 82–98.

7. Liebman, "Training of American Rabbis," p. 108.

INTRODUCTORY NOTE

1. See E. Erikson, p. 251.

CHAPTER SEVEN

1. See Alvin I. Schiff, *The Jewish Day School in America* (New York: Jewish Education Committee Press, 1966); Charles S. Liebman, "Orthodoxy in American Jewish Life," *American Jewish Year Book* 66 (1965): 72–75; Walter I. Ackerman, "Jewish Education—For What?", ibid. 70 (1969): 6–7; William Cutter, "Present Status of Jewish Education," *CCAR Yearbook* (1973): 167–73; and Stanley F. Chyet, "Tomorrow?", *Dimensions in American Judaism*, Winter 1968–69, pp. 61–63.

2. *New York Times,* 26 January 1975.

3. See *Day School Directory: United States and Canada: Elementary, Secondary* (New York: Torah Umesorah, 1971).

4. See Kenneth D. Roseman, "Power in a Midwestern Jewish Community," *American Jewish Archives* 21 (1969): 57–83.

5. See, for instance, Leonard Dinnerstein and Gene Koppel, *Nathan Glazer: A Different Kind of Liberal* (Tucson: University of Arizona, 1973); Nicholas C. Polos, "Black Anti-Semitism in Twentieth Century America: Historical Myth or Reality?", *American Jewish Archives* 27 (1975): 8–31; Nathan Glazer and Daniel P. Moynihan, *Beyond the Melting Pot,* 2d ed. (Cambridge: M.I.T. Press, 1970); Nat Hentoff, *Black Anti-Semitism and Jewish Racism* (New York: Richard W. Baron, 1969); and Harold Saltzman, *Race War in High School* (New Rochelle: Arlington House, 1972). Black-Jewish relations and tensions are central to Bernard Malamud's novel *The Tenants* (New York: Farrar, Straus & Giroux, 1971).

### CHAPTER EIGHT

1. See Alex Inkeles, *What Is Sociology?* (Englewood Cliffs, N.J.: Prentice-Hall, 1964), pp. 6, 79; Kai T. Erikson, "The Sociology of Deviance," in E. C. McDonagh and J. E. Simpson, eds., *Social Problems: Persistent Challenges* (New York: Holt, Rinehart & Winston, 1965), pp. 457–64; idem, *Wayward Puritans: A Study in the Sociology of Deviance* (New York: John Wiley & Sons, 1966); Lewis A. Coser, "Functions of Deviant Behavior," in McDonagh and Simpson, pp. 500–509; Erving Goffman, *Stigma: Notes on the Management of Spoiled Identity* (Englewood Cliffs, N.J.: Prentice-Hall, 1963); and Jack D. Douglas, ed., *Observations of Deviance* (New York: Random House, 1970). The great pioneer of deviant theory was, of course, Emile Durkheim (1858–1917), whose *De la division du travail social* appeared in 1893 and whose *Les règles de la méthode sociologique* appeared in 1895.

2. Nearly two millennia ago normative traditional Judaism already stood for the propositions that Torah study should be a *qeva* (Avot 1:15), and that an *am ha-arets* could never achieve the status of *chasid* (Avot 2:6).

3. See Mintz, pp. 40, 83, 143, 155–58.

4. There is in traditional Judaism nothing really comparable, from the viewpoint of its textual sanctity, to Paul's insistence that "it is better to marry than to burn" (I Cor. 7:9).

5. See, for example, Jacob R. Marcus, *The Colonial American Jew, 1492–1776,* 3 vols. (Detroit: Wayne State University Press, 1970), 2:798; and idem, *Communal Sick-Care in the German Ghetto* (Cincinnati: Hebrew Union College Press, 1947), pp. 121, 177.

6. The "Dulcinea syndrome" (the tendency to be stricken with blindness when something ugly hoves into view), which Shulamit Hareven attributes to Israeli society (*Maariv,* 11 February 1977), is not at all unknown in the American Jewish community.

### CHAPTER NINE

1. James Yaffe offers an engaging summary of the phenomenon in his work *The American Jews* (New York: Random House, 1968), p. 161.

2. See "Birmingham Temple Statement of Principles" (typescript, Nearprint file, American Jewish Archives). See also Sherwin T. Wine's "Word from the Rabbi," *Birmingham Temple Newsletter,* 4 December 1964.

3. Six weeks had passed between the appearance of the new expurgated liturgy and the publicity generated by the meeting. During this early God-less period, only one family resigned its membership in the temple. Following the publicity and the controversy it stirred up within the temple, more than twenty families resigned.

4. *National Jewish Post and Opinion,* 1 January 1965, p. 3. Reprinted with permission.

5. See the *New York Times,* 6 February 1965, p. 17; and the *New York Herald Tribune,* 7 February 1965.

6. See "To the 'Atheist' Rabbi," *Israel Horizons and Labour Israel* 13 (April 1965): 4–5.

## CHAPTER TEN

1. Margaret Mead, *Culture and Commitment* (Garden City: Doubleday & Co., 1970), preface.

2. *Chicago Sun-Times,* 19 September 1974; *Lakeview Press* (Chicago), 25 September 1974.

3. *Chicago Tribune,* 11 December 1974.

4. See Solomon Zeitlin, "The Origin of the Synagogue," in Joseph Gutmann, ed., *The Synagogue: Studies in Origins, Archaeology, and Architecture* (New York: Ktav, 1975), pp. 14–26.

5. Lewis A. Coser, *The Functions of Social Conflict* (New York: Free Press of Glencoe, 1964), p. 60.

6. Neil J. Smelser, *Theory of Collective Behavior* (New York: Free Press, 1962), pp. 14, 67, 382.

## CHAPTER ELEVEN

1. Bishop John A. Robinson, *Honest to God* (Philadelphia: Westminster Press, 1963); and Joseph Fletcher, *Situation Ethics* (Philadelphia: Westminster Press, 1966).

2. See, for example, Harvey Cox, "To Speak in a Secular Fashion of God," in *The Secular City,* rev. ed. (New York: Macmillan, 1966), pp. 211–35.

3. See Solomon B. Freehof, *Contemporary Reform Responsa* (Cincinnati: Hebrew Union College Press, 1974), pp. 23–26; and Freehof et al., "Judaism and Homosexuality," *Central Conference of American Rabbis Journal,* Summer 1973, pp. 31–50.

## CHAPTER TWELVE

1. See, in particular, E. Erikson, *Childhood and Society;* Anna Freud, *The Ego and the Mechanics of Defense* (New York: International Universities Press, 1946): and Heinz Hartmann, *Ego Psychology and the Problem of Adaptation* (1939; rpt., New York: International Universities Press, 1958).

2. I am basing this on a letter that Dr. Arlow addressed to me on 16 May 1974 (copy in American Jewish Archives). See also Jacob A. Arlow, "Ego Psychology and Mythology," *Journal of the American Psychoanalytic Association* 9 (1961): 388.

3. According to Arlow in his letter to me, Yochanan "represents an ego ideal, a character structure to be emulated because [it] was consonant with the conditions for ... Jewish survival for many centuries. Such a character, however, could hardly serve as an ideal personality type for militant Zionists at the end of the 19th and the beginning of the 20th century."

4. In this discussion I often use the word "myth" where others might use "history," and "legend" is often used where others might say "true story." The

reader should take it for granted that myth and legend are intended neither to affirm nor to deny the historicity of the tales analyzed. For makers of myth there is no such distinction.

5. See B. Gittin 56a–b.

6. See, for example, Freud, "A Special Type of Choice of Object Made by Men," *Collected Papers,* 4: 192–202. See also Karl Abraham, "Rescue and Murder of the Father in Neurotic Phantasies," *International Journal of Psychoanalysis* 3 (1922): 467–74. As Jacob Arlow reads the Sleeping Beauty legend, "the dead father re-emerges as the resurrecting prince . . . the fulfillment of oedipal wishes . . ." ("Unconscious Fantasy and Conscious Experience," *Psychoanalytic Quarterly* 38 [1969]: 20).

7. One can, of course, find alternative tales, though they are rarely stressed. In the Bible, for example, Rebekah tricks her husband and gets a blessing for her favorite son (Gen. 27). Queen Esther is prepared to sacrifice herself to save the Jews (Esther 4:16). In the Book of Judges, Deborah saves the men of Israel (Judg. 5:1–31), and Jael slays the enemy general with a tent pin (Judg. 4:21). In the Apocrypha it is Judith, a latter-day Jael, who saves Israel by beheading the enemy warrior Holofernes (Jth. 13:8).

8. B. Gittin 56a–b; Tosefta Berakot 2:6; Tosefta Gittin 3:10; Rosh Hashanah 29b; Shabbat 11a. See also *Jewish Encyclopedia,* 7:18; and Alexander Guttmann, *Rabbinic Judaism in the Making* (Detroit: Wayne State University Press, 1970), pp. 199–200.

9. As examples, see Lloyd Alexander, *The Flagship Hope: Aaron Lopez* (Philadelphia: Jewish Publication Society of America, 1960), pp. 74–82, 115–17, 137–43; and Lee J. Levinger, *A History of the Jews in the United States* (Cincinnati: Union of American Hebrew Congregations, 1944), pp. 113–23.

10. See Hannah Arendt, *Eichmann in Jerusalem* (New York: Viking, 1963); Bruno Bettelheim, *The Informed Heart* (Glencoe, Ill.: Free Press, 1960); Raoul Hilberg, *The Destruction of the European Jews* (Chicago: Quadrangle, 1961); and Isaiah Trunk, *Judenrat* (New York: Macmillan, 1972).

11. See Y. Taanit 4:68d; *Jewish Encyclopedia,* 1:305; Abba H. Silver, *A History of Messianic Speculation in Israel* (New York: Macmillan, 1927), p. 127; and Joseph Klausner, *The Messianic Idea in Israel* (New York: Macmillan, 1955), pp. 398–99.

12. See Shabbat 21b; Meg. Taanit 23. See also Elias Bickerman, *From Ezra to the Last of the Maccabees* (New York: Schocken, 1962), pp. 119–35.

13. See *Jewish Encyclopedia,* 8:378. On Mattathias, see also 1 Macc. 2:1–70. On Hannah and her sons, see 2 Macc. 7:1–41.

14. See, for example, Flavius Josephus, *The Jewish War,* trans. H. St. J. Thackeray (New York: Washington Square Press, 1965), vol. 1, vv. 126–87 (hereafter 1. 126–87). See also Bickerman, pp. 148–52.

15. See Josephus, *Jewish War,* 7. 280–303.

16. See Flavius Josephus, *Vita* v. 9; and Luke 2:46–47.

17. See Josephus, *Vita,* 11–12.

18. See ibid., 13–16.

19. See ibid., 17–417; and Josephus, *Jewish War,* 2. 546–634, 3. 135–595.

20. See Josephus, *Jewish War,* 3. 400–402, 4. 601–63; idem, *Vita,* 414–23; and Suetonius, *Lives of the Caesars,* 8. 5–6. Both Yochanan ben Zaccai and Josephus are credited with predicting Vespasian's succession to the throne. It is intriguing, then, that both the Yavneh and the Masada episodes, otherwise diametrically opposed, trace back to the same Roman general.

21. See Josephus, *Vita,* 358–67; idem, *Jewish War,* vol. 1, Preface; 3. 108; 5. 263–66; and idem, *Antiquities of the Jews,* trans. H. St. J. Thackeray, 9 vols.

(Cambridge: Harvard University Press, 1966), bk. 20, vv. 267–68 (hereafter 20. 267–68).

22. See Josephus, *Antiquities,* 18. 63–64.

23. It is worth noting that the famous German novelist Lion Feuchtwanger diverged sharply from the traditional and anti-Josephan views of Jewish writers. In his trilogy—*Josephus* (1932), *The Jew of Rome* (1936), and *Josephus and the Emperor* (1942)—he paints a very sympathetic portrait of Josephus. It is as if Feuchtwanger were preparing the Jews for the Masada myth by reclaiming Josephus's reputation.

24. See Josephus, *Jewish War,* 7. 280–303.

25. See ibid., 252, 275–79, 304–15, 402–7; see also ibid., 399–401.

26. Ibid., 325–28, 331–36, 381–83, 385–88.

27. Ibid., 389–407.

28. See for example, Yigael Yadin, *The Story of Masada,* Retold for young readers by Gerald Gottlieb (New York: Random House, 1969), chap. 3, "The Traitor Josephus."

29. See, for example, Sklare, *Conservative Judaism,* pp. 254–59; Moshe Davis, *The Emergence of Conservative Judaism* (New York: Jewish Publication Society, 1963), pp. 323–26; and Arthur Hertzberg, "The American Jew and His Religion," in O. Janowsky, ed., *The American Jew: A Reappraisal* (Philadelphia: Jewish Publication Society, 1964), pp. 118–19. See also Solomon Schechter, as quoted in the *Universal Jewish Encyclopedia:* Conservative Judaism is not "a new party, but . . . an old one, which has always existed in this country. . . . I refer to the large number of Jews who, thoroughly American in habits of life and mode of thinking, and, in many cases, imbued with the vast culture of the day, have always maintained conservative principles and remained aloof from . . . Reform" (6:245). Arthur Hertzberg, in *Encyclopaedia Judaica,* says that "the American development [of the Conservative Movement] was parallel to the one in Europe . . . but it was an essentially autonomous development" (5:901).

30. Gottlieb, Foreword to Yadin, *Story of Masada.* Passages from *The Story of Masada,* by Yigael Yadin and Retold for Young Readers by Gerald Gottlieb, copyright © 1969 by Random House, Inc., are reprinted with permission.

31. See Geraldine Rosenfield, *The Heroes of Masada* (New York: United Synagogue Commission on Jewish Education, 1968), pp. 3–4.

32. See *Masada, Struggle for Freedom, and the Finds from the Bar-Kokhba Caves* (New York: Jewish Theological Seminary, 1967). The volume appeared in connection with the Masada exhibition sponsored by the Jewish Museum of the Jewish Theological Seminary of America. The exhibition was held in the Jewish Museum, New York City, between October 1967 and February 1968. It later traveled to Chicago, Dallas, Detroit, Philadelphia, and San Francisco.

33. Yadin, pp. 88–91 (chap. 15, "The Faith of the Zealots").

34. See ibid., pp. 95–98.

35. See ibid., p. 96.

36. Josephus, *Jewish War,* 7. 389.

37. Ibid., 390–98.

38. On the JDL see Ruth A. Buchbinder, "Jewish Vigilantes," *Congress Bi-Weekly,* 26 May 1969, pp. 4–6; Sam Peuzner, "Inside the Jewish Community," *Jewish Currents* 23 (July–August 1969): 33–34; Michael Pousner, "Never Again!", *New York Daily News,* 27 July 1970; Tannah Hirsch, "The JDL: Heroes or Hooligans?", *Jerusalem Post,* 4 March 1970; American Jewish Committee, *Fact Sheet—Jewish Defense League,* February 1970 (updated January 1971), pp. 1–18; and *The Jewish Defense League: Principles and Philosophies* (New York: Jewish Defense League, n.d.). All of the above are located in the Nearprint file of the

American Jewish Archives. See also Meir Kahane, *Never Again! A Program for Survival* (Los Angeles: Nash, 1971), pp. 239–82; and idem, *The Story of the Jewish Defense League* (Radnor, Pa.: Chilton, 1975).

## CHAPTER THIRTEEN

1. Schwartz and Wyden, pp. 1–2.

2. Erica Jong, *Fear of Flying: A Novel* (New York: New American Library, 1974), pp. 27–28.

3. Ibid., pp. 147–52.

4. See Jacob R. Marcus, *The Jew in the Medieval World* (New York: Harper Torchbooks, 1965), pp. 443–44; Mark Zborowski and Elizabeth Herzog, *Life Is with People* (New York: International Universities Press, 1952), pp. 124–41; Solomon Schechter, *Some Aspects of Rabbinic Theology* (New York: Behrman House, 1936), p. 330.

5. See Richard L. Rubenstein, *Power Struggle* (New York: Scribner's, 1974), pp. 9, 43.

6. See, for example, Anzia Yezierska's novel *Bread Givers* (1925; rpt. New York: Braziller, 1975).

7. Abraham Cahan's novel *The Rise of David Levinsky* (1917; rpt. New York: Harper Colophon, 1960) is a classic presentation of this problem.

8. Here Philip Roth's novel *Portnoy's Complaint* (New York: Random House, 1969), with its blurring—if not utter eradication—of the line between reality and fantasy, has become a classic.

## CHAPTER FOURTEEN

1. See Sklare and Greenblum, p. 50; Charles S. Liebman, "The Religion of American Jews," in Marshall Sklare, ed., *The Jew in American Society* (New York: Behrman House, 1974), pp. 241–52; and Sidney Goldstein and Calvin Goldscheider, *Jewish Americans* (Englewood Cliffs, N.J.: Prentice-Hall, 1968), pp. 195–205.

2. See Harvey Swados's novel *On the Line* (Boston: Little, Brown, 1957). See also Robert S. Weiss, Edwin Harwood, and David Riesman, "Work and Automation: Problems and Prospects," in R. K. Merton and R. Nisbet, eds., *Contemporary Social Problems* (New York: Harcourt, Brace, Jovanovich, 1971), pp. 545 ff.; and Rose Giallombardo, ed., *Contemporary Social Issues* (Santa Barbara: Hamilton Publishing Co., 1975), pp. 105 ff. (sec. 3, "Work Ethic, Automation, and Alienation").

3. See Daniel J. Boorstin, *America and the Image of Europe* (New York: Meridian Books, 1960).

4. Norman Mailer, *The Naked and the Dead* (1948; rpt. New York: Signet, 1951), p. 409.

5. Weiss, Harwood, and Riesman, p. 545.

6. Judith R. Kramer and Seymour Leventman, *Children of the Gilded Ghetto* (New Haven: Yale University Press, 1961), pp. 130–31, 199–200.

7. Wallenda is quoted in Erving Goffman, *Interaction Ritual* (Garden City: Anchor Books, 1967), p. 149.

8. See *Negro Family: Case for National Action* (Washington, D.C.: Government Printing Office, 1965).

9. See, for example, Paul Cowan, "World of Our Children," *New York Times Magazine,* 3 April 1977, pp. 64–70.

10. Herbert Marcuse, *Eros and Civilization* (Boston: Beacon Press, 1966), pp. 188–89.

11. Interesting in this connection is Ralph J. Gleason's remark: "For the reality of what's happening today in America, we must go to rock 'n roll, to popular music" ("Like a Rolling Stone," in Harold Jaffe and John Tytell, eds., *The American Experience: A Radical Reader* [New York: Harper & Row, 1970], pp. 332–45).

12. Marcuse, p. 193.

CONCLUSION

1. E. Erikson, pp. 354–57.

2. Robert Jay Lifton, *Boundaries: Psychological Man in Revolution* (New York: Vintage Books, 1970), pp. xi–xii.

# Glossary

| | |
|---|---|
| Ab (Ninth of) | a midsummer fast commemorating the destruction of the Jerusalem temple in antiquity |
| afikomen | matzo hidden during the Passover seder meal, to be found by children and eaten at the meal's conclusion |
| Akedah | the sacrificial binding of Isaac (Gen. 22) |
| *am ha-arets* | a person unlearned in Jewish law and observance |
| Amidah | the benedictions that form the core of the Jewish worship service |
| bat mitzvah | the ceremony, initiated in the twentieth century, by which a Jewish girl assumes religious duties and responsibilities; equivalent to bar mitzvah for a boy |
| Ben Sirah | the author of the Book of Ecclesiasticus in the Apocrypha |
| *bet midrash* | a place set aside for Torah study |
| Biryonim | Jewish anti-Roman activists during the Judean rebellion against Rome (66–71 C.E.) |
| B'nai Abraham, B'nai Yisrael | the descendants of Abraham, Jacob (Israel); the Jews |

| | |
|---|---|
| Borchu | the call to worship in Jewish morning and evening services |
| *brith* | a covenant (specifically, Abraham's covenant with God); often symbolized in circumcision |
| challah | Sabbath bread |
| *chasid* | a person of exceptional piety; a disciple of a charismatic personality |
| *chavurah* (pl. *chavurot*) | a fellowship group focusing on a Jewish purpose |
| *cheder* | a traditional Hebrew school |
| *davening* | the prayer style of Orthodox Jews |
| *Dorf* (pl. *Doerfer*) | the Central European equivalent of the *shtetl* |
| *ferbrangen* | a Hasidic-style get-together |
| *Galgenhumor* | gallows humor |
| *get* | a traditional writ of divorce |
| *goy* | a non-Jew |
| *haimish* | homey |
| *haskalah* | the nineteenth-century Jewish Enlightenment in Central and Eastern Europe |
| Havdalah | a ceremony marking the end of Sabbath and the beginning of the work week |
| *herem* | excommunication, ostracism |
| *hosanoth* | prayers for salvation declaimed on various festivals |
| *hupah* | a bridal canopy |
| Kaddish | a doxology, often the version associated with commemoration of the dead |
| *kasher* | kosher, ritually acceptable |
| *kashrut* | dietary regulations |
| *kiddush* | a sanctification prayer recited over wine |
| *kiddush ha-shem* | martyrdom |
| *kippa* (pl. *kippot*) | a skullcap |

| | |
|---|---|
| *k'lal yisrael* | the entire Jewish people |
| *kohen* | a member of the priestly caste |
| Kol Nidre | the prayer ushering in the atonement fast of Yom Kippur |
| Lubavitcher Hasidim | the followers of the Lubavitcher Rebbe, now domiciled in Brooklyn |
| *makom* | place; sometimes used euphemistically for God |
| *malkoth* | the ritual of shaking the willow branches on Sukkot |
| *maskil* | a proponent of the *haskalah* movement |
| *mazel* | luck |
| Mi Chomocho | a proclamation of God's wondrous power |
| *mikveh* | a ritual bath |
| *minhag* | a custom or folkway |
| *minyan* | a prayer quorum |
| *mitzvah* (pl. *mitzvot*) | a divine command; a good deed |
| *mohel* | a ritual circumciser |
| Moshe Rabbenu | the biblical Moses cast as a rabbi |
| *motzi* | a benediction recited over bread |
| *oneg, oneg Shabbat* | usually a Sabbath festivity |
| *parnoseh* | a living |
| Pesach | Passover |
| Purim | a late winter holiday commemorating Jewish deliverance from persecution |
| *qeva* | a routine |
| Sabbath | the period from sundown Friday to sundown Saturday |
| Shabbat | Hebrew for Sabbath |
| Shabbat Shuvah | the Sabbath of Repentance between Rosh Hashanah (New Year) and Kippur (the Day of Atonement) |
| Shekinah | the feminine aspect of God |
| Shema | the prayer "Hear, O Israel, the Lord our God, the Lord is One" |

| | |
|---|---|
| *shikse* | Yiddish slang for a non-Jewish female |
| *shomer shabbat* | a Sabbath observer |
| *shtetl* (pl. *shtetlach*) | a predominantly Jewish town in Eastern Europe |
| *shul* | a traditional synagogue |
| Simhat Torah | the ritual celebrating the Torah cycle at the conclusion of Sukkot |
| *s'michah* | rabbinical ordination |
| *succah (sukkah)* | the tabernacle or booth constructed during the celebration of the Sukkot festival |
| Sukkot | the autumnal tabernacle festival |
| Tachanun | a petitionary prayer |
| Talmud Torah | a traditional religious school |
| *tfilah* | prayer; often used to mean the Amidah |
| *yeshiva* | a school for rabbinic students |
| *Yiddishkeit* | the Jewish life-style |
| Yom Tov | a Jewish holiday |

# Index

································································